PRAISE FOR *FACING THE BEAST*

"When Western leaders abandoned reason and embraced the ideology of force several years ago, Naomi Wolf was one of few who understood instantly what was happening. She decided to tell the full truth about it all the time, no matter what. The result has been a thrilling inspiration to those of us who've followed it, and for the first time is collected here in one place. Read *Facing the Beast* to understand what bravery looks like."

—TUCKER CARLSON

"In the crisis of our lives and of everything we call civilization, Naomi Wolf has been a prescient observer, a keen analyst, and brave fighter for truth and freedom. Everything in her life and career prepared her for this moment. We all owe her a debt of gratitude for what she has done and continues to do for the great cause. Like her last book, *Facing the Beast* stands as a testament to truth in times gone mad."

—JEFFREY TUCKER, president, Brownstone Institute

"Today's world has been constructed to divide us. Naomi Wolf has seen through the lies and deception. In her personal journey, described in *Facing the Beast*, she unequivocally came to understand the universal principle— that all of humanity is connected. Dr. Wolf fights for our God-given rights and freedoms. I am honored to call her friend."

—EDWARD DOWD, author of *Cause Unknown*

Also by Naomi Wolf

Facing the Beast

Courage, Faith, and Resistance

in a New Dark Age

NAOMI WOLF

Chelsea Green Publishing
White River Junction, Vermont
London, UK

For the noncompliant

Editor: Brianne Goodspeed
Project Manager: Rebecca Springer
Copy Editor: Kerri Landis-Grzybicki
Designer: Melissa Jacobson

Printed in Canada.
First printing November 2023.
10 9 8 7 6 5 4 3 2 1   23 24 25 26 27

Our Commitment to Green Publishing
Chelsea Green sees publishing as a tool for cultural change and ecological stewardship. We strive to align our book manufacturing practices with our editorial mission and to reduce the impact of our business enterprise in the environment. We print our books using vegetable-based inks whenever possible. This book may cost slightly more because it was printed on paper that contains recycled fiber, and we hope you'll agree that it's worth it. *Facing the Beast* was printed on paper supplied by Marquis that is made of recycled materials and other controlled sources.

ISBN 9781645022367 (paperback) | ISBN 9781645022374 (ebook) | 9781645022381 (audiobook)

Library of Congress Control Number: 202394673

Chelsea Green Publishing
White River Junction, Vermont, USA
London, UK

www.chelseagreen.com

MIX
Paper from
responsible sources
FSC   FSC® C103567
www.fsc.org

CONTENTS

Introduction

This story begins in the "Before" world.

"Before" the years 2020 to 2022, when a set of policies based on abject lies posed an existential threat to our democracy and our way of life.

"Before" this likely AI-deployed set of lies, dispensed globally, targeted our West with its core traditions of free speech—and in the US, with its First Amendment—with arrant censorship.

"Before" the Left—the subculture that used to stand for human rights, freedom of speech, real science, critical thinking, and skepticism about Big Government and Big Corporations, let alone about their merger, and that used to fight against discrimination and inequality—fell into a trance in which that same group became champions of censorship, and of a two-tier society in which some people, as the pigs declared in *Animal Farm*, are "more equal" than others; and fell prey to magical thinking and cultlike behavior.

"Before" the media—which used to see itself as the source of investigation of elite powers; which used to ask questions about received narratives; which used to demand that its journalists produce evidence and independent verification before drawing conclusions in print—were bought out by Big Government via the CARES Act, and by Big Pharma directly, and by the Bill and Melinda Gates Foundation, to the extent that almost all legacy media became unquestioning stenographers for interested parties aligned with the global powers who dictated the harmful nonsense.

I miss the "Before Times."

Because I have studied the histories of the overthrowing of past democracies, and learned that many democracies have died incrementally; that tyrants' attacks on liberty are often executed surreptitiously, or attributed to benign motives, and thus succeed in draining people's freedoms; or by enforcing bit by bit tiny compliances that add up to huge compliances, any of which would never have been considered by the same population without revolt, if the curtain was brought down all at once—I thought it was important to keep a kind of journal of these changes as I witnessed them.

This book is a memoir of how our "Before" world—that lasted up until March 2020—became, through a slow boil and through various shocks to its core institutions—this "After" world of tyranny, sadism, and forced inequality.

I have been an activist defending the Constitution for the past three-plus decades. As a result of my work identifying and fighting earlier threats to democracy and free speech, I was able to see, early in 2020, the inevitable implications for our democracy and for our country as a whole, in the rollout of pandemic and lockdown and then mandate narratives and policies.

Given my previous work, it was easy to guess what all these policies would quickly do to us. It was easy for me to foretell that the immediate deployment of mass censorship of critics of these policies; the ramped-up State surveillance; the forced closures of schools, places of worship, and businesses; the unconstitutional declarations that we must not assemble, beyond a certain small number of people, even in private homes; the violation of the Nuremberg Laws and the most basic international human rights laws that guarantee bodily integrity and informed medical consent, represented mRNA vaccine mandates—would utterly transform our nation, and the nations of the West, into post-democratic societies; into societies that may look pretty much the same on the surface (as I argued in my 2008 bestseller *The End of America* that post-democratic societies would)—but that the heart of their freedom would be annihilated, leaving intact pretty-looking vassal states, with no real autonomy left for their citizens, where the nations of the free West so recently prevailed.

I saw early what a dangerous time it was and is: 2020 to 2023.

In my 2008 book about dying democracies, I had described the threats to liberty that prevailed at that time, in the George Bush Jr. era, as deriving primarily from the Right. But even then I was not deceived by partisanship assumptions about fascism, as I learned from my study of earlier totalitarian and fascist regimes and leaders that authoritarians of the Left and the Right are exactly the same; they take the same ten steps to ensure the death of democracies, and do the same things to propagandize their subject people, to silence dissent, to arrest opposition leaders, to create surveillance societies and prisons outside the rule of law, and eventually to bring about emergency law, which is Step Ten.

Since 2020, in America at least, these threats to our country have been deployed largely *from* the Left. Though I come "from the Left," I had no problem recognizing this.

The threats to liberty worldwide had no partisan quality as they were "metapartisan," being handed down from the WEF (World Economic Forum), the WHO (World Health Organization), the CCP (Chinese Communist Party), nongovernment foundations such as Bill Gates's, and allied Big Tech leaders, as I described in my 2022 book *The Bodies of Others.* You could see the exact same pandemic, lockdown, and mandate policies rolled out in conservative-led Australia, in conservative-led UK, in liberal-led Canada, in liberal-led France, and so on.

Other people also spoke up, as the dark shadow of fascism descended on our nation under the cloak of a "public health emergency."

Some others who had been identified with the US Left were also speaking out against the public health response to the pandemic. They also spoke out about the censorship regime that so visibly descended on us. Glenn Greenwald, Bret Weinstein and Heather Heying, Joe Rogan, Robert Kennedy Jr., and others, though identified with the Left, held the principles of the Constitution and basic human rights above partisanship.

Other heroes, too, arose in this dark time, in ways that also transcended partisanship. Many of these were heroes of real medicine, real science, real public health. Some were doctors: Dr. Peter McCullough, Dr. Pierre Kory, Dr. Paul Alexander, Dr. Henry Ealy, Dr. Sherri Tenpenny, and many others. Some were scientists and economists; the signatories and the convener of the Great Barrington Declaration, for instance: Dr. Jay Bhattacharya, Dr. Martin Kulldorff, Dr. Sunetra Gupta, and economist Jeffrey Tucker. These all refused to tolerate, or even accept as settled "science," policies that they knew would destroy schooling, damage the development of children, and lead to mass starvation.

Some heroes for truth came from the world of finance—critics such as Ed Dowd, formerly of BlackRock, who raised an early alarm about data showing excess deaths and disabilities post-mRNA vaccination. Or Steve Kirsch, an entrepreneur who also crunched the numbers on these harms, independently confirming the "democide"—death by government—that Mr. Dowd had found. These critics, whose training was in the world of hard data, perhaps spoke out because they simply could not tolerate the fibs and bad math that undergirded "the narrative"; as well as out of concern for their fellow human beings' health, and even survival.

There were—are—many heroes and heroines.

But not nearly enough.

There were—are—many millions more quislings and colluders, as I learned upon this painful journey.

———

My own life changed utterly, because of my taking actions that would have suited the "Before" world, but that I took in an "After" reality.

Until the COVID era, I had lived a fortunate life. I had been a well-known feminist nonfiction writer for thirty-five years; I'd published eight bestselling books. I had lived in Washington, D.C., and served as a campaign consultant to President Bill Clinton's re-election campaign; I had advised Vice President Al Gore. I'd later moved to a charming apartment in Manhattan's West Village, where I'd eventually, as a single mom, raised a beautiful family. I appeared on every news outlet, wrote for every major media platform, and was a columnist for outlets ranging from the *Guardian*, to the Soros-funded *Project Syndicate*, to the *Sunday Times* of London.

In addition to these professional validations, I was privileged to be part of the cultural "scene" made up of influencers on the progressive Left. It was a satisfying lifestyle: film premieres and art openings, book parties and galas. All these events reassured those of us attending that we were at the center of the universe, and for good reason; and that our worldview was the right one—indeed, the only one.

I had been treated as a media fixture for those thirty-five years, for doing what I had always done—speaking up for civil liberties and the

Introduction

Constitution and reporting on women's health issues—especially on sexual and reproductive health issues, my beat.

During the pandemic and the lockdown, then, I did what I have always done; I investigated the myths and narratives that I saw forming online and in news outlets and asked public questions about them. For me, this was nothing new. By doing so, I realized that many of the diktats of the period were untrue. I saw quickly that the COVID-19 maps on the front pages of the *New York Times,* and the Johns Hopkins University COVID-19 map cited by almost every other news outlet in the US, were all produced without giving the reader any access to the underlying datasets, for example. As a tech CEO whose website specializes in presenting the same kind of government data (application programming interfaces—APIs), I saw immediately that there was no way to trust these COVID-19 maps.

I knew from having written *The End of America* that the fact that we were, in July of 2020, already at Step Ten of the Ten Steps to Fascism—emergency law—represented a very dangerous situation. I knew from having read my way, as a former graduate student, through many of the last 400 years' worth of English memoirs and novels, that waves of infectious diseases, ranging from yellow fever to typhus to cholera, had passed over both Britain and America, but that these diseases had never been treated as we were treating this purportedly serious infectious disease, COVID-19. Never had multiple generations been advised to crowd together into closed indoor spaces, only to be denied light, air, and exercise, during an epidemic. Indeed, from Florence Nightingale in the Crimean War, to the reformers of the Progressive Era, health pioneers knew well that doing this was, in fact, deadly.

So many "truths" of the COVID narrative made no sense to me.

As I have always done with official narratives, I questioned these "truths."

But the world had changed. My questioning, instead of continuing to solidify my cultural status, called forth waves of bots and trolls, threats and harassment. My right-on, progressive friends let me know that they did not approve of the issues that I was raising.

Then came late 2020 and early 2021: the launch of the presentation of the mRNA injections as "the only way out" of the lockdowns. I recall reading Moderna's website, which boasted that the company's mRNA technology, and the spike protein in the vaccine formulation, would enter every cell in the human body.

I am an English major—not a medical doctor or a scientist. But I remember thinking: *Every cell?* In your ovaries? Your heart? Your liver? Your digestive tract? Your *eyelashes*? I have a neurological condition—spina bifida occulta; and I knew from experience how delicate was the nearly miraculous activity of healthy nerve conduction and how easily it could go awry. The *nerves?* I wondered. The *myelin sheaths* of the nerves? And I wondered how that—spike protein and mRNA entering the cells of the myelin sheaths of the nerves—would affect the fragile electrical conduction that allows for healthy nerve processes; and I decided to pass.

This personal, rational decision about my own body—one related to my own private health issues—abruptly thrust me into a new social and even legal category; one that was created in the start of 2021: that of second-class citizen; "anti-vaxxer" (note the trashy double *x*s); dissident; weirdo; "conspiracy theorist"; and, though I remained a classical liberal, "Trumper."

The moment I began asking basic questions on my Twitter feed specifically about the novel mRNA injections—the kinds of questions I had asked for three decades about silicone breast implants; about high estrogen levels in birth control pills; about dangerous IUDs; about vaginal mesh, or industrial hospital birthing practices and high for-profit C-section rates—my bio changed everywhere, online, and all at once. Instead of being described as a leading voice of Third Wave feminism, with a string of honors, degrees, and awards after my name, I was now identified from the first sentence, on Wikipedia and everywhere else, as a "conspiracy theorist." Not being aware yet that AI had already been deployed journalistically, I did not even understand how that overnight change in my reputation had been accomplished.

I began to be left out of the social events that had resumed, in New York, after almost everyone had rushed to get vaccinated; I was cut off the guest lists that had once sought to have me. Hostesses told me that I was no longer welcome, as the hosts were "being careful."

Many journalists who had been my colleagues and some even my friends, and who had had no problem in the "Before" world seeking out favors and book endorsements from me, remained silent as I was portrayed as a lunatic and a QAnon aficionado. Others, who knew me and knew better, even joined in the melee.

———

After President Joe Biden gave his notorious and factually baseless December 2021 speech about how the unvaccinated were bringing "severe illness and death" onto themselves and everyone else, my friends and even some of my relatives began to shun me—and my equally scandalously unvaccinated husband.

> *But it's here now and it's spreading and it's gonna increase. . . .*
> *We are looking at a winter of severe illness and death for the*
> *unvaccinated—for themselves, their families and the hospitals*
> *they'll soon overwhelm.*[1]

There was no place left for us in communities that aligned with nonsense.

We had left New York City at the start of the pandemic and had moved into a little house in the woods in the Hudson Valley. Despite our physical separation from the heart of the culture, this bizarre ostracism really stung. And it went on and on. We were left out of family Thanksgivings. One of my best friends moved out of the city to another country, without saying goodbye; later she explained in an email that she had been "disappointed" in me for my position on the vaccine and the lockdowns. Another one of my oldest friends told me that I could not have dinner with him because "he does not sit indoors with unvaccinated people." A beloved elderly relative told me I could not even see him outside because he "does not sit outside with unvaccinated people." A family Christmas vacation was canceled at the last minute, after the President told all our loved ones that we would kill them with our very presence. No one in that world could hear me when I kept explaining that the vaccines did nothing to affect transmission.

It was as if a hex had been cast over everyone I loved, and over the entire culture in which I had, till so recently, felt so at home.

The nail in the coffin came on about June 19, 2021. I had posted a tweet warning that women were experiencing menstrual dysregulation—to say the least—upon having received mRNA vaccines. You don't have to be a biologist to know that this is a serious signal of something going very wrong with a woman's health. And it was obvious that if women were having horrible problems with their periods in 2021, there would be fertility issues—as there are—in 2023.

But after I posted this tweet, my world turned upside down. I was deplatformed from Twitter, Facebook, and YouTube. A wave of mocking news articles—centering on tweets that did not even *exist*, tweets I had immediately deleted as being badly worded—appeared simultaneously, in multiple languages, around the globe. Editors at the *Sunday Times* of London and the *Guardian* and the *Daily Mail*—editors who had commissioned my work for decades—ran similar hostile stories; some depicted me falsely as interested in QAnon (I barely knew what that was) and others as "unhinged." Matt Gertz of Media Matters and CNN mocked my tweet, and did a hit piece on me, for my daring to speak with Tucker Carlson on Fox News about my concerns regarding women's health. Former *New York Times* journalist Alex Berenson called me "batshit crazy." And so on.

Overnight, my world closed. No editor who had formerly commissioned me took my calls or replied to my emails now. An investor in my company withdrew a six-figure investment. I was persona non grata. And it seemed like a blanket fiat. No one who used to invite me to the glittering events of yesterday dared to contact me; not a single legacy media producer would cross the invisible no-go line that cordoned me off from the culture as a thinker. I was radioactive, for telling the truth; for telling the truth about women, as I have always done; for telling the truth about women—related to something unbelievably important.

When the Missouri and Louisiana attorneys general successfully sued the Biden administration,[2] we learned that this fiat had been so massive and so absolute because the administration—for whom I had voted—had coordinated with Twitter and Facebook attacks on "misinformation" online. The Centers for Disease Control (CDC), the Bureau of the Census, DHS, Twitter, and Facebook had all colluded to review lists that included my poor, brief, important, accurate tweet. Carol Crawford, "Chief, Digital Media Branch" of the CDC, on May 10, 2021, had sent out a "BOLO (Be On the LookOut)" alert about tweets and had included mine. I was put on a "misinformation" hit list. And so the CDC and the biggest tech companies in the world used the millions of dollars and gargantuan power at their disposal to close down my voice, along with other dissidents' voices.[3]

"The below are just some example posts. We do plan to post something shortly to address vaccine shedding and I can send that link soon. Our census team, copied here, has much more info on it if needed. Also, we are standing up a BOLO COVID misinformation meeting and inviting all tech platforms," wrote Ms Crawford.

My tweet, written in response to someone worried about abnormal bleeding post–mRNA vaccination, which Ms Crawford singled out, read: "Well hundreds of women on this page say they are having bleeding/clotting after vaccination or that they bleed oddly being AROUND vaccinated women. Unconfirmed, needs more investigation. But lots of reports."

That warning turned out to be accurate and important.

America First Legal also filed a lawsuit, and in July of 2022, they published documents confirming that my tweet, along with other tweets from other commentators warning women about miscarriages and menstrual damage suffered after mRNA injection, was in the CDC's "BOLO" email alert to tech companies.[4]

This global reputational attack proved to be both a heartbreak and an opportunity. My life completely changed. I thought that no one would ever want to hear from me again; but, paradoxically, conservative, libertarian, and independent news outlets and podcasters—a whole world of citizens who cared, as I did, about the Constitution, and about women and babies—sought me out. My life changed even more powerfully when in early 2022, the Pfizer documents were released via court order—the FDA had asked the court to keep them hidden for seventy-five years—and I was prompted by Steve Bannon on his podcast, *WarRoom*, to organize scientists and physicians into a phalanx of experts to read through the highly technical documents and to write reports explaining what was in them.

I was joined, rather miraculously, by the only person whom I can imagine running such a complex, important undertaking: Amy Kelly, the program director overseeing the dozens and then hundreds and finally thousands of experts who sought to join this historic undertaking. She is also now my company DailyClout's chief operating officer. A petite, lovely woman with shoulder-length blonde curls like those of a heroine in an Edwardian novella, her steely mind and inexplicably effective organizational genius defy every stereotype. She turned thousands of experts into an unstoppable truth machine, capable of confronting and ultimately overcoming phalanxes and battalions of lies.

At last, 3,250 distinguished doctors and scientists, including pathologists, oncologists, radiologists, cardiologists, sports medicine physicians; registered nurses and nurse practitioners; biologists; lab clinicians; medical fraud investigators; biostatisticians; and other experts joined our project. These experts—all working as volunteers, simply for the sake of real science and medicine, and for the good of humanity—produced what I consider to be some of the most important journalism of our time: the eighty-four reports that reveal that Pfizer committed the greatest crime against humanity in recorded history; with a special focus on destroying the reproductive capacity of human females.[5]

"As for you, you meant evil against me, *but* God meant it for good in order to bring about this present result," concludes Joseph, in Genesis 50:20.[6] The highest levels of power in this country sought to silence me; yet I was sent by this cancellation on a journey that brought me new friends, new insights, new questions, and the privilege, along with Amy Kelly and these courageous volunteers, of alerting the world to a danger that put humanity itself in jeopardy.

Today Pfizer has lost 89 percent of its manufacturing demand, and at least a substantial portion of humans are going to survive its assault.

What readers will find in this book is a story of a world that changed, bit by bit, into its dark opposite. I am sure it mirrors many of their own stories.

On looking back, I see that I sought to describe three things. First, I wanted simply to be an accurate and reliable witness to a world in a state of degradation and, I hope, also to testify to seeds of its rebirth. In this task, I bore in mind a work by an "ordinary citizen," a German scholar of French literature, Victor Klemperer, who kept a journal during the descent into barbarism of the Nazi years. It was published as *I Will Bear Witness: A Diary of the Nazi Years, 1933–1941*.[7] When I read that book, I realized how important it was to have such journals, since they record indeed how fascism does not descend overnight, but moment by moment, loss by small loss. I was also very moved by and related to Klemperer's stance squarely in the ideals of the Enlightenment—in his belief that culture and literature, the ideals of civilization, cannot be abandoned and must ultimately surely save us again. His faith in the ideals of the Enlightenment, and of a civilized culture, heightened his shock and outrage when those ideals were trampled before his eyes. I too feel, as I witness the destruction of our world today in the West, that we must cherish the memories of a civilized and literate society if we are to save one another and rebuild. So, one task I set myself was simply to, as Klemperer did, "bear witness."

A second theme that drove the writing of this book was my slow-dawning realization that we were not in a normal time of normal bad human politics and normal bad destructive material choices. I realized gradually that the degradation taking place on the material plane simply reflected or manifested a much larger battle—indeed a spiritual battle; one between Good and Evil themselves, and that God—whom till now I hesitated to mention in public—was of course central to what we were witnessing; and He is central, I slowly realized, to whether or not we will survive.

Lastly—relatedly—this book is about how I realized that the pandemic, lockdown, and mandate policies strove to destroy human love, care, and intimacy; that it was human love, care, and intimacy that have saved us, individually and collectively, and that will save us again, if we are to be saved. And I discovered that it is only in human love, care, and intimacy, ultimately, that God lives, and moves in, and rescues, if they are to be rescued, our lives.

Will we live through this? I have concluded, as you will see, that that is up to choices we now make. The attack on humanity is far from over. Pfizer and Moderna may have crashed as stocks, as I write, in August of 2023,[8] but on the near horizon are other existential threats to our liberty and survival, ranging from GMO mosquitoes bearing malaria released intentionally in Texas and Louisiana, to arson-set or negligence-enhanced wildfires that are destroying communities in Canada and Maui as I write, to explosive derailments on our transport systems, to grid outages, to attacks on our food supplies, to the rollout of a central bank digital currency worldwide that can track our spending and cut us off for "social credit" violations; to the debanking of dissident voices, such as Dr. Joseph Mercola's, recently, by Chase Bank.[9] A drumbeat of scary stories about scary COVID variants is audible as well.

Most alarming of all is the insistence by our leaders of a global adherence to a WHO framework that supersedes national sovereignty; if that goes through, anything can be done to us.

I have long been predicting that all of this would unfold, around now. My predictions of all these kinds of attacks, which I made in public over the past two years, are all coming true, and not because I am prescient. They are inevitable now based simply enough on my reading of past histories. The bad guys are not done with us. Their goal is still a global feudalism.

Despite these horrors, and these escalating dangers, I think you will find as you read that I believe that we are also are in a time in which we may witness and receive incredible potential blessings—and experience incredibly rapid evolution—depending on what we choose to do; morally, and as humans fighting for humanity.

This is the story of my cancellation, my survival, my witnessing of an all-out attack on humanity, and my stumbling into an awareness of what holds us and upholds us all.

And this is an account of the unseen gifts and energies and presences along our way; the help and resources—especially as they derive from within our own hearts, deeds, and consciences, human actions that apparently call forth angels—that I believe, in spite of it all, still can save us.

CHAPTER ONE

A Lost Small Town

In March 2020, my husband and I moved from South Bronx to a picture-perfect region in the country—the Hudson Valley—memorialized by painters and poets; it was a patchwork of green trees and yellow fields, majestic hillsides, storied waterfalls, and little homesteads dotted picturesquely on the slopes of sleepy hamlets.

Little did I know, when we moved there, that it would provide me with an illustration, in miniature, for the damage that the pandemic (or, shall I say, "the pandemic," because, as I proved in other analyses, the data on which this story was told, was always compromised and unverifiable) and the reaction to the pandemic—did to our culture, and to our civic life.

And the damage that it did to our hearts.

Towns in our area look like Norman Rockwell paintings: there is Main Street, Millerton. It has a white nineteenth-century church steeple, and the super-cute and foodie-famous Irving Farm New York cafe, with its excellent curated coffee beans. It has a charming antiques mall, a popular pizzeria.

When you drive to Millerton, it looks like you are driving into the heart of archetypal America. Everything that Woody Guthrie songs memorialize, everything of which American soldiers dreamt when they were far away—all that is decent and pure—is to be found in Hudson Valley towns.

It sure looks that way, anyway.

But now I am obliged to maintain a fervent inner monologue, just so I can pleasantly go about my business in the local hardware store, in the local florist, in the post office.

Because an emotional massacre took place in these little towns, across America. And now we are expected to act as if this has never happened at all.

Psychically, though—emotionally—there is blood flowing in the streets. Bodies are stacked up, invisible, in front of the candy stores, the high-end wine stores, the pretty memorials to the World War Two dead; outside the farmers' market on Saturdays, outside the tapas bars.

So, my quiet, internal mantra, is: "I forgive you."

I forgive you, Millerton movie theater. Your owner, who was interviewed just before the pandemic, saying lovely things in a local paper about how the revamped theater would enhance the local community, posted a sign in 2021 declaring that only vaccinated people could enter. You needed to really hunt out the fine print to ascertain that you *could* walk through those doors if you were unvaccinated, but only if you were bearing a negative PCR test.

I forgive the young ladies who worked behind the popcorn counter for telling me that I could not enter further; that I could not sit down with other human beings in my community, to watch a film alongside my neighbors.

I forgive the young ticket-taker for telling me that I had to go back outside, onto the sidewalk; that I could not even stand in the lobby.

I forgive these young people who just wanted jobs and who had to discriminate in the most heinous and scarring of ways—scarring to me, but also to them, no doubt—in order to keep their jobs.

I forgive them. I forgive them for the mortifying scene they were forced to cause.

I forgive the movie theater owner for shouting at me defensively when I questioned this policy.

I forgive the elderly couple in the lobby; the woman who started shrieking at me alarmingly that she was glad of the policy and that she did not want me anywhere near her. I forgive her. I forgive her silent, embarrassed husband for his silence.

I forgive the employee of the Millerton flower shop who demanded of me, the moment I walked in, "Are you vaccinated?"—when I just wanted some nice-looking flowers, some artificial olive branches, perhaps, like those I had seen in a decorating magazine, to arrange in a vase in my study.

I forgive this employee for having to follow a script that must have been set out by the county or by the State for all the small businesses to follow, in some bizarre, coercive methodology, as this out-of-the-blue, un-American and inappropriate question was posed all at once somehow, in store after store, in my little town, and in the nearby towns, and even in New York City, during a certain moment in the bad year of 2021.

I forgive these store owners for stripping me of a great benefit of a free society—the immeasurable gift of liberty, of America: the right to be dreamy, to have some privacy, and to be preoccupied with one's own thoughts.

I forgive this employee for intruding on my privacy in a way that was startling, ill-mannered, and entirely beside the point, given the fact that she was simply selling flowers, and I was simply trying to buy them.

I forgive her for the way this demand made my adrenaline levels jump, as they do when things are unstable around you. In 2021, you could not tell which employees in which stores would confront you, or with what tone, or when, with that urgent, bullying question—when you happened to wander in, just wanting some toothpaste, or a slice of pizza, or to look at some antiques.

Not expecting an inquisition.

I forgive this flower shop employee for presenting me with this abrupt, invasive question that each time made me, with my clinically diagnosed PTSD from a very old trauma, feel ambushed, violated, and humiliated, all at once. Surely this sense of ambush was felt by trauma survivors everywhere.

Are you vaccinated?

Are you? Vaccinated?

Are you vaccinated?

Are you naked? Are you helpless?

Are you mine? My possession?

The viral clip of the president of international markets at Pfizer, Janine Small, admitting to the European Parliament in October 2022 that the mRNA vaccines were never tested to stop transmission, should have made every one of these moments into sources of deep embarrassment and causes for self-criticism for all those people who inflicted these violations of privacy on others or who excluded in any way their neighbors, their fellow countrymen and women.[1]

They did so, it is clear now to all, based on arrant nonsense.

But meanwhile, I forgive them. I must. Because otherwise the rage and sorrow would exhaust me to death.

I forgive my neighbor who froze when I hugged her.

I forgive my other neighbor, who told me that she was making home-made soup and fresh bread, and that I could join her to have some, *if* I was vaccinated. If I was unvaccinated, however, she explained, someday she might consent to walk outdoors with me.

I forgive the monitor—what else could one call him—surely appointed by the local Board of Health, who told me that I could not go inside a church at an adorable outdoor town festival at the tiny forested hamlet of Mount Washington, to see an exhibit, because I was unmasked. I forgive him for the steely look in his eyes as he remained unmoved when I explained that had a serious neurological condition and thus could not wear a mask. I forgive the nervous lady at the table full of trinkets, who had apparently ratted us out to the Board of Health representative, when we were simply browsing outdoors, surrounded by fresh air, on a peaceful June day, our faces uncovered, at her table.

I forgive them for making a miserable scene about all of this in front of my then-ten-year-old stepson. The unmasked and unvaccinated are eternally accused of having made scenes, but the scenes were made, really, by the actions of those who were conforming and coercing.

I forgive them for forcing us to leave the festival. I forgive their demonstrating a pathetic and indefensible lesson in servility, and in submission to "orders" that made no sense, in front of an impressionable American child.

I forgive the teller at my local bank for throwing a paper napkin at me to cover my face, when I explained respectfully and gently, from twenty feet away from her, why I did not wear a mask.

I forgive the staff at the Walker Hotel, in lower Manhattan, for warning me that they would call the manager, who would then call law enforcement, if I sat at the Blue Bottle Coffee lunch counter with my unvaccinated self.

I forgive my loved ones for keeping us from the Thanksgiving table.

I forgive one of my best friends for leaving the country without saying goodbye to me; the reason was that she was "disappointed" in me for my stance on masks and vaccines. No matter that this was entirely my risk, my body, my decision, my life. Her "disappointment" led her to assume the burden of censuring me for something that had nothing to do with her. I forgive her, though my heart broke.

I forgive the friend whose daughter had a baby, and who would not let me indoors to see the child.

I forgive the friend who said he did not sit indoors with unvaccinated people.

I forgive the family members who pressed my loved one to get one more booster—thus leading directly to her sustaining heart damage.

I forgive them because my soul instructs me that I must.

But I cannot forget.

Are we supposed to just pick up again, as if emotional limbs were not crushed, as if hearts and guts were not pierced as if with sharp objects?

As if there has been no savagery, no massacre here?

All those people—now that athletes are dropping dead, now that those people's own loved ones are sickening and hospitalized, now that the "transmission" is known to be a lie and the vaccines' "efficacy" itself is known to be a lie—are they—sorry? Are they reflecting upon themselves, on their actions, on their consciences; on their immortal souls; on what they have done to others; on their part in this shameful melodrama in American and world history—a time that now can never be erased?

I don't hear it. I don't hear any apologies.

I don't see signs on the Millerton movie theater saying, "Dear Customers. We are so sorry we treated many of you as if we were all living under Jim Crow laws. We did so for no reason at all.

There is no excuse, of course, for such discrimination, then or now. Please forgive us."

Nothing. Have you seen or heard anything like this? I haven't. Not one conversation. Not one sign. Not one article. "My friend, I was a beast. How can you forgive me? I behaved so badly." Have you heard that? No, nothing.

Instead, people have reacted to the fact of their awfulness, of their profound wrongness, of their foolishness, of their ignorance and credulity, like sneaky, guilty dogs. They sidled up.

In the city, they quietly began adding one to the guest list. In the country, they began stopping their cars in the sunny air to have a little chat.

They began calling up just to say "Hi"—after two and a half years.

Two and a half years of brutal, ignorant ostracism.

I can and must forgive all those whom I enumerated. But it is harder to forgive—others.

That personal, inward forgiveness of deluded individuals, or of coerced small business owners, which is my own internal labor—work I do daily between myself and my God, just so that I won't turn to stone—has nothing to do, of course, with the wrongdoers' need on their side of the relationship, truly to self-examine and truly to repent. And it certainly does not avert the grave and terrible accounting of crimes, and the enactment of true justice, for the leaders and spokespeople and institutions who committed evil, that is now utterly necessary.

Without accountability, and truth and reconciliation commissions, and terrible, commensurate levels of justice served up to suit the crimes committed, as South Africa, Sierra Leone, Rwanda, and Germany have all learned to their cost, there is nothing at all to ensure that the exact same crimes won't be committed again.

And yes, I write this with a clear memory of COVID mania apologist Emily Oster's ignorant, self-deluding, and dangerous plea in the *Atlantic* for "amnesty," "Let's Declare a Pandemic Amnesty," published on October 31, 2022:

> *The people who got it right, for whatever reason, may want to gloat. The people who got it wrong, for whatever reason, may feel defensive. . . . Treating pandemic choices as a scorecard on which some people racked up more points than others is preventing us from moving forward. We have to put these fights aside and declare a pandemic amnesty.*[2]

Or, no. It's not about a "scorecard." It is about a series of crimes.

Let there be no misunderstanding. "Amnesty" for crimes of this severity and scale is not an option. There was no group hug after the liberation of Auschwitz.

It is hard to forgive the high school in Chatham that forced a teenager to be mRNA-vaccinated against her wishes, to play basketball, and thus hope for a college scholarship. Those officials must be held accountable.

It is hard to forgive the doctors, the hospitals, the pediatricians, who knew and knew and knew. And bowed their heads, and plunged the needles into the arms of innocents, and committed evil. The doctors who today say, of the horrific side effects brought about by their own hands, their own collusion—"We are baffled. We have no idea."

When did Western doctors, before 2020, *ever* have no idea?

The doctors and hospitals and medical organizations—who were discovered in 2023 to have taken money wholesale from the US Department of Health and Human Services—which they received only if they stuck to the HHS "script"—must be held accountable.[3]

It is hard to forgive the mayors of New York City, Bill de Blasio and Eric Adams, who both drove the brave first responders who did not wish to submit to a dangerous experiment into joblessness, with no income with which to feed their families. They and other political leaders must be held accountable.

It is hard to forgive the Ivy League universities, that took the money from HHS and then delivered the bodies of their students, by forcing almost all the members of their communities to submit to a deadly or dangerous experimental injection—one that will damage the fertility of many young women and will damage the hearts of many young men; one that will kill community members.

They took the money and there is blood on their hands. Have you, parents of college-age children, received a letter of apology? "We are so sorry we forced your son/daughter to submit to an experimental injection that can harm him/her, that may cripple your daughter with bleeding every single month of her childbearing years, and that may lead your son to drop dead on the track field. And one that, it turns out, has nothing to do with transmission. We can't apologize enough. (But the money—it was just such a lot.) Really sorry. Won't do it again, rest assured."

Did you get that letter, America's parents?

The deans and trustees who took the money and "mandated" our kids—and some still do, to this day—must be held accountable.

It is almost impossible to forgive the churches, the synagogues, who took the money and stayed closed. Or who took the money, and then locked their doors at High Holy Day Services against the unvaccinated. (Hi there, Hevreh Synagogue of Southern Berkshire. Shalom. Shabbat Shalom. Good Yom Tov.)

"Please note that we require proof of vaccination upon entry for all High Holy Day Services. Please bring a copy with you. Masks are optional and encouraged for all who are comfortable wearing them."

The rabbis and priests and ministers who took the money and practiced unlawful discrimination, and abandoned their spiritual calling, must be held accountable.

These are great sins.

But meanwhile, you have errands to run. You have books to return to the library and flowers to pick up from the florist; you must go to the kids' soccer game, you must go to the movie theater, the hardware store. Back to church. Back to synagogue.

You must pick up your life again.

You must step around the bodies decomposing invisibly in the charming streets of our nation. You must pick up again as if you were not annihilated in spirit. Or you must pick up again if you were the abuser.

Will you apologize if you did wrong?

Will you forgive if you were wronged?

Can this nation, which fell so far short of its identity and its Founders' intention, ever heal?

Can we heal ourselves?

Forgiveness on an internal level—of coerced or deluded individuals—may help us or heal us as private individuals.

But only the gravest of reckonings, the truth pursued to its limit in every single case, investigations and trials launched according to the beautiful rule of our law, and somber justice then served to leaders, spokespeople, and institutions—hey Dr. Oster—will ever allow us to heal, or even move safely forward together—as a nation.

CHAPTER TWO

Opening Boxes from 2019

I n fall of 2019, when we moved out of what had been my home in the West Village, I thought I was simply moving from one place to another. I was excited to build a new home, this time in the South Bronx.

It turned out that Brian and I lived in the South Bronx for only four months, until March 11, 2020. That day, we looked at one another and realized we had to get into his SUV and keep driving north to Millerton.

Why? Because then-Governor Andrew Cuomo announced that Broadway was closing—just like that, a Chinese Communist Party–style State fiat, not an American-style individuals-dealing-with-an-emergency announcement. We both realized that bad things were coming, though whether natural or political we could not yet tell.

As a result of those two moves, twenty years of my possessions had remained, for the past two and a half years, in a storage unit.

So I was now opening boxes that were not just from another place—as is typical when you move; not just from another time; I was opening boxes that were from literally another world. I don't know that such a thing had happened in quite this way in history before.

Some items memorialized normal life losses and normal change. Others, though, revealed that, between the time they were packed and now that they were being unpacked, long-revered institutions had lost all morality and authority.

Here was a grey sweater that had belonged to my father, who had been a writer. It still had the line of loose threads along the clavicle, the little gaps opening in the sewn-together pieces, characteristic of his distinguished-but-absent-minded-professor look. Dr. Leonard Wolf could wear a moth-eaten sweater on a street in New York City and still look like a Byronic poet preoccupied with his latest sonnet. He looked stylish even when he was bedridden—even when advancing Parkinson's meant he could no longer communicate with words, his treasures; even when gestures failed him, and when my husband, an Irish raconteur, sat by his bedside, telling stories to make him laugh. He managed to have élan even when Brian had to ask him to make a sound to let him know if he wanted the stories to continue, and my dad could only groan: yes, more stories.

The stories have ended now for my father, at least the earthly ones. But the sweater still carries that wintry, breezy scent that was his while he was on this earth, telling us stories, more stories.

I folded my father's sweater for the mending pile.

A small brown dog toy surfaced, chewed so thoroughly in one section that only the white lining remained. The little dog who had enjoyed the toy is no more. His dog tag is nailed to a tree that leans over the river in the woods, near where we now live.

I put the chewed-up toy on the discards pile.

There was the little white wooden armoire I had hand-painted—amateurishly but with love—for a child's room. The armoire was not needed any more. That child—everyone—had grown up.

There were many boxes of what had once been exciting, culturally meaningful CDs and DVDs. I sighed—what to do with these now? The technology itself was obsolete.

Then there were the pillows. Floral pillows, tufted pillows. Even I knew these were tasteless, and I'd known that even at the time that I had bought them. When my loved ones were old enough to notice aesthetics, they would chorus, when I brought home a new find: "Mom! Please! No more *florals!*"

I had been obsessed then with accumulating not only florals, but warm colors—cranberry and scarlet, terra-cotta, apricot, peach.

With the eyes of the present, and now in a happy marriage, I realized what had pushed me in the past to acquire all these redundant soft florals. I had longed for domesticity and warmth but had been, as a single mother then, dating the wrong kind of man if I wished to *get* domesticity and warmth. So I had unconsciously kept choosing softness and coziness in decor because I was missing it in my relationship.

The man, a gifted, mercurial charmer, had also, in the past few years, passed away; young; of a wasting cancer.

I sighed again and put the floral pillows in the donations pile.

————

Other objects in the opened boxes, though, did not speak of organic loss and change, but rather of worlds of authority that had seemed sparkling and real in 2019, but that have revealed themselves since then to be seething with rot.

Here was the brown, pleated, Grecian-style dress, with the bared arms and gathered waist, that I had worn to a wedding on Martha's Vineyard in the early 2000s.

Brown is a color I almost never wear, and I had never worn that Grecian style of formal dress briefly fashionable in the *Friends* era; so I remembered, as I shook it out into the sunlight of two decades later, that I had felt quite daring on that night.

The wedding had been in an event hall nestled in the dunes. Local seafood hors d'oeuvres had been passed on silver trays. The bride had been smoldering and lovely in a white lace Vera Wang (always Vera Wang) dress. All was as it should have been.

The wedding had brought together White House politicos, *Washington Post* op-ed writers and reporters, brash young New York City political speechwriters and campaign managers, and trendy nonfiction writers who were already making names for themselves. We were all in our mid- to late-30s—we were fomenting change, approving of ourselves, making a difference; we were like *The West Wing*, we thought (one of our friends consulted for it)—idealistic, unintentionally a bit chic, madly hopeful.

We *were* the scene.

I almost recoiled now with sorrow and anger. I folded up that dress, thinking about the institutions that had undergirded our optimism on that distant night, when our confidence had rung out onto the languid, salty breezes, along with the sound of the ultra-hip blues band.

The major newspapers? The once-young journalists? The two and a half years beginning in March 2020 had shown them to be shills for genocidal imperial powers. They became media versions of sex workers, scheduling time to deliver blow jobs to whomever would write them the biggest checks.

The once-young, *West Wing*–style politicos? The last two and a half years had shown them willing to become policy wonks for a global march to tyranny that instrumentalized a murderous medical experiment on their fellow humans, on their very constituents.

Where now were those institutions that at that wedding had filled us with pride and a sense of mission as we took our part in building them?

Imploded morally; left without a shred of authority or credibility.

I put the brown dress on the Goodwill pile.

I turned to an old scheduling notebook. It recorded some visits to Oxford. We'd been at a dinner party in North Oxford, hosted by the warden of Rhodes House. It was attended by the vice chancellor of the university and by many other luminaries. Indeed, the evolutionary biologist Dr. Richard Dawkins had been a guest; he'd been pestered, as he no doubt often was, by a dinner attendee who had wanted to talk to him about his atheism.

It had been a sparkling evening. I'd felt privileged to be at a table where some of the greatest minds of my time were gathered and where the leader of a great university was helping to convene us.

I loved Oxford with a pure love. The university had sustained a vibrant commitment to the principles of reason and to freedom of speech for over 900 years. It had supported the asking of questions when it was dangerous to ask questions; from just after what used to be called the Dark Ages; through the High Middle Ages; through the Reformation; through the Enlightenment. It had tended faithfully, through the darkest of times, the unquenchable flame of the wakeful mind of Europe.

The legacy of critical thinking of the West—was Oxford's legacy.

But—in 2021—Oxford University too had complied with a requirement that its students endure "online learning"—a demand that had no basis in reason, or in the natural world.[1]

This damage done to its trusting young people was a travesty of the great innovation that the University of Oxford had given to the world—the tutorial system, in which being physically present with a couple of other students and with a don (professor) in his or her study, opens dimensions of rigorous scholarly discourse in a magical and irreplaceable way.

"Online learning"? At *Oxford*? An institution that had survived plagues and epidemics that dwarfed the respiratory disease of 2020 to 2022, that had survived wars and revolutions, and that had taught students nobly in the face of crises of all kinds?

I did not know if I would ever go back to Oxford; and, if I did, what I would find there or how I would feel. I did not even know if today's Oxford would welcome me back, being, as I was by 2022, a "reputational refugee," having been canceled institutionally in most of what had been my intellectual homes.

My heart hurt once more. I put the old notebook in the storage pile.

I unfolded a tablecloth I had bought in India. I'd visited a literary conference in Tamil Nadu in about 2005 and had brought the fabric home as a souvenir.

A flood of memories surged as I looked at the once-familiar pattern.

I'd hosted so many parties in my little West Village apartment that had centered on that hand-blocked tablecloth. I'd set out a big pot of turkey chili—my go-to option, the only dish I could not ruin; I'd pile cut-up baguettes on platters, and assemble bottles of cheap red wine, all on that tablecloth. Thus, I could, as a broke single mom, affordably entertain.

Those parties were fantastic. Crowded, lively, buzzy, with a sexy, intellectually engaging vibe. Filmmakers, actors, journalists, artists, novelists, academics, poets; a handful of the less-boring venture capitalists; all were crowded together, spilling out into the kitchen, the hallways. At a certain point in the evening, the noise would crescendo (my neighbors were tolerant) into the happy roar of new ideas clashing or merging; new friendships, new contacts, new lovers, connecting and engaging.

In 2019, I had still been part of the New York City social scene. My life, as I noted, was full of events, panels, lectures, the watching of rehearsals and film premieres, and art gallery openings. I thought that my place in the society in which I traveled was unquestioned, and that I was in a world in which this calendar of events, these parties, this community, above all this ethos, would last forever.

Where was that society now? Artists, filmmakers, journalists—all of the people who are supposed to say No to discrimination, No to tyranny—had scattered. They virtually all had cowered and had complied. Indeed, they had groveled.

The same people who had been the avant-garde of a great city had gone right along with a society in which a person such as I am, cannot enter a building.

And I had fed those people. I topped up their drinks with my affordable red wines.

I had welcomed them into my home.

I had supported their careers. I had fostered connections on their behalf. I had blurbed their books and promoted their gallery openings because—we were allies, right? We were *intellectuals*. We were *artists*. We were even *activists*.

And yet these people—these same people—had complied—eagerly! With zero resistance! Immediately! With a regime that is appearing day by day to be about as bad in some ways as that of Marshal Philippe Pétain's in Vichy France.

Unthinkable to me now that I had treated them once as colleagues, as friends.

I had been made into a nonperson, overnight. You will recall, as America First Legal disclosed on July 27, 2022, after a Freedom of Information Act request to the CDC, the CDC had colluded with Twitter officials, in reaction to the tweet of mine calling attention to menstrual problems post-mRNA vaccination, to erase me from the worlds of both legacy media and digital discourse. A smear campaign that was global in its dimensions had been orchestrated after Twitter and Facebook aligned with CDC's digital communications czar Carol Crawford, as internal emails showed.[2] Then, in July 2023, a lawsuit, led by Missouri Attorney General Eric Schmitt and then by Missouri Attorney General Andrew Bailey—*Missouri v. Biden*—which I mentioned above—revealed that the White House itself colluded with Big Tech to censor American citizens; my tweet being in that tranche as well.[3]

As if we were characters in a Lewis Carroll book, the world of meritocracy had been inverted.

The highest level of government collusion was directed at me the minute I did just exactly what I have done for thirty-five years; that is to say, the minute I raised, in summer of 2021, a grave women's health concern. Confusingly, my advocating in exactly this way regarding serious women's health journalism and for proper medical responses to women's sexual and reproductive health issues had made me a media darling for thirty-five years. Indeed, this practice had made me sought-after among those very people, who had eaten my food and drunk my wine, while sitting around this very tablecloth.

But now, when I did the exact same thing for which they had long applauded me, I was cast immediately into social and professional outer darkness.

Why? Because the times had changed.

And because the scale of the revenue generated for them by supporting flat-out lies had changed.

Did any of those right-on people—many of them famous feminists, male and female—speak up for me? Did any of them publicly say, wait a minute, whatever the truth may turn out to be (and I was right, right, right)—this is a serious women's health issue? Let's explore it?

Not. A. One.

The bold, brave, edgy New York City avant-garde, whom I had hosted for twenty years?

They were scared off by *Twitter*.

That world surely shunned me, and made me a nonperson, overnight. The power of the federal government is stunning, especially in collusion with the biggest content companies in the world, when you are on the receiving end of being erased by them.

That world rejected me.

But I rejected it right back.

We live in the woods now. Instead of the din of parties, the chatter of the literati, Brian and I are surrounded by crowds of tall, solemn trees; the excitement of our days centers on sightings of cranes and hawks. The dramas we face involve living alongside coyotes and rattlesnakes and evading while yet marveling at the resident adolescent bear. We are making friends with those who grow food, in anticipation of needing to be self-sufficient. We just picked up from farmer acquaintances, to store in a massive freezer, something that was described with a phrase I had never heard in my previous, DoorDash life: our "quarter of a cow."

I was gifted a .22 by Brian. He bought me a Ruger as well. The world was falling apart even as a new world was emerging. A peaceful person though I am, I realize that we may someday need to hunt for food, or perhaps need, God forbid, to defend our home. I learned to shoot.

The old world, the pre-2019 world, is a scene of wreckage and carnage to me.

The old world I left behind, and that left me behind, is not a post-COVID world.

It is a post-truth world. A post-meritocracy world.

The institutions that supported the world, that existed when these 2019 boxes were packed, have all collapsed: in a welter of corruption, in an abandonment of public mission and public trust. I look at them now the way Persephone looked backward at Hades.

I am living in a new world already—a world that most people can't see yet, as it is still being envisioned and built up—painfully, daringly, laboriously. Though it exists at this point more conceptually and even spiritually than it does materially and politically, it is this new world that is my home.

Who else lives in the new world?

My husband, who was not afraid to fight for America, and who is not afraid to defend me.

A new constellation of friends and allies, who have emerged since these boxes were packed away, and since the worlds that are represented by them have collapsed under the weight of their own rot.

I work and party now with people who love their country and tell the truth. The people with whom I spend time are this era's versions of Thomas Paine, Betsy Ross, Phillis Wheatley, and Ben Franklin. I don't know how these folks vote. I don't know if they know how I vote. I don't care. I know that they are sterling human beings, because they are willing to protect the cherished ideals of this beautiful experiment, America.

Life experiences don't unite the people with whom I hang out now; social status does not unite them—they come from all walks of life, from every "class," and they pay little or no attention to status or class markers. Politics don't unite these people. What unites them in my view is the excellence of their characters.

Oddly, living now in the purple-to-red rural America that my former "people," the blue-state elites, are conditioned to view with suspicion and distrust, I also have more personal freedom than I did as a member of the most privileged class. The most privileged class does not have the greatest privilege of all, that of personal liberty: it is a class that is continually anxious and status-insecure, its members often scanning the room for a more important conversation, its collective mind continually exerting subtle control, both socially and professionally, over other members of the "tribe."

My former elite network paid lip service to "diversity," but there was a deadening sameness and conformity in our demographics, and that conformity also policed our world views, our voting patterns, even our kids' schools and our travel destinations.

In contrast, people here in deep purple-red country, the ones whom we know anyway, give each other the assumed permission to differ, to have uncensored opinions, to be free.

Even my social media community is not of the world I left behind in 2019; I can't even get onto most of those platforms anymore, as I am still extra-super-duper-ultra canceled.

But I don't know if I'd even want to be in those conversations now; the discourse of the elite-Left these days, "my people," seems fearful and in lockstep, scolding and rigid.

Now, my online community is made up of a world of people whom I never knew existed—or rather a world of people I was conditioned ignorantly to stereotype and to fear. I am in contact now with people who care about America, who believe in God or in a greater meaning in this world, people who put family first, and who turn out—who knew?—to be open-minded, civilized, and decent.

I spend time with people who love their communities; speak out for their actual brothers and sisters, meaning humanity; risk themselves to save the lives of strangers; and care about actual fact-based journalism, actual science-based medicine, actual science-based science.

These days I chat online with people who tell me, unfashionably but beautifully, they are praying for me.

Despite fighting an apocalypse every day, how can I help but be so much happier now?

————

I no longer want to sit at a table with people who call themselves journalists, but who deny or trivialize injuries to women at a scale that beggars belief, who give Pfizer and the Food and Drug Administration a pass and ask them no real questions.

I no longer want to sit at a table with people who are okay with the murder of children, the poisoning of breast milk, the burdening of women with the twenty different names in the Pfizer documents that all amount to menstrual pain and agony and the ruination of women's fertility. I don't want to do anything but prosecute the people who took money to cover up the damaging of women by means of "reproductive disorders," at scale.

These people, "my people," who were once so erudite, so witty, so confident, so ethical, so privileged—pretty and well-spoken as they once were, turn out, with the twist of just a couple of years, and just a bucketload or two of bribe money, to be revealed as monsters and barbarians.

I left the rest of the boxes to open another day.

There is no rush. The institutions the boxes memorialize are dead; and maybe they never really existed, as we believed them to be, in the first place.

I put the hand-blocked tablecloth on the "keep" pile. Then I took it home with me.

People who still have their honor intact will sit around our table.

CHAPTER THREE

What Is a Miracle?

Mushroom, our beloved and unbelievably elderly dog, passed away. There was a day when he simply pulled his snout back sharply at the offer of food, and from then on, his decline was rapid.

There was a day when I would come into the house and find him slouched like a little black-and-white parcel in unusual places such as the corners of the dining room, or else I'd see him oddly trying to stand behind the wood stove. There were days during which he lay in his bed, curled in a furry round circle as usual, but scarcely moving; the concern, practically the breath, of angels, was palpably over him.

Brian made broths and tried to feed him with a spoon. At last, the spoon was refused, and we knew we did not have long with him.

We called two vets; both were compassionate, but brisk, and quick to suggest euthanasia. "There's a vet service that comes to your house, very sensitively, to put your dog to sleep," explained one veterinary assistant. "This woman is great—you will love her."

"I don't think I'll love anyone who is coming over to euthanize my dog," I blurted out.

The other vet, a little less alarmingly, said that if we brought Mushroom to them, we could hug him in the back seat of the car while they "put him to sleep."

This directive, that we would arrange for the killing of our own dog inside our own car, may seem odd—it did to me; but at the time, people were not allowed to be with their pets inside veterinary offices, not even to hold them when saying goodbye to them. This brutality was on a spectrum with the diktat that we were not allowed to be with our elders, not even to hold their hands, when they passed away in hospitals or in nursing homes.

With heavy hearts we made the appointment.

That was one of the worst days of my husband's and my life. We both felt such a sense of wrongdoing, of negative, inharmonious, even profane forces around us.

We tried to prepare the car to take Mushroom to the vet, but everything went wrong. We noticed that the car was out of registration. We messed up the timing of the appointment. I forgot my phone and had to turn back. It seemed that we simply could not bring ourselves to pick up our little friend and take him, tucked comfortably in his favorite yellow blanket, curled up in his warm blue dog bed, to arrange for the end of his life.

When Mushroom seemed to rally a bit and accepted a sip of water, I called the vet and canceled. "It's not the right time," I explained.

Brian and I looked at each other with relief. We were each glad the other had reached the same conclusion.

"I just can't take my best friend to be executed," said Brian.

So, we knew that Mushroom would soon die at home, and we tried to make him comfortable and let him know how loved he was.

The days before his decline, I used to take him out to the bend in the river in the woods across the bridge from our house. I would hold him as he looked at the water—a burbling stretch heading toward a little waterfall—and he listened to its roaring music. As he faded, he became measurably lighter in my arms, still wrapped in his favorite yellow blanket.

Finally, he grew so weak that he could only look at the water for a short time, and then his head would sink, as his neck could no longer hold it up. But still he seemed to love that place, and I think he loved being there with me.

The day before he lay down in his bed without getting up, I was amazed at what I saw in the river: as he and I looked at his usual favorite place in the water, there was a single long-stemmed red rose, just hovering right under the surface of the water, perfectly horizontal. I am not kidding, and I am not exaggerating; it was an archetypal bright red rose just in bud, with a long green stem stripped of thorns; the kind of classic red rose that looks as if taken from a bouquet in a 1960s musical set in Paris.

What Is a Miracle?

I looked around. From where could it have come? Did someone drop trash from the bridge—and would a single rose have been among it and survived, in perfect condition like this? I saw a bit of detritus, so thought that must be the answer, and I called to Brian to come over. "Did someone dump their trash in our river, and this rose somehow was captured in this place in the water? Or is it a miracle?" I half-jokingly asked him.

He looked at the perfect bloom hovering just under the water, unmoving, though powerful currents poured around it. "What's a miracle?" he asked.

Every day I went down to the river as Mushroom was sinking, and then as he was dying. To my astonishment, the rose stayed just where it was, just under the surface of the water, for ten full days.

There were rains, and snow, and hail. The rose stayed put. The cold water must have kept it from decaying, because while its petals slowly opened, they did not bruise, tear, or fade. Two branches, improbably, formed the shape of a cross over the hovering, water-held rose.

On the last night of Mushroom's life, I had stayed upstairs. We both had murmured to him our different messages of comfort and of farewell. I had whispered into the soft, barely warm fur on top of his head that it was okay, he had been such a good dog, that Rosa and Joe were big now, that he had taken such good care of us all, and that we loved him, and that he could go now if he needed to.

Brian was tending to Mushroom. I fell asleep upstairs at last. At a few minutes past midnight, I felt Brian's hand on my shoulder: "He's gone."

———

The days after that were painful. There was an aching quality to the house. We awaited his ashes from the vet, and we planned to scatter them by the place where he used to love to look at the water.

Brian took the bone-shaped nametag that read "Mushroom" and nailed it to the tree that overlooked that bend in the river. He put Mushroom's blue plastic bowl down at the foot of the tree, weighted it with glass marbles, and filled it with water. Deer now came out of the woods, delicately, to drink from the blue bowl.

A day or so after Mushroom's passing, the rose was still in the water. But now, it started to release its petals. I am telling the truth.

The second night after Mushroom died, I had that horrible feeling you have when you are a mom, and you dream that you have misplaced your baby. I had cared for Mushroom for so long, and then Brian had joined me in caring for him, and now we could not care for him in any way. I started to tear up and tried to pray. "God, please take care of my little dog," I began, but that did not sound right. It felt like the wrong job description. God is super busy.

I am Jewish, and I have no idea who Mary really is, but some time ago I stopped trying to fit spiritual needs into boxes with labels. It just came to me in that moment to try again; so, I prayed, "Mother Mary, please look after my little dog."

And I wept and wept but felt comforted. Surely, she would.

That night I dreamt that Mary showed me the empty physical body of Mushroom, truly spent, almost broken with age. It was not a kindness to wish him back inside that body. And she then showed me with a gesture a lovely sight—Mushroom, but in a just-grown-past-puppy body, sleeping peacefully, the warmth of health and youth on him again. Wherever he was, he was fine.

"What's a miracle?" Did my subconscious produce a meaningless wish fulfillment, a fairy tale for me, just when I needed one, as Dr. Freud would have maintained? Maybe. Did an answer from the universe produce itself, making use of a symbol system that brought me comfort, just when I needed it to do so? Maybe.

Did a neighbor dump trash in our river that led to a rose hovering just under the water for ten days while our dog was dying? Maybe. Did the universe show us a symbol of perfect resilience, renewal, and beauty, just when we needed it? Maybe.

Why must these possibilities be dichotomous? Why must it be either/or? Perhaps the world in which we live is one in which all these things can be true at once.

The rose had teased my consciousness; the mystery of its appearance led me to look at saints, and at Mary figures bearing roses. I learned that Saint Therese is "the Little Flower," and that many believe that Saint Therese and Mother Mary will grace a petitioner with an unexpected rose, in response to prayer. Seeing the images online, when I searched, of beautiful saintly women, or of the Divine Mother herself, holding roses in their arms, was a balm.

As someone who had nurtured a little being, I needed to see a Divine Mother caring for us, and maybe even caring for the little creatures of this world, helping them into the next.

My own faith tradition did not have this kind of figure. But did that really matter? Are these divisions even relevant anymore? Was the miracle the rose itself—or the fact that I noticed it enough to learn about other ways the Divine Mother may possibly manifest in this suffering world?

A few weeks before Mushroom had started to fade, I was walking down our rural street; I was wrestling with the vast crimes committed against humanity—by pharma, by Davos, by tech, perhaps by Satan Himself; crimes whose documentation are the work I do every day, these days.

I felt overwhelmed; that any strength or skills I had were insignificant against the monumental powers arrayed against humanity. I could not see a way to victory, let alone to the survival of all the things we hold dear as free men and women. I was at the end of my ability to see a way ahead. "How can we ever overcome such adversaries?" I asked—Whoever was out there.

The road had been dark, as evening was falling, and the Taconic mountain range had been in shadow. But as I glanced up, the entire massive range of mountains lit up slowly, from one end to the other, with a blazing golden light. Half-a-state's length of pure gold light overspread the entire face of the mountain range and extended hundreds of feet high into the evening sky.

I started laughing.

It was as if God was saying, "Don't be so silly. Just look at me."

Was the depth of my despair answered by a massive blaze of gold, just when I needed a miracle?

Or was the miracle simply that I happened to look up and notice something I usually overlook—that miracles are simply all around us?

Or could it be both?

What *is* a miracle?

CHAPTER FOUR

Principalities and Powers

In the depths of lockdown, I spoke at a gathering for medical freedom advocates in a little community center in the Hudson River Valley. I cherish this group of activists: they had steadfastly continued to gather, and they kept on gathering, undaunted. By joining their relaxed potluck dinners around unidentifiable but delicious salads and chewy homemade breads, I was able to remember what it meant to be part of a sane human community.

Children played—as normal—frolicking around and speaking and laughing and breathing freely; not suffocating in masks like little zombies or warned by terrified adults to keep from touching other human children. Dogs were petted. Neighbors spoke to one another at normal distances, without fear or phobias. Bands played much-loved folk songs or cool little indie rock numbers they had written themselves, and no one, graceful or awkward, feared dancing. People sat on the house's steps shoulder to shoulder, in human warmth, and chatted over glasses of wine or homemade cider. No one asked anyone personal medical questions.

Meanwhile, what had been human community outside of that little group, and outside other isolated normal communities—and outside of a handful of normal states in America—became more and more surreal, terrifying, and unrecognizable.

The rest of the world, at least on the progressive side in the United States, became increasingly cultlike and insular in its thinking. As the months starting from March of 2020 passed, friends and colleagues of mine who were highly educated, and who had been lifelong critical thinkers, journalists, editors, researchers, doctors, philanthropists, teachers, psychologists—began to repeat only talking points from MSNBC and CNN, and soon overtly refused to look at any sources—even peer-reviewed sources in medical journals—even CDC data—that contradicted those talking points. These people literally said to me, when I offered primary-source evidence that challenged their views, "I don't want to see that; don't show it to me." Eventually they started to say, "This debate is over." Eventually they would storm off, or hang up, when I persisted.

It became clear soon enough that if they absorbed information contradictory to "the narrative" that was consolidating, they risked losing social status, maybe even jobs; doors would close, opportunities would be lost. One well-educated woman told me she did not want to see any unsanctioned information because she was afraid of being disinvited from her bridge group. Hence the refrain: "I don't want to see that; don't show it to me."

Friends and colleagues of mine who had been skeptical their whole adult lives of Big Agriculture—who only shopped at Whole Foods, who would never let their kids eat sugar or processed meat, or ingest a hint of Red Dye No. 2 in candy, or eat candy itself, for that matter, in some cases—lined up to inject into their bodies, and then offered up the bodies of their minor children for the same reason, an mRNA gene-therapy injection, whose clinical trials would not end for two more years. These parents announced on social media proudly that they had done this with the bodies of their children. When I pointed out gently that the trials would not end till 2023, they yelled at me and blocked me.

The progressive "woke" part of the ideological world—my people, my "tribe," my whole life—became more and more uncritical, less and less able to reason. Friends and colleagues who were wellness-oriented, and who, their whole adult lives, had known the dangers of Big Pharma—and who would only use Burt's Bees on their babies' bottoms and sunscreen with no endocrine-disrupting additives on themselves—lined up to take an experimental gene therapy; why not? And worse, they crowded around, like the stone throwers in Shirley Jackson's short story "The Lottery," to lash out at and to shun anyone who raised the most basic questions about Big Pharma and its highly compensated spokesmodels. Their critical thinking, but worse, their entire knowledge base about that industry, seemed to have evaporated magically into the ether.

Whole belief systems were abandoned painlessly overnight as if these communities were in the grip of a collective hallucination, like the witch craze of the fifteenth to seventeenth centuries in Northern Europe. Intelligent, informed people suddenly saw things that were not there, and were unable to see things that were before their faces.

Feminist health activists, who knew perfectly well the histories of how the pharmaceutical and medical industries had experimented on the bodies of women with disastrous results, lined up to take an injection that, by 2021, women were reporting was wreaking painful havoc on the female menstrual cycle. These same feminist health activists had spoken out earlier, as they should have, about Big Pharma's and Big Medicine's colonization of women's reproductive health processes. They had spoken out about issues ranging from women's access to safe contraception to abortion rights, to the rights of mothers to a midwife delivery or to a birthing room, to women's rights to labor without being rushed into unnecessary C-sections, to women's rights to store breast milk at work or to breastfeed their babies in public.

But these formerly reliable custodians of medical skepticism and of women's health rights were silent as such voices as former HHS official Dr. Paul Alexander warned that spike protein from mRNA vaccines accumulated in the ovaries (and testes), and as vaccinated women reported hemorrhagic menses—double-digit percentages in a Norwegian study reporting heavier bleeding.[1] Many women also reported blood clotting. Women even reported post-menopausal bleeding; mothers reported their vaccinated twelve-year-old girls suddenly got their periods upon being injected—but some young girls endured two periods a month.

Almost no one out of the luminaries of feminist health activism who had spent decades speaking out on behalf of women's health and female bodies, raised a peep above the parapet. Those two or three of us who did were very visibly smeared, in some cases threatened, and in many ways silenced.

When I broke this story of menstrual dysregulation post-vaccination on Twitter in summer of 2021, I was suspended, as I described earlier. Matt Gertz works at CNN and Media Matters. The former is a channel on which

I had appeared for decades; the latter, a group whose leadership members I've known for years, and in one instance, with whom I've worked.

Despite both of his employers having sought out professional association with me, Matt Gertz publicly called me a "pandemic conspiracy theorist" upon my first having warned of vaccinated women's reports of menstrual dysregulation, and elsewhere on social media accused me of "crack-pottery."[2]

Shame on me for doing journalism. I broke the post-vaccination menstrual dysregulation story by doing what I always do: by using the same methodology that I used in writing *The Beauty Myth* (about eating disorders) and *Misconceptions* (about obstetrics), and *Vagina* (about female sexual health).

I listened to women: that radical act.

The *New York Times* rebroke my story of menstrual dysregulation ten months later, January 2022, *in a different year*, after millions of women readers were physically harmed by the *Times's* lack of decent reporting any earlier, and by the newspaper's uncritical acceptance of soundbites from captured regulatory authorities.[3] There has been no retraction or apology from Mr. Gertz, from the *New York Times*, or from other news outlets such as DailyMail.co.uk, who did not challenge the consensus calling me crazy in 2021, but then began reporting my story as if it were their own.[4]

Feminist health advocates—who know about routine hysterectomies at menopause; about vaginal mesh that had to be surgically removed; about silicone breast implants that leaked or burst and had to be recalled or replaced; about Mirena IUDs that had to be removed as they caused perforated organs or fluid buildup in the skull; about the thalidomide that deformed babies' limbs in utero; about birth control pills at hormonal doses that heightened heart attack risks and stroke risks and that lowered women's libidos; about routine C-sections to speed up turnover at hospitals; about the sterilization of low-income women and girls, and women and girls of color, without informed consent—were silent now about the unproven nature of mRNA vaccines, and about coercive policies to force injections, that violated the Nuremberg Code and other laws. They were silent as a whole generation of young women who have not yet had their babies was forced to take an mRNA vaccine (and sometimes second vaccine and booster) with what would be catastrophic effects on their reproductive health, in order simply to return to campus or to get or to keep a job. The Our Bodies, Ourselves website? From the legendary women's health advocates, you can now learn "All About Orgasms" and find out anything you need to know about "chestfeeding," but there is not a peep about the dangers to fertility or menstrual health in the subject categories that address those topics.[5] NARAL Pro-Choice America? Where were they? Crickets. The author of the pregnancy bible *What to Expect When You're Expecting*, Heidi Murkoff, who warned pregnant women not to drink, smoke or eat sushi? This is from an ad for a book of hers, *Eating Well When You're Expecting*[6]:

> At the heart of the book are hundreds of pressing questions every mother-to-be has: Is it true I shouldn't eat any food cooked with alcohol? Will the caffeine in coffee cross into my baby's bloodstream? . . . Is all sushi off limits? . . . I keep dreaming about a hot fudge sundae—can I indulge?

What was this woman doing now—this woman, trusted by millions of moms-to-be, who knew perfectly well that what a mother ingests, crosses into the baby's bloodstream?

She was having a cozy sit-down chat with CDC director Dr. Rochelle Walensky, for her What to Expect Project website. In that chat, Murkoff's prior sober caution about introducing any potentially dangerous substance into an expecting mother's body had flown out of the window: "The two discuss everything from why the COVID-19 vaccine is safe for pregnant women to the risks of not getting vaccinated."[7]

Where were all the responsible feminist health activists, in the face of this global, unconsenting, uninforming, illegal experimentation on women's bodies, and then on children, and then on babies?

People who had been up in arms for decades about eating disorders or about the coercive social standards that led to—horrors—leg shaving, were silent about an untested injection that was minting billions for Big Pharma; an injection that entered, according to Moderna's own press material, every cell in the body, which would thus include the uterus, ovaries, endometrium.

The amnesia extended to feminist legal theory. Feminist jurists such as Justice Sonia Sotomayor and Justice Elena Kagan debated President Biden's vaccine mandates on the week of January 7, 2022—as if they had never heard of the legal claims for *Roe v Wade*: privacy law. Both Justice Kagan and Justice Sotomayor have long, distinguished histories as defendants of bodily autonomy and privacy rights—at least for women when it comes to abortion. As *Politico* reported of Justice Kagan,

> *The Supreme Court's ruling on privacy rights served as a basis for its later decision,* Roe v Wade *and as former Sen[ator] Barbara Boxer had stated, "I have no reason to think anything else except that [Kagan] would be a very strong supporter of privacy rights because everyone she worked for held that view."*[8]

Except . . . when it came to vaccine mandates, the two justices aren't "strong supporter[s] of privacy rights." With medical mandates, there are no privacy rights for anyone, ever.

Indeed, Justice Kagan seemed suddenly, after decades of supporting privacy rights, to not see a contradiction. Her career-long philosophical foundation that had resulted in a consistent view, when it came to abortion rights, that citizens had a right to physical privacy in medical decision-making—"My body, my choice"—"It is between a woman and her doctor"—vanished abruptly, along with her expensive education and all of her knowledge of the Constitution.

Justice Sotomayor, for her part, said, on December 10, 2021, that it was "madness" that the state of Texas wanted to "substantially suspend[ed] a constitutional guarantee: a pregnant woman's right to control her own body." Her tone was one of high dudgeon at the thought that anyone might override this right. But when it came to Justice Sotomayor's discussion on January 7, 2022, less than four weeks later, of President Biden's vaccine mandates, that awareness of a clear constitutional right to privacy was nowhere to be seen; it too had vanished into the ether, along with Heidi Murkoff's understanding of placentas and blood circulation. Part of Justice Sotomayor's brain seems to have simply shut down at the word "vaccines." Though it was the same woman in the same court, with the same Constitution before her, the justice could no longer manage the Kantian imperative of consistent reasoning.[9]

Lifelong activists for justice, for the Constitution, human rights, and the rule of law—friends and colleagues of mine who are LGBTQ rights activists; the American Civil Liberties Union itself; activists for racial equality; constitutional lawyers who teach at all the major universities and who run the law reviews; activists who argue against excluding anyone from any profession or access based on gender; almost all of them, at least on the progressive side of the spectrum—were silent; as a comprehensive, systematic, cruel, titanic discrimination society was erected in a matter of months in such cities as New York City, formerly the great melting pot and equalizer; and as whole states such as California adopted a system much like apartheid systems based on other physical characteristics, in regimes that these same proud advocates for equality and inclusion had boycotted in college.

And yet now these former heroes for human rights, and for equal justice under law, stood by calmly or even enthusiastically as a massive edifice of discrimination was constructed. And then they colluded. Without even a fight or a murmur.

And they had their "vaccinated-only" parties, and their segregated fashion galas, and their nonprofit-hosted discussions in medically segregated New York City midtown hotels over expensive lunches served by staffers in masks—lunches celebrating luminaries of the civil rights movement or of the LGBTQ rights movement or the immigrants' rights movement, or the movement to help girls in Afghanistan get access to schools that they had been prevented from attending—invitations which I received, but of which I could not make use, because—I was prevented from attending.

And these elite justice advocates enjoyed the celebrations of their virtues and of their values and did not notice that they had become—in less than a year—exactly what they had spent their adult lives professing most to hate.

The bottom line, though, is that this infection of the soul, this abandonment of modern civilization's most cherished postwar ideals—this edifice of evil was too massive, too quickly erected, to complex, and too elegant, to assign only to human awfulness and inventiveness. This sudden dropping of post-Enlightenment norms of critical thinking, this dilution of even parents' sense of protectiveness over the bodies and futures of their helpless children, this acceptance of a world in which people can't gather to worship; these structures themselves that had built up this demonic world in less than two years and imposed it on everyone else, these heads of state and heads of the American Medical Association and heads of school boards and these teachers; these heads of unions and these national leaders and the state-level leaders and the town hall level functionaries, all the way down to the men or women who disinvited a relative from Thanksgiving due to social pressure, because of a medical status which was no one's business and which affected no one—this edifice of evil was too massive, too quickly erected, too complex, and too elegant, to assign only to human awfulness and inventiveness.

Months before, I had asked a renowned medical freedom activist how he stayed strong in his mission as his name was besmirched, and as he faced career attacks and social ostracism. He replied with Ephesians 6:12: "For we wrestle not against flesh and blood, but against principalities, against powers, against the rulers of the darkness of this world, against spiritual wickedness in high places."[10]

I had thought of that response often in the intervening time. It made more and more sense to me.

I confessed, at that gathering in the woods with the health freedom community, that I had started to pray again. This was after many years of thinking that my spiritual life was not that important, and certainly very personal, almost embarrassingly so, and that thus it was not something I should mention in public.

I told the group that I was now willing to speak about God publicly, because I had looked at what had descended on us from every angle, using my normal critical training and faculties, and I had concluded that it was so elaborate in its construction, so comprehensive, and so cruel, with an almost superhuman, baroque imagination made out of the essence of cruelty itself—that I could not see that it had been accomplished by mere humans working on the bumbling human level in the dumb political space.

I felt all around us, in the majestic nature of the evil encompassing us, the presence of "principalities and powers"—awe-inspiring levels of darkness and of inhuman, anti-human forces. In the policies unfolding around us I saw anti-human outcomes being consistently generated: policies aimed at killing children's joy; at literally suffocating children, restricting their breath, speech, and laughter; at killing school; at killing ties between families and extended families; at killing churches and synagogues and mosques; and, from the highest levels, from the President's own bully pulpit down, demands for people to collude in excluding, rejecting, dismissing, shunning, hating their neighbors and loved ones and friends.

I have seen bad politics all my life, and this drama unfolding around us went beyond bad politics, which is silly and manageable and not that scary. This—was metaphysically scary. In contrast to hapless human mismanagement, this darkness had the tinge of the elemental evil that underlay and gave such hideous beauty to the theatrics of Nazism; it was the same nasty glamour that surrounded Leni Riefenstahl films.

In short, I don't think humans are smart or powerful enough to have come up with this horror all alone.

So I told the group in the woods that the very impressiveness of evil all around was leading me to believe in a newly literal and immediate way in the presence, the possibility, the necessity of a countervailing force—that of a God. It was a negative proof: an evil this large must mean that there is a God at which it is aiming its malevolence.

And that is a huge leap for me to take, as a classical Liberal writer in a postwar world; to say these things out loud,

Grounded postmodern intellectuals are not supposed to talk about spiritual matters—at least not in public. We are supposed to be shy about referencing God Himself and certainly are not supposed to talk about evil, or the forces of darkness.

As a Jew I come from a tradition in which hell (or *gehenom*) is not the Miltonic hell of the later Western imagination, but rather a quieter, interim spiritual place. "The Satan" exists in our literature (in Job for example), but this is not the Catholic or the Miltonic Satan, that rock star, but a figure more modestly known to us as "the accuser."

We who are Jews, though, do have a history and literature that lets us talk about spiritual battles between the forces of God and negative forces that debase, that profane, that seek to ensnare our souls. We have seen this drama before, and not that long ago; about eighty years ago.

Other faith traditions also have ways to discuss and understand the spiritual battle taking place through humans, and through human leaders, here on earth.

It was not always the case that Western intellectuals were supposed to keep quiet in public about spiritual fears and questions. Indeed, in the West, poets and musicians, dramatists and essayists and philosophers, talked about God, and even about evil, for millennia. These contesting powers were seen as being at the core of their understanding of the world and as forming the basis of their art and of their intellectual missions. This was true right through the nineteenth century and into the first quarter of the twentieth, a period when some of our greatest intellectuals—from Charles Darwin to Sigmund Freud to Carl Jung—wrestled often and in public with questions of how the divine, or its counterpart, manifested in the subjects they examined.

It was not until after World War Two and then after the rise of Existentialism—the glorification of a worldview in which the true intellectual showed his or her mettle by facing up to the absence of God and to our essential aloneness—that smart people were expected to shut up in public about God.

So, it's not wacky or eccentric, if you know history, for intellectuals to talk in public about God, and even about God's adversary, and to worry about the fate of human souls. Mind and soul are not in fact at odds; and the body is not in fact at odds with either of these. And this acceptance of our three-part, integrated nature is part of our Western heritage. This is a truth that was only recently obscured or forgotten; this memory of our integrity as human beings has been, only for the last seventy years or so, under attack.

So I am going to start talking about God, when I need to do so, and about my spiritual questions in this dark time. Because I have always told my readers the truth of what I felt and saw. This may be why they have come with me on a journey now of almost forty years, and why they keep seeking me out, though I have in the last couple of years—after I wrote a book that described how nineteenth-century pandemics were exploited by the British State to take away everyone's liberty—been pulped, deplatformed, canceled, recanceled, deplatformed again, and called insane, by dozens of the same news outlets that had commissioned me steadily for decades.

It is time to start talking about spiritual combat again. Because I think that that is what we are in, and the forces of darkness are so big that we need help.

What is the object of this spiritual battle?

It seems to be for nothing short of the human soul.

One side seems to be wrestling for the human soul by targeting the human body that houses it; a body made in God's likeness; the temple of God.

I am not confident. I don't have enough faith. Truth is, I am scared to death. I just don't think humans alone can solve this one or win this one on their own.

I do think we need to call—as John Milton did, as William Shakespeare did, as Emily Dickinson did—on help from elsewhere; on what could be called angels and archangels, if you will; on higher powers, whatever they may be; on better principalities, on whatever intercessors may hear us, on Divine Providence—whatever you want to call whomever it is you can hope for and imagine. As I often say, I'll take any faith tradition. I'll talk to God in any language. I don't think forms matter. I think intention is everything.

I can't say for sure that God and God's helpers exist; I can't. Who can?

But I do think we are at an unheard-of moment in human history—globally—in which I personally believe we have no other choice but to ask for assistance from beings—or from a Being—better armed to fight true darkness than we ourselves are alone. We'll find out if they exist, if He or She exists, perhaps, if we ask for God's help.

At least that's my hope.

Which I guess is a kind of prayer.

CHAPTER FIVE

Thinking Like a Tyrant

We can't fully understand where we were, and potentially still are, in this thicket of unknowing, unless we are willing to face the nature and sources of this evil.

Something that is slowing down many people from fully grasping what is upon us, is that they are making mistakes in their reasoning about events, because they are engaged, naturally enough, in what intelligence analysts call "mirror imaging." That is, because most of us are decent people with basic compassion at our cores, and are not sociopaths or psychopaths, we tend to "mirror image" in assuming that others are also driven by basic human motivations such as empathy, altruism, and kindness—or even just by the notion that other human beings are also deserving of life, self-determination, and dignity. How can such brutality be imposed on us? How could others be at the helm of such vicious policies?

But this assumption, that those who influence events and make certain key decisions are "like us"—is a fatal error.

To understand how a brutal tyranny could be enacted upon us in lock-step globally, by many otherwise familiar and formerly benign-seeming Western leaders and philanthropists and investors—men and women we thought we knew—we must begin to "think like a tyrant."

I am not talking about anything arcane or occult. I am not talking about a QAnon fantasy of a few elites running the world.

I am talking, rather, about the global elites whom I know and among whom I have lived for forty years, and about events that I have witnessed.

I am talking about what the German-Jewish philosopher of totalitarianism Hannah Arendt called the "banality of evil":

> *Evil comes from a failure to think. It defies thought for as soon as thought tries to engage itself with evil and examine the premises and principles from which it originates, it is frustrated because it finds nothing there. That is the banality of evil.*[1]

To understand the global lockstep of tyranny (at one point, I would have said, "toward tyranny"), we have to understand that certain subcultures, certain leaders, and certain ideologies simply don't have these core values at heart; and we must face the fact that these monsters are not just Nazis long dead, or members of the CCP far away, taking out their brutality on their own distant, silenced populations. Some monsters are very near to us; some are wearing lovely suits and chatting away about their kids, or about their renovation hurdles, at dinner parties; and some kinds of monstrosity and sociopathy are actively cultivated by the norms and networks that are all around us, albeit half hidden at elite levels, and systematized and accepted at very high levels.

One source of the kind of global cruelty we observed so acutely in the medical fascism of the pandemic derives from a postwar stratum of power. I'll explain.

Paradoxically, metanational organizations such as the European Union and the United Nations, agreements such as the Trans-Pacific Partnership, and global corporate and investment communities, founded after the carnage of the Second World War, served to create a class of global elite policymakers, nonprofit leaders, and bureaucrats who are able to engage in cruel and oppressive policymaking precisely because they are no longer part of the communities whose lives are affected by what they have done.

These metanational organizations purported to foster a more peaceful, cooperative world—one that would blunt enmity between historical adversaries (such as France and Germany). Most made the case that this metanational organizational structure would far more greatly benefit ordinary men and women in the street than did the poor, battered, dysfunctional nation-state, with its rotten history and its bloody impulses.

The first half of the twentieth century, with its two catastrophic World Wars, seemed indeed to reveal to the world the dark side of nationalism and the tragic limits of the nation-state; the period seemed like a textbook lesson in how decision-making at the level of nation-states led inexorably to bloodshed and to racist, cruel jingoisms.

The problem, though, as it turned out, is that you can't have accountability to citizens or a real democracy if you do not have a democratic nation-state. Another problem is that it spawned a class of distant, unaccountable deciders.

As faulty and limited as the post-1848 modern secular parliamentary nation-state is, it is the most perfect form of government yet created, in its accountability to a set group of people—that is, to the citizenry of a constitutional democracy bounded by national borders. As Winston Churchill famously said, democracy is the worst form of government, except for all those other forms that have been tried.

Metanational organizations rapidly created superstructures that made decisions above the heads of citizens of democratic nation-states. Quickly, the unelected deciders of the EU became more powerful than were the parliamentary leaders at the national level in Greece or Portugal or Spain. Quickly, citizens of various European countries lost the skills of understanding how their local and national levers of power worked; EU citizens were encouraged to leave it all to the bureaucrats at a level high above that of national parliaments.

But nationalism within a bounded nation-state, though it can surely be excessive or perverted to the dark side, also has constructive and protective aspects. Positive nationalism, within an accountable, constitutional nation-state, allows people to care about and act on their own futures; to be motivated by allegiance to their own families, communities, landscapes, histories, and cultures. And leaders must face their citizenry.

Seeing the positive aspect of nation-states does not in any way have to be a racist or an anti-immigrant position. America at its best, as a "melting pot," welcomed people of all backgrounds and faiths as citizens. But then, American citizenship had responsibilities and rights.

By the same token, it is not necessarily racist to celebrate what is brightest about French culture and history, if one is French; to revel in Dutch holidays and cuisine and rituals, if one is Dutch; to celebrate the beautiful culture and unique history of Morocco, if one is Moroccan. If "French" or "Dutch" or "Moroccan" or "American" are defined as citizenship rather than as race, then the culture expands and welcomes the new; and what is "French" or "Dutch" or "Moroccan" or "American," for that matter, evolves.

But a discourse was propagated—by global elites, who benefited from it—that shamed well-intended, anti-racist people, especially in the West, for being in the least bit proud of or loyal to their nation-state or national culture. And a discourse was propagated that shamed any right-on member of any nation-state, also in the West, for worrying about what might happen if there were any limits at all on national borders.

But just as you cannot have a constitutional democracy unless you have a discrete citizenry, of whatever background, race, or faith, who are initiated into that nation's culture, language, history, rights, and responsibilities, so you cannot have a functioning, accountable parliamentary democracy if you have open borders and voting by noncitizens. Simply as a practical matter, you can't. You have something nebulous, but it is no longer a representative democracy within a nation-state, and it absolutely dissolves the accountability of ever-more-distant leaders to the people.

The effort to hand over voting rights to a million noncitizens in New York in January 2022[2] seemed, superficially, like a right-on blow for "equity" and for anti-racism; but it is, as are fully open borders, a tyrant's dream; as the effect is to dilute the power of citizens and the accountability of leaders to a discrete set of citizens, within the boundaries of a nation-state.

By the same token, the democratic nation-state is by necessity accountable to its people in a way that meta-national organizations simply are not. The people in a nation-state can vote out corrupt leaders. They can change course when it comes to bad policies. They can put corrupt leaders in prison, or in the case of the United States, they can execute leaders who have engaged in espionage or committed treason to the nation-state.

Their leaders must, in short, whether they wish to or not, see their own people and worry about their reactions. There is thus a natural limit on the levels of cruelty and oppression that an elected leader in a constitutional nation-state can get away with.

Not so with leaders in the world of metanational organizations and global nonprofits. Nothing need constrain their cruelty once they go bad. The same is true for economic global elites: on the economic level, too, global networks and alliances also left national allegiances and national accountability behind.

What happened, in the seventy-plus years since the end of the Second World War, is that an elite international class of technocrats, EU bureaucrats, global nonprofit leaders, and international investors has developed, in which allegiance to the relationships, programs, profits, and outcomes of that global class is more immediate and important to its members than are any of the relationships, allegiances, rights, property, and outrage of their fellow countrymen and women.

To these people, the nation-state—even one's own nation-state of origin—is an artifact; a secondary, sentimental add-on. What really matters are other global elites in one's social circle and business network, and the valuable relationships one can create with them. One's "ordinary" countrymen and women recede and become theoretical. And the constant message one receives from one's peers and from the elite metanational culture is that those "ordinary" men and women simply are not as smart or well-educated as one's metanational peers, and so it would be a disaster to let them make their own decisions. One is saving them from their own fecklessness, ignorance, and shortsightedness, by deciding for them.

What does this have to do with cruelty?

Stanley Milgram, a Yale University psychologist, devised an experiment in 1963 that revealed that most ordinary people—as he found, 65 percent—would administer what they believed were shocks to innocent victims, up to what they believed could be lethal shocks, if they were told to do so by an authority figure.[3] As the Milgram experiments showed, if you are shielded from the victim whom you are harming and you have an authoritative directive to harm that victim, then easily enough, "normal" people conveniently become monsters and abusers.

With this in mind, you can understand how many global elites—who are lovely one-on-one, nice to their kids, and so on—can execute vast cruelty without even noticing.

That is the situation of the new elite class and the cultural and economic environment I am describing. It set the groundwork for the extraordinary global cruelty from these metanational elites to men and women in the street. It set the stage for the cruelty of the lockstep COVID-19 policy in which we suddenly found ourselves.

————

I will never forget being in a company car in 2015, heading to the BBC's political flagship show. It was driven by the BBC's longtime driver. As a reporter, I always talk to drivers in those circumstances, because the elite men and women whom I described above, often literally do not "see" drivers, waitstaff, cleaners, and other mere mortals. So drivers and waitstaff and cleaners tend to hear everything and know everything.

It was an important week, in which the people of Greece, who were distraught at having had policies of "austerity" forced upon them by the EU, were about to engage in a referendum. The papers were full of elderly Greek men and women who were weeping or in despair because the proposed policies would wipe away their retirement savings. As is common, the European newspapers were portraying the people of Greece who opposed austerity as spendthrifts, as ignorant, as having brought their economic disaster upon themselves, and as needing to be rescued by the policies of those wiser heads above the level of their national leaders' decision-making.

I couldn't help thinking: maybe it will be the case that rejecting "austerity" policies will turn out to be an economic mistake for the people of Greece. But I knew about referenda. If there is a majority vote in a referendum, it is by law the will of the people, and in a democracy, their decision must be enacted. So you can have your opinion about whether austerity would be smart or not in this context, but if the people have a real nation-state, their referendum will, willy-nilly, determine what happens in their country; and if the people's decision turns out to be a mistake—well, it is their mistake to make, with their own country, in their own parliament.

"Oh, no," explained the driver. "The EU ministers were in this car before you. The referendum is purely cosmetic. It will be ignored. Whatever happens, they are going ahead with austerity."

I was dumbfounded.

As it turned out, the BBC driver was exactly right. The people of Greece voted against austerity. But they were not to get their wish.

Later that week, back in New York City, I was at a dinner party. It was hosted by a major hedge fund manager. His clients were Chinese, Russian, Ukrainian, and other international investment funds. At the party were his colleagues: British, Swedish, Chinese, French, and Belgian hedge fund managers and investors.

My host, an otherwise lovely guy, trained of course in the Ivies, was apoplectic—*furious*—at the rank-and-file men and women of Greece. He did not yet know what the EU ministers knew. He knew that the people of Greece had rejected austerity, but that he had hedged in the opposite direction. Now he was *enraged* at those weeping grandmas and grandpas, and at their resistant, angry sons and daughters, for having temporarily messed up his bet on austerity. He was literally pale with fury. His fists clenched as he spoke about the Greek referendum. How dare they, was his attitude. The fools.

The mansion where we all gathered that night had been built by a robber baron at the end of the nineteenth century. The dining room was staffed by beautiful actors/waiters and actresses/waitresses in black pants and spotless white shirts. They served us charmingly a lovely plaice in white sauce dinner, with sides of grilled asparagus and heirloom beets. The ceilings were twenty feet high and wreathed in shadows. The walls were adorned with images of Italian Renaissance princelings, luscious still lifes from the sixteenth-century Netherlands, and portraits of late-nineteenth-century American society doyennes.

The conversation was sprightly. To my right, a Norwegian investor spoke about the play that was the latest avant-garde sensation on Broadway. To my left, an artist friend of the host and hostess described movements in the New York art market. Everyone was educated, pleasant, and cultured. The money guys were all agreeing with the host about the perfidy and "bad" behavior of the stubborn people of Greece. The wine flowed, red and white; it was beyond excellent. No one at that table was visibly evil. There were no secret signs, or shadowy gatherings, here. If this were a movie, you could not identify a villain. No one was part of a "cabal."

These people did not need to gather in the shadows or to be part of a cabal. Why would this group need a secret sign or a secret meeting? They simply owned the global stratum in which they operated, and they were accountable only to one another.

Neither did anyone there, expressing his or her views about the events of the week, think there was anything wrong with wishing to override and ignore the democratically expressed will of an entire nation of citizens who had articulated their wishes lawfully.

Thus, the whole nation, all the people of Greece, were being treated with extraordinary cruelty and contempt by these distant, non-Greek men and women—in part because these men and women would never see them or have to face them or ever answer to them.

At the end of the evening, I was introduced to a brilliant young woman, a protégée of my host's. She was from a small, poor democracy in the Global South; she had been educated in the Ivy League. My host showed off the young lady's knowledge and acumen about financial markets, in the context of a discussion about the "reckless" behavior of the Greeks and their nonsensical referendum.

Did she think her own fellow countrymen and women should have a say in outcomes about their economic futures? I asked her gently. I truly wondered what her views would be.

"No; the ordinary people of any given country don't have the skills to make the right economic decisions for themselves or their nations. We should be deciding for them," she explained to me calmly, with all the confidence and certainty of a now-privileged twenty-something.

"That's right," my host confirmed proudly.

The Greeks never got their referendum outcome. There was a famous U-turn, and austerity was imposed against the wishes of the people. Many elderly Greek men and women were driven into abject poverty in their retirement. Many businesses were lost.

Not much later, I was at another dinner hosted by the same man and attended by roughly the same group of people. Among the guests, though, now, was someone new: a former Greek politician who until very recently had been at the center, first, of the fight to reject austerity, and then, of the baffling U-turn.

He looked flushed, proud, and ashamed at once, and he was being introduced around like a captured prize.

Who knows what promises were made, what arrangements attended this outcome, this new alliance? But that former national leader must have seen a level of influence and wealth far above what mere allegiance to his fellow citizens, mere decency, could have gotten him.

And my host—he and his colleagues got, in the end, the outcome on which they had placed such a big bet.

That's why I am often called a "conspiracy theorist"—I have simply been, my whole adult life, in those rooms in which the very rich or the very powerful quietly arrange that chance and other—legitimate—stakeholders can never harm their prospects.

That night the wine continued to flow—and a new constellation was part of the social mix.

Too bad about the hundreds of thousands of "ordinary" Greeks, many of them elderly, now ruined for the rest of their lives.

This is just one example of how great evil—evil at a national level—can easily be done: by distance, and by condescension, and by the creation of a metanational community whose members see and hear and are answerable only to each other; but who do not see, or in any way respect, the rights of nations; or the rights of self-determination of elders, of voters, of property; of you or of me.

So—evil is not what you think. It need not be a goose-stepping soldier, or an official knocking at your door, wearing jackboots. To understand how COVID policy can be so coordinated and so cruel and so neo-fascistic, we need to understand these realities.

Evil can come in the form of a well-dressed man or woman, far from any traditional loyalties or decencies, passing you the sherry.

CHAPTER SIX

The Subtlety of Monsters

So there emerged during the pandemic a metaphysical, seemingly a satanic, level of evil. We are not done with it, though we'd like to take a breath and assume that the worst is behind us. It is gathering force and mutating in form.

Vaccines did not manage to wipe out humanity's ability to reproduce, though live births are down 13 to 20 percent: so the same darkness is coming at us in late 2023, via central bank digital currency plans; and via Fifteen-Minute Cities; via the all-in surveillance of Smart Cities, and the Internet of Things; via the confiscation of land of Dutch farmers; via the debanking of well-known figures in both the UK and the US, for no other crime than their political or medical views; via climate-related lockdowns or restrictions that are still under discussion—all of these plans are now underway, or else they are gleams in the eyes of the World Health Organization and the World Economic Forum and their allies. Neuralink, a "brain-computer interface," is bearing down on us; ChatGPT was unveiled; the transhumanist world used to be a catchphrase that suggested the very margins of discourse if not sanity, and now it's clear that there really are powerful people planning a future in which humans and machines have merged. We see patterns in the eruptions of fires in food processing plants in North America and Europe; in attacks on our food supply; in the plans to inject mRNA into cattle; in the propagandizing of shifting from meat to lab-grown "meat" to insects; in the efforts in every nation to manipulate wedge issues, such as artificially inflated rhetoric around racial issues or indigenous rights, to divide the people and destroy unity. We see in every Western nation attacks on the role of the family; attacks on the very idea of biological gender, though it is not a cultural construct; the sexualization of children and the darkening of culture.

No, evil is not done with us.

I sought to explain how people raised to know about human rights and the rule of law could go about their days doing evil, with whole hearts. I sought to understand how otherwise nice people—and indeed Western people, who grew up with post-Enlightenment norms—could suppress the respiration of children; how they could consign friends and colleagues to eat in the street like outcasts, or send cops to arrest a woman and terrify a nine-year-old child, whose crimes were that they tried to visit the Museum of Natural History in New York without "papers."

How could "nice" people in the humane West, have put on the agenda in Washington State in January 2022, plans to retain regulations that allow those exposed to a "contagious disease" to be placed in forcible quarantine, without charge or trial.

All of this happened in America—in the land of people who, since the Civil Rights Act of 1964, have had the principle of equality governing human relations as a matter of law; a nation that had passed laws against the abuse of or corporal punishment of children in public schools in the 1970s in virtually every state; and a people who have been raised in a culture of freedom and civility compared with lawless or totalitarian regimes, that led them, for the most part, to be, on the scale of decency to cruelty, until a few years ago, very decent people.

There are lessons from history that we must learn, or relearn, and quickly.

Some leaders and commentators (including myself) have passionately and publicly been comparing these years, 2020 to 2022, in the West and in Australia, to the early years of Nazi leadership. Though we face criticism for doing so, I won't be silenced about this. The similarities must urgently be addressed.

People need to reread their Nazi history. They are getting it wrong in demanding, "How dare you compare?"

While the popular imagination of the Nazi era is familiar with death camps, and think of them when Nazi policy is invoked, the fact is that many years led up to that horror. Germany invaded Poland in 1939. The extermination camps were established years into the Nazi drama, in 1941.[1] Dr. Josef Mengele, "The Angel of Death," began his medical experiments in Auschwitz after 1943.[2]

No one sensible is comparing the COVID years to those years and those horrors.

Rather, the vivid similarities between our moment in the West since 2020, and the earliest years of Nazi Germany's civil society policies, are to the years 1931 to 1933, when so many vicious norms and policies were set in place. But these were often culturally or professionally policed, rather than being policed by camp patrols. That's the point that better-informed analysts of these similarities are making.

During these years, mass societal cruelty, and a two-tier society itself that perpetuated this cruelty, was built up and policed, as today, by polite civil society institutions tasked with snarling and baring their teeth.

Casual, escalating cruelty, a culture of degradation of the "othered," and a two-tier society were built up in those years, certainly at the behest of Nazi social policy. But the construction of a world of evil out of what had been a modern civil society, if a fragile one, was also endorsed and even policed by doctors, by medical associations, by journalists, by famous composers and filmmakers, by universities; by neighbors, by teachers, by shopkeepers—for years before the death camp guards were tasked with their own far more heinous cruelty.

Amos Elon's poignant history, *The Pity of It All: A History of the Jews in Germany, 1743–1933*, reveals how many Jewish civil society leaders warned about the imperceptible shifts day by day in the direction of evil. In 1931, street violence was directed against Jewish storefronts, and led to smashed-in windows. In other contexts, Jews were beaten upon leaving synagogues. At the time, commentator Theodor Wolff warned, "This simply cannot continue. All decent people, irrespective of party, must form a common front." But Wolff's call to action was to no avail. Wolff's publisher told him to "tone down his warnings in the interest of advertising and circulation."[3] As we saw during the pandemic, those issuing alarms were also suppressed and censored.

"Hitler wanted full powers like Mussolini's in Italy," writes Elon. "He knew exactly what was needed to turn a government into a 'legal' dictatorship: emergency powers under Article 48.”[4] As we saw during the pandemic, emergency laws then were the benchmarks that would allow democracy to collapse.

In late 2021, forty-seven US states were operating with emergency measures, which suspended or bypassed normal legislative checks and balances, including New York, the state in which I live. Under emergency measures, pretty much anything can be done. When you are living under emergency measures, you no longer have a functioning democracy. See if you notice any echoes here.

In Germany, to move back in time, the demonically intelligent incrementalism of Nazi policy continued. In 1933, the year Adolph Hitler was appointed chancellor of a new cabinet, Hitler gave his word that “the Nazis would remain a minority in any future cabinet.” Even in 1933, though, some prominent Jews still believed that “nothing can happen to us.”[5]

But “Theodor Wolff was one of the few who warned that Hitler’s appointment was merely the first stage of a *coup d’etat in installments.* [italics mine] . . . Wolff predicted that ‘a cabinet whose members have been proclaiming for weeks and months that salvation—by which they mean their own—is at hand, in the form of a *coup d’etat*, a breach of the constitution, the elimination of the Reichstag, the muzzling of the opposition, and in unbridled dictatorial rule . . . will do everything in its power to intimidate and silence its opponents.’”[6]

“For millions of Berliners,” writes Elon, “nothing seemed to have changed at first. . . . Few seemed aware of the watershed they had just passed.”[7]

“Few seemed aware . . .”

Let me just summarize where we are right now in America, as well as in the West, in case you have gotten too used to it to see it clearly. I warned in *The End of America* that democracies usually do not die with a cinematic scene of goose-stepping Brownshirts suddenly in the streets. They tend to die, rather, just as Elon described—incrementally, day by day. Just because the settings are familiar to us now, does not mean that a 1931-like reality, if not yet a 1933-like reality, isn’t upon us.

In this country, citizens were forced to take their second or third experimental gene-therapy injection in order to go back to school or to keep their jobs as truckers crossing borders, or as soldiers and sailors and military pilots and hospital workers.[8] Millions of other workers narrowly escaped this coercion; and millions did not escape this coercive experiment, in effect, upon them, in parts of Europe.[9]

Minors were forced to submit to this experimental gene therapy simply to keep playing high school basketball or tennis.

Thousands of adverse events have been recorded in Vaccine Adverse Events Reporting System (VAERS), including deaths shortly after vaccination, but the forcing of injections continued, against all existing laws, despite their having no effect on transmission.

Voices of opposition to tyrannical overreach were censored en masse; payment processors declined to process funds of entities offering medical therapeutics. *The View*, that formerly cozy group of TV-talk-show gals, called for the censorship of podcaster Joe Rogan. Musician Neil Young also called for music streaming service Spotify to censor Rogan's "misinformation."[10] Calls for censorship of opposition voices echoed across the internet. Dissident platforms such as Parler were deplatformed from their hosting services or from their payment processors, a digital version of boycotting businesses.[11]

Leaders called for one group of citizens to be denied health care; in some areas of Canada, leaders told grocers that it was optional to allow this group to buy food. Children in Canada were told, "No mask, no voice." In New York, children as young as two were subjected, by a smiling new governor, a woman, to facial coverings that restrict their breathing, that impair their ability to acquire language, to bond with other children, and to recognize and express emotions.

Certain citizens, set apart as "other," falsely called infectious and positioned as "unclean," were not permitted to enter buildings or restaurants in New York; in Washington, D.C.; in San Francisco; in Los Angeles. Everyone was asked to hate and resent them, and irrationally to blame them for the nation's predicament.

People were asked to join a cult and offer up their bodies; if they didn't, they were ostracized and denied social life and professional advancement.

Small businesses, restaurants, and movies theaters; small hotels and venues; small real estate holdings; entire livelihoods, were crushed by arbitrary dicta, by the unrestrained powers of boards of health and the CDC to crush whole sectors and thus to destroy, or in effect to transfer, entire classes of assets from one targeted group into the hands of another group: to institutional investors, or shall we say, to allies of the current oligarchs.

In Washington State, proposals were put forward—like those that have been enacted in Australia and elsewhere—to turn the boards of health into entities with the equivalent of police powers; to provide detention powers to unelected, unaccountable boards of health. "Fact-checkers" claimed that this was not true, but it was true.[12]

Reports proliferated of the unvaccinated being treated abusively in hospitals, and therapeutics were withheld, via government agencies' pressure, from an entire population, leading to countless avoidable deaths. A class of therapeutics—monoclonal antibodies—were withdrawn by the FDA from ill people's access.[13] Medical entities such as the formerly respected Mayo Clinic were sued for refusing to give treatment, for which his wife begged, to a dying man.[14]

What do you call all of this, if not an early Nazi-like set of practices?

In the early years of Nazi policy, as Robert Proctor's magisterial 1988 *Racial Hygiene: Medicine Under the Nazis* points out, it was doctors who were tasked by the State, and given special status and authority, with singling out "life unworthy of life" and elaborating racially based policies that separated the "clean" and privileged, from the "unclean" or "degenerate" and restricted. In 1933, doctors began to sterilize the unfit. As Michael Grodin, Erin Miller, and Jonathan Miller point out, in "The Nazi Physicians as Leaders in Eugenics and 'Euthanasia': Lessons for Today":

> *A series of recurrent themes arose in Nazi medicine as physicians undertook the mission of cleansing the State: the devaluation and dehumanization of segments of the community, medicalization of social and political problems, training of physicians to identify with the political goals of the government, fear of consequences of refusing to cooperate with civil authority, bureaucratization of the medical role, and the lack of concern for medical ethics and human rights.*[15]

Half of Germany's physicians joined the Nazi party.

"The devaluing and dehumanization of segments of the community . . ."

Proctor shows how medical associations embraced the rise in the status and authority of physicians, and how "public health" was the anodyne label under which the early structure of emerging horrors was erected. He shows how doctors led the way.

The author even addresses the "health pass" that was established by Nazi public health policy, a pass that separated those who could participate fully in Nazi society from those who were singled out for deprivation and disgust.

Proctor tracks how eugenics allowed for increasing arguments, like those being resuscitated today, that "useless eaters" or the "unfit" do not deserve food, or are a burden on public resources, and should not be a drag on hospitals or receive medical care.

Proctor shows what a short slide it was from public health officials identifying "life unworthy of life," these "useless eaters," to the same officials using the language of "hygiene" and public safety, to setting up the first Nazi euthanasia programs—programs targeting those who were identified as "less than," or in some way impaired.

Then as now, anodyne language—"public health" and "racial hygiene" in the 1930s, and "public health," "safety," and "harm reduction" today—conceals the true nature of what should be a visible, nauseating, daily spreading evil.

Historians such as Proctor have argued that gloss of public health language, the invocation of medical authority, compartmentalization, and bureaucratization permitted evil in the early Nazi past to flourish, in spite of its taking root in what was still supposed to have been a modern civil society.

I'd argue that the same exact things in similar guises, cloaked in similar language, recurred in the years 2020 to 2022.

If we don't wake up, see exactly where we stand, and quickly read back in history about a demonic time that overtly mirrors, and in many ways foreshadows, where we are—then most of us will be fools, even as some of us are already monsters.

If we don't forcibly and immediately call out monsters where we see them—where they walk among us—whether they wear nice earrings and sit demurely at the helm of the CDC, or whether they gather in white coats, in all their authority, at the Mayo Clinic, standing between a dying man and his desperate wife—we will fail forever to deserve the blessing of the Constitution, and of the rule of law, that are supposed to be our heritage.

And no doubt: the next chapter will surely be for us, as it was for others in the past, darker still.

CHAPTER SEVEN

White Feathers

After it became clear that the "pandemic" crisis, the lockdown crisis, was never about "the virus" but rather about a global bid to kill off our free world and suppress all of our freedoms—since I and many others had been publicly vocal about this danger and were doing all we could to alert our communities—that is to say, humanity—I started to receive a lot of private direct messages (DMs). And they were all kind of similar. And they grossed me out.

In the DMs, people whom I know socially or professionally—people from journalism, from politics, from medicine, from science; most of them upper-middle-class "men in suits"—said something like, "Naomi, I really respect your actions right now. I totally agree with what you are saying. But of course, I can't say anything publicly because [fill in the nonsensical, craven reason]."

These people—privileged people, who had the power and resources to help in ways that many other people couldn't—instead expended their time and energy to justify their monumental, world-changing cowardice, at a time when we all needed to be at least somewhat brave.

The nonsensical and craven reason that followed this shameful message was typically something along the lines of, "My boss will get mad at me" or "My professional peers will have a problem with my speaking up." It's never even, "I have bills to pay."

Your boss will get mad at you, Oh, you who DM?

Do you understand what is at stake? If you comply and collude with a tyrannical oligopoly, your kids will live as slaves and as serfs forever.

The DMs insist that I am "brave." But I am not "brave," I thought; you're just a p—y.

Don't get me wrong. I understand the gender politics around ever using the epithet above. Everyone who has read my work knows that, being myself a woman, I have great respect for women, and for their bodies; I understand that one does not throw around this epithet lightly or in a misogynist way.

But in such a moment of historic-level cowardice among some privileged and influential people, no other epithet will do.

I was initially baffled by these DMs. Why would I be getting these? What did these people want? Why did they think I needed their excuses? I asked other, braver people WTF this was.

They laughed and said, "They want you to tell them that it is okay."

So I am saying publicly: this is not okay.

I am exasperated by those who stay in the shadows, agreeing with the risk-taking of others, who admire their "courage." This is a form of othering that dehumanizes and exploits those speaking out.

It casts the people who do take risks for the wellbeing of others as being somehow naturally better fitted for this difficult job than is the speaker. It's a form of offloading one's own responsibility guiltlessly onto a subgroup that is assigned the status of somehow liking the battle, or of being somehow better suited to combat, by nature, than is the speaker himself.

It's like all those guys I knew in college who never did the dishes after dinner because they said they were bad at it.

I don't know anyone truly heroic who likes the battle. But I think that most could not live with themselves if they walked away from doing what they know they could do to help—in a moment in which obvious right and wrong have not been clearer since 1941.

Dr. Patrick Phillips—a Canadian ER doctor who spoke out early against the harms of lockdowns, when many fellow doctors remained silent—said something like, "I realized that many of my peers were silent because they were worried about their careers. But I also realized that if I didn't speak out, soon I would have no career worth saving."[1] Dr. Jay Bhattacharya said, when asked about having been vilified, smeared, attacked, and hounded professionally for eighteen months—for having been *right* about the harms of lockdowns—something like: "If I didn't speak up now, what is the point of my career?"[2]

Dr. Peter McCullough, who, in the middle of fighting for everyone, took time to text me a way to help my loved ones who had COVID, said on television something like, "They can arrest me for saying this. Just don't give these mRNA vaccines to your child." He also wryly commented at another time that those opposed to his message were trying to erase, one by one, the professional credentials after his name. But those dangers, and those forms of bullying, have not stopped him.

In March 2022, I interviewed Edward Dowd, the investor who was a portfolio manager at BlackRock. He warned the world about Pfizer's fraud, and was, for sure, going against "principalities and powers." He cautioned his peers in the investment community that betting on the Pfizers of the world is a bet against freedom forever. I asked him where he got his personal courage. He said something like, "I will keep going till we either win our freedoms back or I am in a gulag."[3]

The "pandemic" was a time in history that hammered out heroes and heroines in the forge of crisis.

It was also a time of unprecedented cowardice, when those who chose collusion, when they knew better, allowed their souls to shrivel in that same heat.

There was, at that time, no room left to equivocate; there was no room left to moon about in the middle.

At that point, there was no middle.

I watched the bravest men and women of our time forced to hurtle into battle. The women leaders were certainly as courageous as the men (though they got less airtime): I watched Jenin Younes, then of New Civil Liberties Alliance, realize she had to speak up publicly against unlawful lockdowns, even though she would endure professional opposition. Leslie Manookian of Health Freedom Defense Fund, early on, sued coercive governors and governments, and won. I followed Tiffany Justice of Moms for Liberty as she was shadowed and faced down by a security guard when she insisted on accompanying her maskless child into a context of school bullying and mask coercion. This intimidation did not stop her; it made her more determined to defend the kids. Lori Roman, of the American Constitutional Rights Union (ACRU), took every single email I forwarded from desperate parents trying to protect a young adult daughter or son, often a soldier, or a pregnant government employee, or a student, from forced mRNA vaccination.

The warrior queens Stephanie Locricchio and Aimee Villella, then of Children's Health Defense, rallied thousands of moms and dads to confront their abusive governors and the cruel, forced-masking, forced-vaccinating schools; these moms, along with other parents, put their bodies between middle-schoolers and medical vans that were parked in the schoolyards—vans seeking to inject minors against their parents' wishes with an experimental product; a product that turns out to have been generated via fraud and via the concealment of serious harms.

But that is exactly where parents' bodies should be, in such a dangerous situation for the minors.

The real question is not, What drives such parents to put their bodies between the van and the kids? But rather, Where are all the other parents?

I watched Dr. Paul Alexander race into the thick of a peaceful trucker protest in Canada that was being targeted by Canadian authorities, to send back defiant—nonviolent—dispatches from the front; I listened as he spoke up on stage and in press conferences in support of the truckers' lawful rights to freedoms of speech. I read his accounts when the brutal regime in Canada floated frightening rumors of an arrest warrant being issued for him to intimidate him. He did not stop. Next, he stood with the *American* truckers.

I watched Dr. Martin Kulldorff, Dr. Sunetra Gupta, and Dr. Bhattacharya, along with Jeffrey Tucker—the signatories and the convener of the Great Barrington Declaration—tell the truth about lockdowns early and consistently in the face of continual whirlwinds of institutional and media blowback. Dr. Harvey Risch dared to say that we had attained herd immunity—at a time when people were being professionally ostracized for doing so.

The reporters who showed courage? I can count them on two hands. Stephen K. Bannon kept producing reports on the advances of attacks on liberty in the face of government legal scrutiny. Natalie Winters and

The National Pulse team reported on government malfeasance regarding COVID when the President was saber-rattling personally and scarily against purveyors of "misinformation." The legacy media? My former publishers, the *Guardian*, the *New York Times*, the *Washington Post*? Silent about dangers or colluding with lies.

Nonreporters were doing the jobs of AWOL or cowering reporters: Dr. Henry Ealy, a nutritional healer, and two Oregon state senators, Dennis Linthicum and Kim Thatcher, broke a massive story of CDC malfeasance regarding government data.

These heroines and heroes did not take these actions because it was fun or easy, or because they were already warriors for liberty as career choices. These are not entertaining, lucrative, status-filled paths.

Most such heroes and heroines, and other less-known peaceful warriors aligned with liberties right now, would surely rather be back in the classroom, or polishing essays on any number of other subjects, or in the lab, or enjoying their families, free of the need to face down bullies and to stand up to security guards.

But unlike most of us, they understood that they were called to rise to this moment.

The thing is—we *all* are called, similarly.

This is why you always hear heroes, when questioned about their heroism, saying "I had no choice" or "I was just doing my job." Heroes and heroines are right. They *are* just doing their jobs. They are doing their jobs *as human beings*, with responsibilities to others.

The cowardly, affluent men who DM me for my exoneration (it is pretty much always men; I think women are more aware of when they have chosen silence, and don't try to justify it) make the lives of all the heroes and heroines of this moment, named and unnamed, harder.

The work of heroes and heroines is more difficult, the more that others seek to stay in the comfortable shadows, and eventually, when it is safe, to ride out on the wave of change that was painfully generated by those out front.

The problem is that it really matters that a lot of people resist all at once. This decision whether to speak up makes the difference, when it scales, between freedom or servitude forever.

Tyrannies only fall when there is mass resistance. History is clear on this. When it is just a few—well, they are marginalized, silenced, smeared, or, when things go far enough, arrested.

So, to you who DMed me: *thanks.*

———

In the spring of 2022, the Democrats in power received a political consultant's memo telling them that a majority of voters were sick of "restrictions," and that the opposition's message of restoring freedom was a winning message. This memo caused the nauseating, immediate about-face on "restrictions"—attributed of course to "the data" and not to the obvious politics.

It took the voices of dozens and then hundreds of brave folks, speaking at first contrary to a mass of propaganda, and facing deplatforming, professional cancellation, and worse to change that cultural atmosphere.

Watching these brave people made me braver than I would have been myself.

Shortly before the Democrat volte-face, I was in New York City. I could no longer bear the fact that my hotel, the Walker Hotel Tribeca, had a cafe and a restaurant in the lobby with signs stating that these facilities were for "vaccinated only." I am unvaccinated, for reasons that should be, of course, no one's business but my own.

So on day three of my stay, I politely informed the staff at the Blue Bottle Cafe that I was unvaccinated, and that I would now take my small coffee and my overnight oats to the forbidden lunch counter, and I would sit there peacefully, but that I would not comply with the New York City directive for the cafe to discriminate against me.

The staff informed me stertorously—doing their jobs—that my doing so was against NYC mandate. I said that I understood, but that I was nonetheless choosing not to comply. They warned that they would call the manager. I said that I understood that as well.

I then sat down at the illegal lunch counter, texted my lawyer to be on standby, posted publicly to Governor Hochul and to New York City mayor Eric Adams that I was currently intentionally violating the discriminatory New York City mandate that prevented unvaccinated people from being seated in cafes and restaurants, and that I was at the Walker Hotel Tribeca Cafe lunch counter at that very moment if they wished to arrest me.

Then I waited for an hour, heart pounding, to be arrested.

Do you know what happened?

Nothing.

Later that day I was at Grand Central Station. Almost all of the lower-level food court was roped off for the vaccinated, and there was nowhere for an unvaccinated New Yorker to sit down, let alone to eat lunch. In a restricted seating area, a heavyset bouncer in a mask was demanding people's digital vaccination cards along with—unprecedented in my experience—their IDs, just to enter.

I explained that I wished to enter, and that I was unvaccinated and had no "Key to NYC" pass.

Two cops appeared at once. "Look at the other seating area (over there, far away) saved for the unvaccinated," they said nicely. I explained that the strength of New York City, and of America for that matter, was its diversity and its equal treatment of all, and that if people had refused to comply with other forms of discrimination and forced separate accommodations, discriminatory rules would have ended sooner. I stated for the second time that day I intended peacefully not to comply.

A third police officer, their senior, appeared. He explained that I would be given a summons for trespassing.

The cop with the notebook that contained the summons form took as long as he possibly could to write it out. No one wanted to arrest me or to give me a summons.

Finally, the three cops surrounded me and firmly escorted me to the upper level. I was quite scared, but I told myself not to give in.

On the upper level, I waited to be arrested. I was braced for the handcuffs again. Once again, my heart was racing. I have been arrested before in NYC, and it is frightening and uncomfortable.

But when I asked if I could now walk away and take my train—no one stopped me.

The takeaway? When I refused to comply with these unlawful mandates that have burnt out the soul of a once-great city, nothing happened.

The bullies, Governor Hochul and Mayor Adams, who put these scary-sounding, Dear Leaderesque "edicts" in place, and forced free people to act against their wishes like petty tyrants, were all bluster, like the Great and Mighty Oz.

When the city and state leaders were called on it, there was nothing there.

It turned out the police were not instructed to impose the law against resisters to "the mandates"—because the law would be unsustainable.

But it took those awful, frightening moments of pressing against those terrifying sounding mandates to prove, at least to myself, that they were meaningless.

Other people's courage builds possibilities in this world.

The heroes and heroines whom I know gave me the courage to prove, that day, something that I believed was important for me to take a risk to demonstrate. I would not have known how to be brave without having witnessed their greater bravery.

———

There is also an ugly class divide emerging in terms of who showed real, scaled-up courage in the face of tyranny.

Who were the majority of those who stood up, speaking out and taking risks against tyranny? Overwhelmingly, it was not the "Zoom class," for all their virtue-signaling about social justice. It was working people. It was truckers. Moms. Firefighters and cops.

When I spoke at a rally against forcing injections on first responders in NYC, the audience was made up mostly of working people. The people who march for every other cause in NYC—my affluent, liberal "tribe"—sat that one out.

The first responders put their bodies in harm's way for the safety of my colleagues and acquaintances; but the "Zoom class" did not reciprocate with courage of their own, to protect the bodies of first responders from coercion and from harm.

We are not all equally brave, to say the least.

———

An old friend—an affluent, educated man, who works at the Pasteur Institute—trolled me relentlessly on social media for the duration of the pandemic, to assail me for my warnings about harms from mRNA vaccines.

As the news emerged of fraud in Pfizer's internal trials, and news emerged of more deaths in the vaccinated group than the control, his trolling abruptly ceased.

Then, shortly after, on Facebook, he sent me news of his admittedly very pretty golden retriever.

In the run-up to the First World War, when brave men were signing up to fight, women handed out white feathers to healthy young men who had not enlisted in the war effort.

There is a metaphorical white feather to be given out these days, to those who try to change the subject—from the damage done by their "side" to the bodies of children, to evidence of the charm of their golden retrievers.

———————

One of my favorite quotations is this, from the late poet Audre Lorde: "My silences had not protected me. Your silence will not protect you."[4]

Danger, if we meet it, also gives each of us a God-given opportunity to serve our kind. In the process we become immeasurably more than we had been before.

Maybe while forcing ourselves to act bravely, we do become brave.

———————

Someday all our kids and grandkids will ask each of us directly: Why did you stand by? Why did you not help me?

I could not breathe. Or God forbid: Now I have these health problems.

Or else they will say: Thank you so much for speaking for me, when I was too little to speak.

They will ask—Dad, Mom—Grandma, Grandpa: What did you do in the war?

Well.

What *did* you do?

CHAPTER EIGHT

Rethinking the Second Amendment

In 2021 and 2022, as the lights went off all over Europe—and Australia, and Canada—via lockdowns and vaccine passports and the forced control of the movements, commerce, and education of formerly free people—the last thing that was keeping us in America free was, yes, the Second Amendment.

I can't believe I wrote those words. But I stand by them.

I am a child of the peace movement. A daughter of the Left, of a dashingly bearded proto-beatnik poet (my late dad) and of a Summer of Love activist/cultural anthropologist (my lovely mom). We are a lineage of anti-war, longhaired folks who believe in talking things out.

By the time I was growing up in California in the 1960s and 1970s, weapons were supposed to have become passé. When I played at friends' houses in our neighborhood in San Francisco, there were posters on the walls: "War is not healthy for children and other living things." Protesters had iconically placed daisies in the rifle barrels of unhip-looking National Guardsmen.

We were obviously supposed to side with the daisies.

Weapons were archaic, benighted—tacky. A general peace was surely to prevail, in the dawning Age of Aquarius.

My young adulthood, too, unfolded in a context that reviled all guns all the time. The media was seared with images of gun mayhem. Drive-by shootings devastated inner cities. Gun violence was glorified in hip-hop videos, which, in turn, was rightly denounced by leaders of victimized communities.

As I grew older, the catastrophes related to lawless gun violence in this country did not abate: Columbine, Virginia Tech, Sandy Hook—the horrors were endless. After every burst of violence, the same question was asked: How can we allow anyone access to any weapons such as these when they cause such devastation?

Because there were mass shootings and criminal gun violence in America, and because Americans, unlike citizens of other nations, owned and had access to firearms, guns themselves were identified, uncritically, in my progressive circles (or perhaps I should say, in my former progressive circles) as being the scourge. My liberal community generally reacted to gun violence with a simple, literal arithmetic. Surely the sensible reaction to these catastrophic scenes was simply to *remove the guns*. End of problem.

The catastrophic scenes of gun violence were connected, in my former circles, directly to all gun owners, but without much equivocation or nuance. And since none of us knew people who *owned* firearms, or had ever asked such people why they did so, it was easy to believe in broad generalizations and crude, even racist stereotypes: All gun owners or National Rifle Association members, for instance, we were sure, were unexploded emotional landmines—any one of them could become a mass murderer in a heartbeat. All gun owners or NRA members were surely, we believed, one cheap beer or one fentanyl hit away from spraying a church or workplace or parade with bullets.

It was hard for us to conceive that anyone might own guns and be law-abiding, responsible, and peaceful.

My former progressive circles even saw hunting not as a symbol of conservatorship of the land nor a means of sustainable food sourcing, and a relatively humane one compared with the harvesting of animals in factory farms, but as a sign of the bloodlust of backwoods yokels straight out of *Deliverance*.

We assumed all gun owners were driven by fear or by rage.

It certainly did not occur to us that anyone might enjoy marksmanship, or like being a collector, and that thus there might be good reasons to own more than one firearm.

We always interpreted the ownership of multiple weapons as a sign of mental instability. Obviously! Who would need more than one gun, we asked one another, even if we conceded that anyone needed a gun at all?

Living in safe (wealthy) neighborhoods, assuming that a stable democracy would last forever, and relying, with our costly educations, on talking above all, we could not fathom the "need" for guns or for gun rights.

We used to roll our eyes at the claims made by supporters of the Second Amendment. In my former circles, "2A" was often interpreted, even by constitutional scholars and certainly by the news outlets that we read, as applying only to government-run militias such as the US Army or the National Guard. I was told more times than I could count that the Second Amendment was never meant to apply to individuals' ownership of guns; and I believed that.

Grammar, too, was used to make the case against individual gun ownership. Often, commentators in our circles described the phrasing of the Second Amendment as being so twisted and archaic that no one today could ever truly confirm the Founders' intentions regarding gun ownership by individuals.

Indeed, I heard these truisms so often, that when I sat down and read the Second Amendment carefully—as I was writing *The End of America*—I was startled: because the Second Amendment wasn't unclear at all.

> *A well-regulated Militia, being necessary to the security of a free State, the right of the people to keep and bear Arms, shall not be infringed.*[1]

Critics of individual gun rights on the Left often described this sentence as being opaque because it has two clauses, and two commas prior to the final clause, so they read the first two sections as relating unclearly to the last assertion.

But if you are familiar with late-eighteenth-century rhetoric and sentence construction, the meaning of this sentence is transparent.

The construction of this sentence is typical of late-eighteenth into early-nineteenth-century English grammar, in which there can be quite a few dependent clauses, gerunds, and commas that come before the verb, and the object of, the sentence.

Thus, the correct way to read the Second Amendment, if you understand eighteenth-century English grammar, is:

> *A well-regulated Militia being necessary to the security of a free State,*
> *the right of the people to keep and bear arms shall not be infringed.*

Or, translated into modern English construction: "*Because* a well-regulated militia is necessary to the security of a free State, therefore the right of the people to keep and bear arms shall not be infringed."

Here is another example of many dependent clauses, commas, and gerunds prior to the verb and object of the sentence, from the second paragraph of Thomas Paine's pamphlet *Common Sense* (1776):

> *As a long and violent abuse of power is generally the means of call-*
> *ing the right of it in question, (and in matters too which might never*
> *have been thought of, had not the sufferers been aggravated into the*
> *inquiry,) and as the King of England hath undertaken in his own*
> *right, to support the Parliament in what he calls Theirs, and as*
> *the good People of this Country are grievously oppressed by the*
> *Combination, they have an undoubted privilege to enquire into the*
> *Pretensions of both, and equally to reject the Usurpation of either.*[2]

This would translate into modern English: "The good people of this Country are grievously oppressed by the combination of a long and violent abuse of power and of the King of England's support of Parliament in what he calls his rights and theirs. Thus, the [good people of this country] have an undoubted privilege to enquire into [ask about] the Pretension [claims] of both [King and Parliament], and by the same token to reject the Usurpation [of rights] of either." The logic of the sentence, with its multiple clauses, gerunds, and commas before the final verb and object of the sentence, is perfectly clear to anyone who is familiar with eighteenth-century rhetoric.

Here is the famous first sentence of Jane Austen's *Pride and Prejudice*, with the similar construction—common still in 1813, though uncommon today—of two commas and two clauses prior to the verb and object of the sentence: "It is a truth universally acknowledged, that a single man in possession of a good fortune, must be in want of a wife."[3]

So: there is no ambiguity whatsoever about the Second Amendment to readers of Paine and Austen. The Second Amendment says with zero ambiguity, in the English grammar of 1791, that Americans have an absolute right ("shall not be infringed") to keep ("own") and bear ("carry") arms because they as individuals may be summoned to become a "well-regulated militia." In the grammar of the eighteenth century, it's the militia that is "well-regulated"—orderly, with a clear chain of command, not a chaotic mob—and not the guns.

Why do I raise all of this?

In part because I have evolved my view about firearms, and I understand that doing so is in fact in alignment with the Constitution. And the thing about really supporting the Constitution is that you do not get to pick and choose. I can't choose my favorite amendment, the easy one, the First Amendment, and then shy away from the glass-clear directive of the Second Amendment, simply as a result of my own cultural discomfort. You have to stand up for it all, if you are to call yourself a supporter of the Constitution.

In part I am addressing this difficult, tender topic because I now *know* people who "keep and bear arms." And they do not match the stereotypes I had long taken for granted.

I met my husband, as many know, because I was receiving death threats and I needed protection. He was highly trained in the use of firearms via eleven years in active-duty service with the US Army—in military intelligence, seven years of which he spent assigned to two Special Forces groups—and another ten years working in various defense and intelligence roles as a contractor. The fact is, I was relieved to have someone who could physically protect me during a time that felt dangerous to me. I'd be a hypocrite if I pretended that that was not the case.

Reader, I married him.

I have recently become a firearm owner myself.

Nonetheless, my old resistances died hard.

For years, I remained jumpy knowing he had weapons in our home. People from my cultural background are taught to think of firearms as being innately incredibly dangerous; as being always loaded, always half an inch away from causing a fatal accident indoors. I had no idea, until Brian showed me, of how safely one can responsibly store a weapon; or of the many layers of prevention, from storing ammunition separately, to the safety mechanism on the firearm itself, that should keep accidents from happening in conscientious homes. I also did not know, until I met responsible gun owners, that they do not in fact want mentally ill or unstable people to have access to arsenals at will; most support reasonable restrictions such as required safety classes and background checks.

Nonetheless, for years, I had intense anxiety when Brian would keep his Glock in the glove compartment of his vehicle, or when he had his weapon on his person. When we arrived at our country home late at night after being away, if something seemed "off"—a light on, or a screen door open, for example—he would check the perimeter of the property to make sure all was safe, armed with a flashlight, and with his gun ready to be drawn. I would lock myself in the car and look away, heart racing. But I was . . . glad that it would be safe.

And then . . . there was the day a relative took us shooting, and I was carefully taught to fire a pistol against a deserted hillside in the Pacific Northwest. It terrified me, and I vowed never to do it again.

And then . . . there was the day, a bit later, that the same relative took me back to the hillside, and carefully taught me to fire a Galil ACE assault rifle. I leaned into it as instructed, and I shot the target and hit it; and I felt that the weapon was not a chaotic animal that could turn on me or another, creating havoc, but rather that it was an instrument of power that I could control and use with direction and will.

And then . . . there was the night Brian had to be away from home, and he showed me how to shoot his 12-gauge Mossberg shotgun that he kept in a safe. I was scared—but then I was not scared. I prepared to go to sleep with it within arm's reach, in a safe place in the bedroom.

I thought of the many nights when I had been a single mother in that house, when any sound outside, especially sounds of footsteps—animal footsteps often sound human—would turn me rigid from fear in my bed, wondering what to do. Back then I'd have been nearly helpless if an intruder, armed or unarmed, had, God forbid, tried to come in and harm my family.

But that night, after I'd gotten used to the shotgun being in my bed-room, I fell asleep; and then I slept the sweetest sleep I'd ever slept out of all the nights I'd spent alone, or with small children to protect, in that house.

When I awoke, I thought: Could it have been this easy the whole time? And then I thought: I was irresponsible, as a single mother, not to have been trained and not to have been armed.

And then . . . there was the day when I went to a gun shop with Brian, because we were possibly about to lose our national sovereignty, and he wanted to make sure I could protect myself, God forbid, if needed. In the gun shop, a smart, pleasant, woman in her late twenties, named Nadine, showed me what she recommended for me—a handgun that would fit nicely in a woman's hand and that would not have too much of a kick. She showed me the size of the bullets that would stop an intruder. And she showed me a holster, designed by a woman, with soft edges that fit around one's hips and tucked into the waistband of one's jeans. If your blouse is a bit loose, no one knows you are carrying a weapon.

She demonstrated, hitching the holster around her own hips and tucking the handgun under the waistband of her jeans. Her light cotton summer blouse did indeed conceal it.

She looked like any slight young woman who was ready to go out to a concert or a club. But she was secretly armed, and therefore protected.

I thought of all the young women I knew who were harmed—badly— at concerts, at clubs, in alleyways. I thought about what would happen to rapists and abusers if young women—if women in general—were armed or even if many were *reputed* to be armed. And I thought of my decades of struggling with the issue of female victimization: the existential vul-nerability of women who are always in danger from anyone bigger and stronger who wished to injure or exploit them.

And I thought: Could it always have been this easy?

Could women resist and deter victimization—by simply owning, and knowing how to use, firearms?

Obviously.

How had this issue escaped me so long, as a rape survivor myself, and as a feminist? The rape survivor in me longed, on an animal level, for a weapon. Longed, on an animal level, to deter any future attacker. The rape survivor in me wanted a weapon the way an injured creature wants teeth and claws.

I did not buy the handgun, as I needed first to take a safety class and procure a permit and four references. But I did buy a .22 Rossi Rimfire rifle.

Brian assembled it. When I came downstairs in the morning, he had attached a bipod and had positioned it above my computer on my writing desk (with a safety lock and no ammunition nearby, of course). An assortment of dried flowers in a vase, and the stacks of books from my research, surrounded it.

I started laughing at the contrast: the elegant diagonal line of the sleek black weapon, stabilized and ready to be placed into defensive use, standing guard over my computer.

It was nonetheless a powerful symbol—as powerful as had been the image of the holster tucked low around the hips of the no-longer-vulnerable young woman.

I thought not only of rape survivors. I thought, too, when I saw the rifle on my desk, of writers, of journalists, of critics of the State, of dissidents. I thought of reporters around the world hauled off to prison by the minions of tyrants. I thought of our own recently created Ministry of Truth, and of the armed men who might make note of what was emerging from the computers of American writers.

What would happen to tyrants—to threats of violence and arrests for free speech—if writers, too, were defensively trained and armed? What if words themselves had a defense against violent tyranny, one that was always ready for action?

The writers of our nation's birth—they were armed. The writers who forged our country's founding documents were armed *because* they were writers. In Britain, when our nation was born, the crime of "seditious libel" punished criticism of the government.

Sedition was defined broadly: "The common law of seditious libel prohibits all writings and other utterances which tend to bring about hatred or contempt for the king, the Government or the constitution as by law established. Sedition consists of any act done or word spoken or written and published which has a seditious tendency, and done or spoken or written and published with a seditious intent."[4]

As historian Clare Feikert-Ahalt described in a Library of Congress blog post: "The punishments for this offense were rather steep—up to life imprisonment and/or a fine. . . . The earlier punishments were significantly more severe in which perpetrators would have their ears cut off for a first offense and recidivism was punishable by death."[5]

King George III issued a Royal Proclamation in which the authorities were charged with seeking out the authors and printers of "wicked and seditious writings" and reporting to government on radical activities.[6] Thomas Paine and his book *Rights of Man* were targeted.[7]

> *To the ruling class Paine's proposals spelled "bloody revolution," and the government ordered the book banned and the publisher jailed. . . . Paine was tried in absentia, found guilty of seditious libel, and declared an outlaw, and* Rights of Man *was ordered permanently suppressed.*[8]

I am also reexamining my reflexes about the Second Amendment because I believe that we are at a moment that our Founders, in their nearly prophetic wisdom, knew might come to pass. We are at the kind of moment for which the Second Amendment may have been written in just the clear, unequivocal way that it was.

Tyranny is descending all around the formerly free nations of the world. I say these days that the coup in America has already taken place—a stealthy, sneaky coup, mounted without a shot being fired.

In February 2022, President Biden extended emergency powers due to COVID.[9] A few months later, in May of 2023, he extended them due to the situation in Iraq.[10]

In June 2023, he extended emergency powers again—due to the Balkans—and I didn't see this massive news covered anywhere.[11]

At which point we must ask, since it is almost comical: who writes his material?

Many states around the country, such as New York State, where I live, existed under continually renewed emergency laws. Governor Andrew Cuomo declared a COVID state of emergency in March of 2020 and did not end it till June of 2021.[12] But that was not the end of emergency powers! Cuomo declared a state of emergency on July 6, 2021, due to "gun violence."[13] The next New York governor, Kathy Hochul, extended the emergency law month after month. On May 16, 2023, she extended it again—due to "gun violence."[14] On August 13, 2023, she extended it again.[15] Due to gun violence.

Even when there was no "disaster emergency," of this or any other kind, in New York.

Emergency orders strip citizens of our usual protections provided by legislative actions and leave us vulnerable to future depredations: the return of lockdowns, of forcible quarantines such as we saw in Shanghai, of confiscations of our property, of mandated masks and injections, and of indeed far worse. That is the nature of emergency laws in history. They are almost never given up willingly. They eventually, almost always, lead to the imprisonment or terrorization of the now-subject people.

The democratic protections of the so-called free nations of the world—Canada, the Republic of Ireland, the United Kingdom, Australia, New Zealand—were shut down with the ease of someone switching off a light, and with almost no resistance from citizens. Yes, there have been protests, and there were petitions and innumerable complaints online, and a few brave legislators spoke up, if only to echoing chambers.

But the fact remains that when the unidentifiable police or mercenary forces, as in Canada, are violent, and the protesters have nothing but the moral high ground with which to deter their violence, then even the bravest of resistances is fleeting.

In Australia, citizens were arrested when they sought to escape forcible quarantine. Police in Melbourne, in 2021, shot citizens who were protesting against Draconian lockdowns, with rubber bullets.[16] This happened to this formerly robust democracy, so easily. Australians yielded 650,000 privately owned guns in a mandatory gun buyback program in 1996 and 1997.[17] Australians are weaker now in deterring violence against them by the State. New Zealanders handed in more than 50,000 weapons in their own country's gun buyback program in 2019—right before the global pandemic.[18] New Zealanders were attacked with sound canons during the pandemic years and suffered one of the worst of the lockdowns.

The unarmed people of China had nothing with which to deter the way their own State leaders dealt with the COVID pandemic. From 2020 onward, in the name of public health, authorities welded shut the doors of Chinese citizens suspected of having infections.[19] Leaders used mass incarceration—"a strict lockdown"—against the inhabitants of Shanghai.[20] Neither can the unarmed citizens of China deter the transportation of ethnic minorities into detention camps, or organ harvesting, or forced abortions. About half a million Shanghai residents who "tested positive" for COVID were sent to quarantine camps.[21]

You can hate guns. I have hated guns most of my life. I hate violence. I hate gun violence. I hate the slaughter of innocents. I am a peaceful person.

But it is becoming obvious, even to us pacifists, vegans, and tree huggers, that formerly free people who are unarmed are defenseless against the criminal tyrannies exerting massive violence and control upon them.

And it is becoming obvious that similar tyrannical moves against the people of the United States have been thwarted in advance or deterred— and only state by state—pretty much only because the people of the United States have the right to own and carry weapons, and because many do so.

This question of who has access to firearms became more serious as the war against the US and the free world ramped up. In May 2022, the mostly Bill Gates– and CCP-funded World Health Organization planned to try to drain sovereignty from sovereign nations, in the name of Global Health and the prospect of future pandemics.

This power grab was delayed. It is not off the table. The demand for a Global WHO accord returns every six months. It returned to the US when the WEF pushed the treaty in 2023. The WHO anticipates its ratification by 2024.[22]

Who then will be the armed men at your door? They can easily be private mercenaries, sent by WHO Director-General Tedros Ghebreyesus; mercenaries sent to lock you in your home or take you to a quarantine camp against your will, under the guise of a "public health emergency."

What will stop this, if not states' refusal to comply, and if not the weapons of citizens?

Bill Gates has been making the case for just this structure of transnational power for a long time. He has long advocated for a transnational power structure to take over global decision-making, under the guise of protecting public health. In a 2018 speech to the Massachusetts Medical Society, Gates said:

> This [past work on pandemics] includes simulations and other preparedness exercises so we can better understand how diseases will spread and how to deal with things like quarantine and communications to minimize panic. We need better coordination with military forces to ensure we can draw on their mobilization capacity to transport people, equipment, and supplies on a mass scale.[23]

Bill Gates is still trying to have his psychotic fantasies come true, worldwide; but now it appears that he—and his potential allies—may be able to do so in the future with his own private One Health army.[24] He won't give up, nor will the WEF and the WHO. There are mercenary armies available, with a phone call, to private individuals and nonprofit entities around the world. The Second Amendment alone, along with our sovereignty, protects us from them.

This realization is hard to accept. But the risks of criminal gun violence, while always tragic, are risks that sadly can't be done away with altogether, if we are to secure a more fundamental safety for more people and more lives; the right, as a nation of 335 million people, to deter massive planned violence, criminal detentions, lockdowns, theft of assets, and violent crimes at the State, and now at metastate, levels, against our lives and freedoms and yes, against our children.

Without the brilliantly conceived and clearly worded Second Amendment, without the deterrent to state and transnational violence of responsible, lawful, careful, and defensive firearms ownership in the United States of America, it is clear that nothing at all will save our citizens from the current fates of the people of China, Australia, and Canada, including the children, who may be facing—unarmed, defenseless as their parents sadly are—even worse fates still ahead.

CHAPTER NINE

The Next Thing

For a few days in late April 2022, I began feeling an uneasy sense of grief. At first, I could not figure out the cause of it.

Nothing unusual was wrong in my personal life. My loved ones were safe and well, thank God. The battle for liberty was ongoing, as it had been for two years, but I was used to the stresses of that. What was the matter?

I was driving with Brian over the Taconic foothills, and through the vast early spring expanses of the beautiful Hudson Valley. The sun was shining. Daffodils, creamy white and bright yellow, displayed their trumpets in shadowy recesses under old ash trees with wide-spreading boughs. The lighter-yellow forsythia dotted the roadsides in a fury of color.

We'd just been talking to a realtor acquaintance who described how the area had changed when the city people fled their Brooklyn apartments at the start of the pandemic, to sit out the crisis in the gracious, creaky old farmhouses that they could purchase for a relative song.

We'd driven through reopened businesses flush with this newly transplanted money. An old railroad car diner had been revamped and now offered curated organic-beef hash, and tasty, if ironic, egg creams.

We drove past little 1960s ranch houses with some land around them, now being redone with costly cedar shingles and white trim, for the farmhouse look that the ex-Brooklynites liked. Sotheby's signs were out on the lawns already, in preparation for the lucrative flipping.

On driveway after driveway of the ex-Brooklynites, the former weekend people (and I confess that I too was once a weekend person, but something had happened to me over the course of the past two years that changed me even more than my change of home address), there were now Ukrainian flags. Not American flags. No one cared or even asked about the American town halls that had been closed for the past two years. Tyranny overseas was more pressing than the rights that had been suspended just up the road.

Otherwise, most things were almost back to normal! Almost pre-2020 normal!

The masks had recently come off. Hudson, New York, and Great Barrington, Massachusetts, the two cities nearest us, and, by chance, both left-leaning, had also been two of the maskiest and most coercive of places when it came to pandemic policies and cultures. Now businesses were being permitted to reopen.

(I'd been rejected from my Great Barrington synagogue—literally, they had returned my membership fee—because I'd dared to invite people over to my house at the depth of the pandemic—if they had wanted, as adults, to join me—to watch the Zoom Friday evening Shabbat service together. Shocking behavior on my part, I know.)

As if a switch had been flicked, now the cruel moral judgments, the two-tier society, the mandates, the coercions, the nasty looks, the desperate masked children with their laboring breath, the loneliness, the desolate centrally planned economies—were no more.

That memo from the political consultancy had gone out to the DNC, warning about how these policies spelled defeat in the midterms, and *poof!*—a whole retinue of mandates messaged as if they had been matters of life and death, a raft of Board of Health demands, a plethora of social strictures, and baroque instructions on how and when to discriminate against one's fellow Americans—vanished, like the smoke from an unwelcome cigarette on a breezy veranda.

Overnight, a new concern, a new moral signifier, was presented, wholly formed: and it involved a conflict area half a world away. Now, war is always bad, and invasions are always cruel, but I could not help noticing that there are wars, refugees, invasions, and conflict areas around the world, and that only this *one* demanded the attentions of my irksomely cultish and uncritical former "tribe." I could not help noticing that the dozens of devastated conflict areas and war zones being totally ignored by the ex-Brooklynites—from Ethiopia, where there had been 50,000 deaths since September 2021; to Sri Lanka, with its catastrophic food shortages; to Mexico's drug war, which has led to 300,000 deaths; to Afghanistan, where since 2021 women have been, and still are being, rounded up and detained, or their movements restricted, and where child brides are forced into marriage and where the Taliban has not stopped its attacks on civilians[1]—do not involve white people who look like the ex-Brooklynites. These many, severe conflicts, for these and other reasons, are not attracting a lot of television cameras.

You'd think the ex-Brooklynites, with their expensive educations, would bear the complexities of these other conflicts in mind. But no; the ex-Brooklynites are so easily led, when it comes to anyone invoking their moral high ground.

When they are directed to pay attention to one conflict out of dozens and ignore the rest, no matter how dire the rest may be, they do so. Just as, when they were instructed to present their bodies uncritically to an untried mRNA injection and to offer up the bodies of their minor children, they did so. When they were asked to shun, and to discriminate against, their blameless neighbors, they did so.

So the great apparatus of messaging about COVID was switched off, almost overnight, as the politics clearly soured and as Republicans consolidated an increasingly popular, multiracially inclusive, trans-partisan-appealing freedom message; and the mainstream comms apparatus simply replaced the COVID drama with a new, equally gripping European-conflict drama.

These dramas are real, of course, but they are also highly messaged; a fact about politics that adults, such as these are, would do well to understand at last.

But—when politics required it—Look over there!

So, as I was driving through the sunny valley that looked and felt like it was becoming America again, with freedom coursing through the towns and rural areas like blood slowly returning to a limb that had been asleep—I started to realize what the source of my sorrow really was.

People who had joined school boards that had masked ten-year-olds—their lives were back to normal! People who had told family members that they were unwelcome at Thanksgiving dinner—their lives were back to normal!

Huzzah.

On MSNBC that morning, Dr. Anthony Fauci, that entangled mass of compromised spiritual matter who had presided over the intentional wastelands of the pandemic; who had for two years delivered in his nasal Brooklyn cadences its lie-based soundbites, with their dearth of scientific studies, that wrecked livelihoods, destroyed kids' educations, and that drove whole communities into destitution—had declared, as if he were God Himself, that the pandemic was over.

Well—okay then!

I realized, as we drove, that my grief was not actually grief. As any pop psychologist will tell you, just beneath depression is rage.

I realized: I was furious.

Brian and I had been fighting, side by side, relentlessly, for over two years, in a bitter, exhausting war to return America—simply to normal; to its historic status as a great, free society, in which people could enjoy their constitutional liberties.

We were part of a loose community of people braver and more dedicated than we; of what you might call a liberty movement. But these heroes and heroines alongside whom we fought were all pitiably few. There were maybe hundreds; maybe a few thousand. Many more perhaps were in sympathy with us, but our energies were still spread very thin. As I noted earlier, these heroes and heroines risked medical licenses and livelihoods. They were smeared and mocked by their peers and were stripped of credentials. They staked their savings and lost them as their incomes were taken away.

But they burned, as the rebels in 1775 had burned, to defend our way of life and our institutions. They would not let the dream of America die.

They were the miserably few real doctors and real reporters, real activists and real lawyers; the truck drivers; teachers, cops, and firefighters.

They were patriots.

They did not have easy lives.

You know who had easier lives over the past two years? The quislings.

The people who stayed at the cocktail parties and who mocked the unvaccinated. The doctors who were silent about vaccine harms when teens presented with heart damage, because they might lose their licenses if they breathed a word of what they knew. The ex-Brooklynites who were supposed to be journalists but who smeared and attacked the medical freedom movement instead of reporting on Pfizer's internal documents showing massive undisclosed medical catastrophes, in one of the great corporate cover-ups of our generation.

I realized the source of my rage: the labor and nightmares and isolation and persecution and money worries and awful battles waged by us few hundreds, few thousands, had helped these quislings and collaborators have back what—we had wanted them to have back; indeed, what we had wanted us all to have back.

Our America. That treasure.

The fight was not over—it would not be over till open-ended emergency law was made impossible by new legislation, and until every criminal was charged and tried; but hey, the folks who had gone along with it all, they were, in many ways, getting their America back.

I thought of the phrase from Matthew 5:45: "for He maketh his sun to rise on the evil and on the good, and sendeth rain on the just and on the unjust."[2]

But I wanted justice.

I wanted, as I blurted out to Brian, some kind of closure. Some kind of Nuremberg Trials. A Truth and Reconciliation Commission—the South African kind, not the CCP kind. I wanted people to face what they had been, what they had done.

"It's like the partisans after the end of the war—or the revolutionaries after the fall of the Bastille. I want to shave people's heads and march them through the town square," I said to Brian, uncharitably.

I am not proud of that. But there is a reason that societies display their collaborators and quislings and traitors for public shaming. There is a reason that treason is a capital offense. There is a reason fraud and coercion, battery and child abuse, unlawful detainment and theft and child endangerment, all which were committed on mass scale "in the pandemic," are criminal offenses.

To have healing, there must be justice.

To have a free society, we must have a history. In this major historical moment, we had a massive betrayal of the social contract; one committed by millions. The social contract cannot be reknit without public account-ability, trials, public confrontations, and sentencing.

Let the school board members who masked the children be sued in civil court. Let them do community service in bright orange vests. Let them pick up trash along the sides of the roads. "I MASKED YOUR CHILD FOR NO REASON" their vests should read, as furious parents honk at them in passing.

Let the members of the Boards of Health who shut down their neighbors' businesses for no reason, face civil charges. Let their names be published in the newspapers. Let them be hounded out of their communities.

Let those who shunned the unvaccinated and disinvited them from their galas and dinner parties, experience for themselves what that feels like, and face the fact that they were hateful and engaged in hate.

Let the deans who took millions of dollars from nonprofits to adopt policies to mandate vaccines for healthy young college students—vaccines that disrupted the cycles and damaged the hearts of perfectly healthy young women and men in their charge—face trials for racketeering and trafficking, for reckless endangerment and coercion. Let the pharma exec-utives and the heads of the FDA be tried for fraud and battery.

Let the trials begin.

For people to be part of a healthy society they need to face themselves. These quislings and collaborators must be confronted with what they did.

Will I let it go? Will I forget? Will I forgive? On another morning, maybe, I pray that I will.

But not yet. Not this morning.

Amos promised: "Let judgment run down as waters, and righteous-ness as a mighty stream."[3]

Jesus said, in the gospel of Matthew, "Think not that I am come to bring peace on earth: I came not to send peace, but a sword."[4]

Maybe they meant that there are times to make amends, but there are other times when it is necessary to overturn the tables of the corrupt.

I am angry that beautiful America is mostly back, mostly free again, overnight, just because a shameless creature who should never have had the power to suspend our liberties in the first place *said* so; just because the whiny-voiced evildoers, once evidence of their fraud and coercion emerged irrevocably to light, wanted to tiptoe away from the scenes of their massive crimes.

I say: Not so fast.

Freedom is not free, as many veterans have said.

I never really understood what that meant except superficially.

But you don't get freedom back so easily if you yourself committed massive crimes.

Freedom is not free. You don't get to take away the freedom of others and enjoy it, without penalty, for yourselves.

The people you harmed, the parents of the children you harmed—they are coming. Not violently, not vengefully; but with the righteous sword of justice in hand.

Don't rest too easy, leaders who did wrong, in this bright American sunlight. You don't get America back as if nothing happened.

You cannot yet know that it's over—just because you said so.

The Statue of Liberty holds up a torch.

Crimes must be illuminated.

You cannot yet know that you will never be unmasked—revealed to all—in the bright sun of the town square.

CHAPTER TEN

The Pfizer Documents

I didn't write, or publish, or podcast much in the weeks following that drive through the Taconic foothills with Brian, as I simmered with rage. It wasn't due to the maddening DMs, or to the trauma of my visit to a once-great city where Jim Crow–style laws creating a two-tier society had been put back in place. Rather, I was rendered almost speechless by the unenviable task of trying to announce to the world that indeed, a genocide—or what I've called, clumsily but urgently, a "baby die-off"—was underway.

The WarRoom/DailyClout Pfizer Documents Analysis Volunteers, that group of 3,250 highly credentialed doctors, registered nurses, nurse practitioners, biostatisticians, medical fraud investigators, lab clinicians, and research scientists, began turning out report after report, to tell the world what is in the 450,000 internal Pfizer documents that the FDA had asked a court to keep under wraps for seventy-five years. By court order, these documents were forcibly disclosed.[1] And our experts began serving humanity by reading through these documents and explaining them in laymen's terms.

The lies they revealed are stunning.[2]

The WarRoom/DailyClout Volunteers have confirmed: that Pfizer (and thus the FDA) knew by December 2020 that the mRNA vaccines did not work—that they "waned in efficacy" and presented "vaccine failure." One side effect of getting vaccinated, as they knew by one month after the mass 2020 rollout, was "COVID-19."

Pfizer knew in May of 2021 that thirty-five minors' hearts had been damaged a week after mRNA injection—but the FDA rolled out the emergency use authorization (EUA) for teens a month later anyway, and parents did not get a press release from the US government about heart harms till August 2021, after hundreds of thousands if not millions of teens and young adults were mRNA-vaccinated.[3]

Pfizer (and thus the FDA; many of the documents say "FDA: CONFIDENTIAL" at the lower boundary) knew that, contrary to what the highly paid spokesmodels and bought-off physicians were assuring people, the mRNA, spike protein, and lipid nanoparticles did not stay in the injection site in the deltoid but rather went, within 48 hours, into the bloodstream, from there to lodge in the liver, spleen, adrenals, lymph nodes, and, if you are a woman, in the ovaries.[4]

Pfizer (and thus the FDA) knew that the Moderna vaccine had 100 mcg of mRNA, lipid nanoparticles, and spike protein, which was more than three times the 30 mcg of the adult Pfizer dose. The company's internal documents show a higher rate of adverse events with the 100-mcg dose, so they stopped experimenting with that amount internally due to its "reactogenicity"—Pfizer's words. But no one told the millions of Americans who all got the first and second 100-mcg Moderna dose *and the boosters.*

Pfizer skewed the trial subjects so that almost three-quarters were female—a sex that is less prone to cardiac damage. Pfizer *lost* the records of what became of hundreds of their trial subjects.

In the post-marketing period, which spanned just three months from December 1, 2020, to February 28, 2021, there were over 42,000 adverse event cases (patients), over 158,000 adverse events, and more than 1,200 people died. Four of the people who died, *died on the day they were injected.*[5]

Adverse events tallied up in the internal Pfizer documents are completely different from those reported on the CDC website or announced by corrupted physicians and medical organizations and hospitals. These include reports of joint pain; muscle pain (myalgia); neurological effects including multiple sclerosis, Guillain-Barré, and Bell's palsy; encephalopathy; every iteration possible of blood clotting, thrombocytopenia at scale, strokes, hemorrhages, and many kinds of ruptures of membranes throughout the human body. The side effects, about which Pfizer and the FDA knew but you did not, include skin blistering, rashes, shingles, and herpetic conditions. They include strokes, brain damage, kidney damage, liver damage, and a vast range of neurological problems including tremors, epilepsy, paralysis, and dementia.

The internal documents show that Pfizer (and thus the FDA) knew that angry red welts or hives were a common reaction to the PEG (a petroleum-derived allergen) in the vaccine. PEG is an allergen so severe that many people can go into anaphylactic shock if they are exposed to it. But people with a PEG allergy were not warned away from the vaccines or even carefully watched by their doctors, EpiPen in hand. They were left to their shock.

Pfizer knew that "exposure" to the vaccine was defined—in their own words—as skin contact, including sexual contact at the time of conception; inhalation; or lactation.[6] "Fact-checkers" can deny this all they want. The documents speak for themselves.

Of course, people who have tried to raise any of these issues have been deplatformed, scolded by the president, called insane, and roundly punished.

I was able to process all of this and keep simply reporting. But then the horror overcame me. Because the Volunteers have confirmed that there is a genocide underway, intentionally driven or not.

Israeli journalist Etana Hecht added her own superb analysis in a May 25, 2022, post to her Substack. Ms Hecht found that live births were indeed dropping at key sites around the world.[7]

Reproduction itself is targeted by the mRNA vaccines. And if you know that reproduction is harmed, and babies and fetuses are harmed, and you know that this is at scale, which everyone at Pfizer and at the FDA who read these documents, knew—and if you do not stop—then does that not ultimately become a genocide?

The WarRoom/DailyClout volunteers have confirmed that lipid nanoparticles, the tiny hard fatty casings that contain the mRNA, traverse the amniotic membrane. Pfizer's biodistribution study, approved by the FDA in November 2020, shows that the vaccine ingredients go almost everywhere in the human body and collect in organs, bone marrow, and so on.[8] That means that they enter the fetal environment. (They also traverse the blood-brain barrier, which may help explain the post-mRNA vaccination strokes and cognitive issues we are seeing.) The Volunteers drilled deep into the Pfizer documents' reports about pregnancy and found that the assurance that the vaccine is "safe and effective" for pregnant women was based on a study of forty-four French rats, followed for forty-two days (the scientists who ran the study are shareholders or employees of BioNTech).[9]

The Volunteers found that while pregnant women were excluded from the internal studies, and thus from the EUA on which basis all pregnant women were assured the vaccine was "safe and effective," nonetheless about 270 women were reported as pregnant in Pfizer's post-marketing report. More than 230 of them were lost somehow to history. But of the 32 pregnant women whose outcomes were followed—*28 lost their babies.*

That is more than 80 percent.

The Volunteers found that a baby died after nursing from a vaccinated lactating mother and was found to have had an inflamed liver. Many babies nursing from vaccinated mothers showed agitation, gastrointestinal distress, failure to thrive (to grow), and were inconsolable.

I have heard anecdotal reports of these symptoms in babies nursing from vaccinated mothers, now, from across the country. The Pfizer documents also show that some vaccinated mothers had suppressed lactation or could produce no milk at all.

Doctors, of course, were stumped by all this. Stumped.

The National Institutes of Health (NIH) database has a preprint study making the case that there is PEG in the breast milk of vaccinated women.[10]

But what does it mean that a petroleum product is appearing in mother's milk, when you are a tiny newborn, just arriving in the world? The NIH preprint itself reported higher levels of GI distress and sleeplessness in the infants studied, and one mother had elevated PEG levels in breast milk. The fine print concludes that more study is needed:

> *Larger studies are needed to increase our understanding of transfer of PEG into human milk, and potential effects after ingestion by the infant. Although expert consensus states there is minimal or no potential risk for the infant from maternal COVID-19 vaccination,*

the minor symptoms that were reported (sleep changes and gas-trointestinal symptoms) could be further investigated in future studies to determine if they are related to vaccination.[11]

Since no babies *died* in the brief time frame of the tiny NIH study, the study concluded that nursing babies suffered no real ill effects from vaccinated mothers. But the study did not follow these poor babies, with their acknowledged sleeplessness and their confirmed GI distress, to see if they "thrived"—gained weight and developed normally.

A later report by the Volunteers found that in a different section of the Pfizer documents, two babies died in utero; and that Pfizer concluded that these babies died due to transplacental exposure to the vaccine. Pfizer also had a chart that shows various ways that babies were harmed from nursing from vaccinated mothers: edema (tissue swelling), agitation, crying, sleeplessness, vomiting, fevers—all these tortured babies are calmly, carefully documented in the chart. On April 20, 2021, this report, including the information about the dead babies, was approved by the FDA. On April 23, 2021, three days later, CDC head Dr. Rochelle Walensky gave a press conference declaring that the mRNA vaccines were safe and effective for pregnant women and their babies and that there was no bad time for women planning to give birth to receive the mRNA vaccines—before, during, or after their pregnancies.[12]

With such murderous, white-washed "science" were women assured that the vaccines were "safe and effective" for them and their nursing babies.

Four of the lactating vaccinated women in the Pfizer documents reported "blue-green" breast milk. I am not making this up. And the nursing baby who died, with an inflamed liver—the case has been buried and has not made headlines.

Coincidentally—or not—the *same* FDA that turned a blind eye to vast harms to humans, and to the subcategory of moms and babies, in the Pfizer documents, declared that Abbott, a major producer of baby formula in the US, had to close its factory.[13]

Coincidentally, with little formula available and with some or many (we don't know) vaccinated moms having compromised breast milk, it turns out that Bill Gates, Jeff Bezos, Richard Branson, and Mark Zucker-berg have all invested in a start-up called "BIOMILQ"—which produces lab-grown breast milk from mammary cells.[14] Reports of this start-up include this Frankenstein-like language *as if this is normal*: "The BIO-MILQ team creates its product from cells taken from human breast tissue and milk, donated by women in the local community, who get a Target gift card in return."[15]

As if all of this is not horrific enough, Ms Hecht drew studies from three countries—Canada, Scotland, and Israel—to show that babies were dying disproportionately, during and after 2021, in highly vaccinated countries, and that newborns were dying disproportionately if they have vaccinated mothers versus unvaccinated mothers.

In highly vaccinated Scotland, almost twice the number of babies died in 2021 as died in baseline numbers.[16] Ontario, Canada, has seen a rise in stillbirths, an issue a brave parliamentarian brought to Parliament.[17]

In Israel, at Rambam Hospital in Haifa, there were 34 percent more spontaneous abortions and stillbirths from vaccinated women compared with unvaccinated women.[18]

Ms Hecht also notes that menstrual dysregulation in vaccinated women was fully confirmed by many studies, with an average of one extra day of bleeding a month (a side effect I warned about in 2021, as you recall).

You don't have to know more than eighth-grade biology to know that a dysregulated menstrual cycle; not to mention spike protein accumulating in the ovaries; not to mention the traversing of the bodies' membranes, including the amniotic sac, by tiny hard fatty lipid nanoparticles; not to mention PEG in breast milk—are all going to affect fertility, fetal health, childbirth, and babies' GI wellbeing or distress, and thus their ability or failure to thrive, let alone to bond.

And now, the babies are dying. Now scale the data from Canada, Scot-land, and Israel to all the vaccinated nations in the world.

What do we do with all of this?

Knowing as I do, that Pfizer and the FDA knew, just by looking at their own internal records, that babies were dying and mothers' milk was dis-coloring; knowing as I do that they did not alert anyone let alone stop what they were doing, and that to this day Pfizer, the FDA, and other demonic "public health" entities are pushing to mRNA-vaccinate pregnant women; knowing that they are about to force this on women in Africa and other lower-income nations who are not seeking the mRNA vaccines[19]; knowing that Pfizer and Moderna pushed for and received FDA authorization for injecting babies six months old, to four-year-old children—I was forced to conclude that we were looking into an abyss of evil humanity has not seen since 1945.[20]

I must switch gears, with this kind of knowledge, to another kind of discourse.

I am not saying that this is exactly like finding evidence of Dr. Mengele's experiments. I am saying that now, with these findings, the comparison is not excessive. These anti-humans at Pfizer, speaking at the WEF; these anti-humans at the FDA; knowing what they know—targeted the miraculous female body, with its ability to conceive, gestate, birth, and nurture life. They targeted the female body's ability to sustain a newborn human being with nothing but itself. They targeted the amniotic membrane, the ovaries that release the ovum, they targeted the lymph and blood that help support the building up of mother's milk, they targeted the fetus in utero, helpless. And they have not relented once.

They targeted the human fetus' very environment, one of the most sacred spaces on this earth, if not the most sacred.

And they knew it.

I am not proselytizing, but in those apocalyptic days, I turned to prayer. I started to say in public, once I had to face the fact of the die-off of the babies, that this was a Biblical time; and I mean Old-Testament Biblical.

I mean a time like that of the construction of the Tower of Babel—of massive arrogance against divine plans. Men such as Bill Gates tamper with and seek to outdo God's best works in lab after lab, and tech bros "disrupt" the human competition for their unsought-after goods and services by targeting human processes and by ruining the bodies made in the image of God. They tried to inject their way into destroying the health and reproductive powers of humanity, and now that Pfizer's manufacturing demand has dropped 89 percent—in part because we relentlessly reported what the Volunteers were finding—the same tech bros have moved on to attacking humanity's freedom and bodily integrity in other ways.

And the babies continue to die. I interviewed Dr. James Thorp, a fetal-maternal medicine specialist who was fired by his hospital in 2023, though he was said to be the most published of the obstetricians and to have brought in the highest revenue. I interviewed two independent midwives. And all confirmed that they are seeing unprecedented horrors in the birthing rooms: compromised placentas with networks of calcifications, probably caused by the lipid nanoparticles traversing that membrane; placentas that are shrunken, or flat, so that the babies cannot grow normally and must be delivered prematurely; babies with congenital malformations. Babies with breathing problems—air sacs between their chest walls and their lungs, which condition was identified in the Pfizer documents. Deaths in childbirth are up 40 percent, as women are endangered by amniotic sacs that fall apart and cause bleeding. Women have been returned to the unsafe childbirth conditions of the nineteenth century.

It is a time like that when the ten plagues assailed the Egyptians in Exodus, and the Lord said to Moses:

> *About midnight I will go throughout Egypt. Every firstborn son in Egypt will die, from the firstborn son of Pharaoh, who sits on the throne, to the firstborn son of the female slave, who is at her hand mill, and all the firstborn of the cattle as well. There will be loud wailing throughout Egypt—worse than there has ever been or ever will be again.*[21]

This was the worst plague of all, the slaying of the firstborn.

It is a time of *ha-satan*—Satan. In the book of Job, Satan told the Lord that he was "roaming throughout the earth, going back and forth on it."[22]

That description, that vibe, felt familiar.

It is a time of demons sauntering around in human spaces, though they look human enough themselves, smug in their Italian suits on panels at the World Economic Forum.

Ha-satan and his armies: ruining the conception, the milk, the menses, the touch, the cradling of the infant by its mother, ruining the feeding of the infant; ruining the babies themselves.

I read the prophets a lot as the Pfizer revelations emerged—because how could I not? I was looking for what writer Anne Lamott called "operating instructions." What do you do when humanity itself is threatened? When there are professional battalions and bureaucratic departments of people who act with anathema toward humanity?

Surely there must be a clue.

So I reread the story of Noah, and the Book of Esther; I reread Jeremiah.

We've been here before. Embarrassingly often, when it comes to that.

The story is always the same, at least in the Hebrew Bible (in the New Testament, of course, God skips to the end and upends the plot).

In the Hebrew Bible, God is always trying to get our attention, always, it seems, simply asking us just to walk alongside Him; simply asking us to keep His not-too-challenging commandments; not, indeed, asking a lot. As the Lord said to Jeremiah: "I will pronounce my judgments on my people because of their wickedness in forsaking me, in burning incense to other gods and in worshiping what their hands have made."[23]

In the Hebrew Bible, anyway, the math is simple. We turn, we listen, and we are saved; or we carry on heedlessly, worshipping what our own hands have made, sluts to other gods—to "the science," to media lies; to the narcissism of convention, these days, one might say—and thus we are lost.

We have been nearly lost, time after time after time.

This time, these monsters in the labs, on the transnational panels, are so very skillful; and so powerful; and their dark work is so extensive.

If God is there—again—after all the times that we have tried His patience—and who indeed knows?—will we reach out a hand to Him in return? Will we take hold in the last moment out of this abyss, and simply find a way somehow to walk alongside Him?

Or will we, in losing the babies, and heedlessly carrying on nonetheless—be truly lost ourselves?

CHAPTER ELEVEN

Facing the Beast

I was relaxing in our screened porch at our little cottage in the forest, feeling rather pleased with myself. It had been an arduous week of the usual combat for liberty. But there had been victories.

I was reading a decorating magazine (we all have our vices). The grass was dewy; birds were loud. The morning was glorious.

I was feeling pioneerish and independent. I was alone in the house; Brian was traveling. I enjoyed the narrative moment: "Lady in the woods."

Then I heard a thump about eight feet away, behind my head. It was an exasperated thump, like a teenager slamming the door to his room. Like, "Really??"

I glanced behind me and saw the enormous ears and forehead of a sizable brown bear, who was ducking insolently, clearly aware of me, to lower himself behind the trash cans.

I sped indoors, locking the door. I grabbed a weapon out of the hall closet. In my haste, I grabbed the weapon that looked like a rifle instead of the actual rifle, which was in a case. Thus I found myself locked in an upstairs bathroom, cowering, armed with a BB gun.

I sort of knew this bear. Brian had captured him on his outdoor wildlife camera about a year ago; what must have been this bear and his brother or sister, when the little ones were just adorable cubs. One of the cubs had nuzzled the trail cam till the mom had batted it away, urging her little ones to follow her deeper into the woods, far from the dangerous things of men. One of the cubs had now turned into this massive creature, what bear-watchers call a "sub-adult."

I saw, peering fearfully out of the window, that he was no longer cute and fat. He was thin, but massively muscled, and looked disoriented. He must have been eight feet long.

I raced into the upstairs bedroom and secured the windows. The bear left the garbage cans and followed me around the corner of the house. I could now see him pacing and sniffing directly opposite the bedroom windows, though on the ground level. There were windows all around the house on that level. Bears have been known to break into homes.

I looked under the bed: hiding there could not save me if the bear made it into the house. I realized I was holding a BB gun and felt ridiculous. Even if I managed to shoot him, this would do nothing but enrage him. The thin bedroom doors, that I had thought so rustic and charming, could be broken down in no time by an angry animal of that size.

My heart pounded as I realized that he was not leaving; he continued pacing and circling, no matter where I went.

I went back into the bathroom and locked that door with its flimsy lock.

There he was *again*, outside on *that* side of the house, as if he was spotting me or as if he could scent me. Surely, he could smell my fear.

I cowered behind the bathroom curtain. The bear paused in his ransacking of the trash, stood up again on hind legs, looked right at me—or smelled right at me—and bared his long, sharp yellow teeth.

If I had had sympathy for the hungry teenager abandoned by his mom (or "emancipated" by his mom, as the bear-watching sites explain), it evaporated.

I was on the phone with Brian, frozen with fear.

"Make yourself big! Shout at him!" Brian instructed. That was impossible. I could not move. I could hardly breathe.

That would be it, surely, I thought, after the bear had exhausted the trash bag. He'd leave now, surely. But no. He came back toward me again like a nightmare and headed once more to circle the house.

I called the sheriff's office.

Twice they told me that nothing could be done, and to stay inside. I don't blame the Columbia County Sheriffs. They have issues to deal with more serious than a former city lady trapped in her house by a hungry bear.

But the bear kept circling right up against the walls of the house. This went on for an hour. Adrenaline poured through my bloodstream. I did wonder if I would die that day.

When I called back in spite of myself and begged the police for help, they told me to call again only if he managed to break into the house. (Thank you, "Defund the Police" advocates.)

At certain points of extreme stress, I could not even bring myself to look outside to see where the bear was. What if I looked and couldn't see him because he was already in the house? I went right into a place that is familiar to those of us with PTSD—a traumatized place where you freeze and where you engage in magical thinking.

If I don't look at the bear he won't be there. If I don't meet his gaze he won't see me or smell me. I am somewhere else. I am not really here.

After an hour I was saved when brave colleagues of mine, who had been meeting nearby, drove down our wooded driveway, blowing their car horns. I raced down the steps, never so happy to see people in my life. Had the sound scared the bear away? He was now nowhere to be seen. My friend Reinette laughed at the sight of me scrambling to open the door to welcome them—still carrying my useless BB gun.

I think I was coherent, but I was in shock. An officer from the sheriff's department arrived at the same time, bless him. Humans saved me. The aggressor, the wild animal, had been scared away, and not by me. I'd been a wreck, hopeless.

For days, I ruminated about the sharp yellow teeth of that bear, exposed as he raised his snout into the air, sniffing, like a scene from a horrifying fairy tale.

Why do I tell this story?

Because—the bear had been growing more and more comfortable emerging from the woods; he grew more and more comfortable exploring our trash, and then he took over territory by exploring our lawn. He was "habituated" ultimately, as bear-watchers say; he had ownership of the lawn and was circling the house to mark his territory. He was comfortable at last in stalking the homeowners.

He was here because I had done nothing to stop him. He was here because I let him slowly take over our home.

My not being able to look directly at the bear did not make me any safer. My denial put me in greater danger.

This all, of course, really happened. But that does not mean it is not also a metaphor.

The same week that this happened, I also finalized my reporting about the Pfizer vaccines, showing—what I knew for months I would eventually find.

The heart of the manufacture and distribution of millions of doses of the mRNA vaccines that have caused such a swath of death and destruction throughout North America and Western Europe is enmeshed with the plans, methods, and manufacturing infrastructure of our existential adversary.

The enemy is within our very bodies.

Since I first started reading the reports produced by the 3,250 medical and scientific experts of the WarRoom/DailyClout Pfizer Documents Analysis Volunteers team, based on the 450,000 Pfizer documents released under court order, I knew I was seeing not just medicine gone wrong, not just a greedy pharmaceutical company and a regulatory agency that was fully corrupted, but rather, or additionally, I was seeing a massive act of war.

When I saw the eighteen months' worth of sudden deaths, slow deaths, encephalopathy, strokes, heart attacks, pericarditis, myocarditis, Guillain-Barré, Bell's palsy, multiple sclerosis, blood clots, lung clots, leg clots, blue-green breast milk, spontaneous abortions, stillbirths, neonatal seizures, neonatal multiorgan system failure, liver damage, kidney damage, suppressed lactation, suppressed sperm count, disrupted menses, all detailed in the Pfizer documents; when I saw the fact that 34,000 plus of the 42,000 plus "adverse events" case reports—meaning "patients"—itemized in the first three months of the rollout of the Pfizer injections were in the US—with the next largest group being in Western Europe—and that the fifty-six countries around the world that also had Pfizer injections rolled out amounted to only a bit over 7,000 case reports total—I knew I was seeing not just medicine gone wrong on a massive scale, but rather that I was seeing an act of war.

When I saw the doubling of neonatal deaths in country after country, the rise of 34 percent above normal in stillbirths and spontaneous abortions for vaccinated versus unvaccinated mothers; when I saw that 3,816 vaccinated women in the Vaccine Adverse Events Reporting System (VAERS) database lost their babies—57 percent of all the neonatal deaths in all the time that VAERS records had been kept[1]; when I saw that of 32 pregnancies followed in the Pfizer documents, 28 of the unborn babies *died*[2]; when I saw the rise of 40 percent in maternal death rates[3] and the shocking rise in cases of disability in the West[4]—I knew I was not seeing just medicine gone wrong on a massive scale, but that I was witnessing an act of war.

When I saw that you could boost the lethality or the damage caused by the injection by simply changing how dilute the solution is, or simply by reassigning which brand you use—with Moderna (100 mcg) far more damaging than Pfizer (30 mcg)—I knew that I was seeing not just medicine gone wrong on massive scale, but an act of war.

When I saw a study out of Hong Kong in 2021—a study that, of course, was answerable to the CCP—that revealed that a second dose (a "booster") into the bloodstreams of mice resulted in visibly enlarged hearts with white patches that could be seen by the naked eye, as well as cytokine storms and liver damage, I realized that the two-dose regime and then the "boosters" were slow but progressive ways to damage and then destroy the health of Western patients. The study concluded: "Post-vaccination myopericarditis is reported after immunization with coronavirus disease 2019 (COVID-19) messenger RNA (mRNA) vaccines."[5]

And yet with this CCP-overseen finding, that by injecting mammals with the mRNA vaccine, their hearts were visibly damaged, the worldwide injection program kept going—I knew that I was seeing not just medicine gone wrong on massive scale, but an act of war.

We were told that Pfizer/BioNTech is a German collaboration. But it is actually a German-Chinese company. Since I first found that Pfizer/BioNTech had an MOU (memorandum of understanding) with Fosun Pharmaceuticals, a major CCP-linked pharmaceutical company based in Shanghai, to make the Pfizer/BioNTech mRNA vaccines,[6] I knew that with a bit more digging I would find China at the heart of these acts of war.

Indeed, Fosun is not separate from the CCP; it *is* the CCP: Fosun acquired almost half of Sinopharm.[7] Sinopharm is owned, in turn, directly by the Chinese state and thus reports directly to the CCP. The initial BioNTech/Fosun MOU seems to imply that all of the BioNTech/Fosun joint ventures' activity is in China, or in regions aligned with or close to China. But is that now the case? Fosun Pharma did not stay in China. It came here. Fosun Pharmaceuticals is now also Fosun Pharmaceuticals USA, with branches for R&D and product formulation in Boston and Princeton, New Jersey. In other words, it is producing formulations and products in the US for distribution in the US and around the world.

Fosun Pharma USA offers potential partners: "A global reach with a focus on the United States and China markets." It offers "US Rights" and "Global Rights" as well as "China Rights."[8] The FDA filing for the Fosun Pharma USA facility says the facility is authorized to "develop specifications," including for the PCR tests and antigen tests it creates, and that the facility can also have US agents.[9]

This is crucial. Fosun Pharmaceuticals does not just partner with Pfizer/BioNTech to make the COVID-19 vaccines, they make, as noted, the PCR tests that are the one primary metric that determines the scale of the pandemic in North America and Western Europe and thus the lockdowns of whole countries, whole industrial sectors.

A CCP-run company, and CCP-created product, thus, decides—who can go to work or school, who must close his or her shop, who can or cannot travel—in Europe and the US. A CCP-run company decides the formulation of the PCR and antigen tests that have gone deep into the nasopharyngeal cavities of Westerners who were forced, week after week, to test and test and test with these products.

This CCP-owned hybrid entity is creating the diagnostic instruments that determine the scale of pandemics in the West. The CCP can thus dial it up or down.

It also makes millions of the Pfizer/BioNTech mRNA injections, the Merck COVID-19 pill Molnupiravir, the Pfizer COVID-19 pill Paxlovid—for which Pfizer CEO Albert Bourla signed a contract with the US government to provide 10 million doses for $5.29 *billion* in 2022—all this for the US and for ten other countries including those in the EU.[10]

These are all formulated and distributed by a company leading directly to the Chinese Communist Party.

When President Biden does a deal with Pfizer/BioNTech in the millions of dollars, with our tax money, he is giving a substantial portion of the funds *to China.* When he spends tax dollars via omnibus bills for PPE, including millions for PCR and antigen tests, he is writing checks to—China.

Is Fosun a squeaky clean CCP-run pharma enterprise? In 2018 a whistleblower—and in China, that is courageous thing to be—broke a scandal revealing that Fosun Pharmaceuticals had "massively" faked its data and also bribed regulators. Its facilities were so chaotic that the US FDA sent the company a stern letter.[11]

BioNTech's SEC filing reports as, 100 percent achieved, a tech transfer to—China. Not to a "Chinese company" or a "Chinese individual" but to the country of—China.[12]

Further, the SEC filing explains that it will affect the "technology transfer with China" after marketing approval has been granted. I don't know what "technology transfer" means in this SEC filing. SEC filing experts who have reviewed it for me have suggested that this can mean intellectual property, manufacturing methodologies, formulas, data, or all four. But surely it is significant that the company BioNTech has declared as 100 percent complete or in process, a "technology transfer" to *China.* It was not "sharing" the tech or "licensing" the tech—it *transferred* the tech. That means that in some capacity, China is in charge of some aspect of BioNTech's technology.

So take all of the above, and map it against the 158,000-plus adverse events in the Pfizer documents, the deadly harms to reproduction, the babies in seizures; map it against the population drop, the rise in disabilities; map it against the rigid, cruel vaccine mandates aimed at Western defense forces (Canada's, and Australia's, and all of Western Europe's, as well as at the most powerful military in the world, that of the United States)—map it against the vaccine mandates aimed at our police, our health care workers, our firefighters, our pilots, our first responders, our kids, our babies—all this done by a White House that is captive, via Hunter Biden's laptop, to the Chinese Communist Party; that laptop contained evidence of millions of dollars changing hands from high level CCP-connected executives, to members of the Biden family. As the *Washington Post* reported:

Over the course of 14 months, the Chinese energy conglomerate and its executives paid $4.8 million to entities controlled by Hunter Biden and his uncle, according to government records, court documents and newly disclosed bank statements, as well as emails contained on a copy of a laptop hard drive that purportedly once belonged to Hunter Biden.[13]

Add to all of this the evidence of birth rates declining, especially in the West, by 13 to 20 percent.[14] Statistician Igor Chudov began in 2022 to track government databases regarding live births—and consistently found that a drop of this scale in live births was taking place after women in those nations had received mRNA vaccines. He found a "dramatic decline" in live births in Germany in 2022. Chudov drilled into individual databases and found that births had dropped 9.5 percent for one month in Germany; Sweden's live births were down 13 percent for the month of October 2022; the UK in 2022 saw a 15.3 percent decline in live births (that country stopped counting after June of 2022); and California saw a drop of 5 percent year on year by 2022.[15]

How better to cripple the world's other superpower than by destroying our American front lines and our American next generation, with tainted, murderous vaccines, flowed easily enough into the West via (not even that many) shell companies and cutouts? How easy to do the same to Western Europe, to Canada and Australia, as a whole?

Take all of the above and consider that the virus originated in China; and now all of the testing apparatuses, as well as millions of the vaccines, the catastrophically damaging or lethal "solutions" to the virus, also all originate from the same folks—the same leadership cadre that brought the world forced abortions, citizens welded into their homes, Uighur concentration camps, and organ harvesting.

I made the case in my book *The Bodies of Others* that a transnational group of bad actors—including the WEF, the WHO, the Bill and Melinda Gates Foundation, tech companies, and the CCP—used the pandemic to crush humanity and to destroy the West.

With the provenance of the vaccines and tests, you can see yet another mechanism, yet another core methodology of this warfare.

Mapping these points of evidence, I think you may start to see what I see. This all means, of course, that we are staring into the abyss right now. Traumatized or not, we all need to snap out of denial.

We let our adversary come too close to us. Into our very bloodstreams.

What does it mean, to "face the beast"? Does it mean to face at last the role of China—and of the WEF, the WHO, and of our own formerly democratic government and those of others'—in this catastrophic past three years?

Does it mean facing the fact that evil on an unimaginable, even super-natural scale is having its way with our world?

Or does it mean: facing the mirror; facing the ugliness, the hatred, the credulity that manifested so hideously from inside the very selves of so many of us?

You decide.

Meanwhile, we need to turn and face the ravening beast.

CHAPTER TWELVE

Thanksgiving Gathering

I n November 2022, I traveled to Florida, to do research for a new book. I stayed in a hotel for almost a week, in a modest, touristy town, a few miles from the beach.

We were able to be in Florida at that time because for the second year, we had not been invited to Thanksgiving celebrations with our relatives.

Two years in, I had stopped hoping that we would be, and my pain had scarred over into angry dismissiveness; and anger at myself that I still wanted so badly to rejoin my people, my nearest ones.

I tried not to think about this at all. It never did not hurt.

For anyone who may have forgotten, Florida and New York were, at that time, essentially different countries. Florida Governor Ron DeSantis was giving press conferences showcasing the fact that he had not closed down local businesses, and that his economy was thriving. Public health in Florida, as he pointed out, was about the same as in lockdown states. But New York governor Kathy Hochul, on the other hand, was persevering with policies that shocked even some diehard lockdown militants. She sought to create quarantine camps, and when a judge objected and struck down her bid, she appealed. And she insisted on keeping schools and businesses compliant with disabling mRNA injection mandates and with forced COVID measures.

Every day, when I was in the hotel in the friendly, little, whimsically tacky beach town, from the moment I opened my eyes till the moment I settled into my cool hotel sheets, my heart exulted with indescribable happiness.

Thanksgiving Gathering

You know those dreams in which a loved one who is dead appears to you, in full youth and health and vigor? You say to that person, in the dream, with tears of joy streaming down your cheeks, Oh my God—*you are not dead!* But then you wake up, and that person is still dead.

It was that dream.

But for a nation.

In Florida I was in a delirium of happiness mixed with nostalgia mixed with grief—because it felt like America.

That is, it felt the way I remember America to have felt, pre-2020.

The malls, the cookie-cutter townhouse developments, the chain stores and auto body shops, churches and sports bars, were the same as they were anywhere in the country.

But the people were entirely different. The culture was entirely different.

Everywhere I went I saw people who were—proud, and confident, and relaxed.

It did not matter who they were, or from where they had come. This was a universal birthright, it seemed, in that part of America.

The very young bartender/busboy, who had recently immigrated from Thailand, was proud, confident, and relaxed. The multigenerational family reunion groups, families who had lived for generations in the region, were proud, confident, and relaxed. The suburban moms walking to their vans in the mall parking lot, were proud, confident, and relaxed. My Uber driver, a former special operator whose wife had opened a Filipino food truck in the downtown area, was proud, confident, and relaxed. The pretty forty-something bartender with one side of her head shaved and with a flowering vine tattooed down one arm, who showed me pictures of her two adult sons—one, she explained, who had autism—the young men standing on either side of their mom, hugging her tight, and all of them grinning; she, too, was proud, confident, and relaxed.

And so on. African American, Caucasian, Latino, whatever, male, female, aged, and young; this was a quality that united everyone.

There was a big, colorful sign—a piece of public art—in the little green park flanking the mall. People stood in front of it to take photos for Instagram.

It read, "You Are Deeply Loved."

Once, when I was walking back to my hotel, I passed a small group of people—three or four of them—with their arms around each other, heads bowed, in a huddle. Colleagues? Friends? A family?

I realized that they were unselfconsciously, publicly, praying.

The pride in themselves, and the calm sense of security of people everywhere around me, simply being who they were, and gladly, openly, showing others who they were, really struck me.

I remembered this quality from the Before Era, as being generally true of Americans.

It was this once-American quality that had formerly so fascinated the rest of the world—the broken, fearful, inhibited rest of the world.

Whether it was the admiration in ravaged 1950s Europe of the proud, relaxed gunslinger John Wayne, or the French marveling in the 1960s at the unabashedly goofy Jerry Lewis, or the appreciation worldwide in the 1970s of beat poet Allen Ginsberg sharing his wild free verse with rapt college audiences while seated on a meditation pillow, Americans were once magnetically attractive because we were once so proud—of ourselves, our speech, our liberties—in a nation in which our individuality was protected by an intact Constitution.

We were relaxed, compared to other peoples, because our rights were inviolable.

The lure of America was not that "the streets were paved with gold" or that one could make a fortune in a generation, though that was attractive, no doubt, to many; the true magnetism of Americans was that we acted like free people.

It was that charismatic quality that everyone still had in Florida, and that had been lost—dramatically in some cases and imperceptibly in others—in the lockdown and mandate states. I did not realize how bad it felt in New York State day by day, till I left it.

Because people in Florida felt relaxed, proud, and confident, and because they had never been held indoors against their will, told where to stand, stripped of their holidays, or forced into submitting to poisonous unchosen injections, there was a rhythm to social life there still. People from all walks of life chatted away with one another; the lady who wrapped up the sandals I bought chatted away with me, she chatted with all who came in; the chiropractor I visited chatted away with his customers; the salad shop workers chatted with the people who dropped off the bagels; the lady moving her grocery cart around me made a jolly, friendly remark. All this complexity took place in a peaceful, almost measurable rhythm.

When social scientists have done stop-motion videos of people moving around a city intersection, they prove that humans move in a perceptible rhythm; by the same token, newborns sync their breathing and nervous systems with their moms' and vice versa, and happy couples' respiration and even heartbeats align when they sit near one another.

Whole communities unconsciously align with one another in creating complex rhythms.

I had been feeling, strongly, that something was discordant, jarring, in how we in the lockdown states were relating to each other as 2022 was drawing to a close. The contrast with Florida showed me what it is: we had had our community rhythms broken off, our human music silenced.

Then, as we started up our lives again, our interactions became tentative, awkward, erratic. Do we chat with the checkout girl? Do we not, as she is just trying to breathe behind her mask? Did she get out of the habit of chatting, if unmasked now? Do we drop in on a friend? Or do we Zoom now forever? Do we hug, shake hands; not hug, not shake hands?

Or do we never again just embrace, just kiss, just stop by?

It was all smashed to smithereens.

But in Florida, I saw from the richness of those little social moments that these were a people who had not lost two years of church, of knitting clubs, of Rotary, of synagogue, of playdates, of ballroom dancing, of after-work happy hours, of bowling, of fishing, of brunch, of poker games, of christenings, of bar mitzvahs.

So the myriad, invisible bonds that are created with every human interaction and woven tight by kindness and mutual enjoyment and shared mission—had never been severed. That continuity allowed for the restful, elegant human rhythm I saw all around me.

How lovely it was; how heavenly.

If you want the Kingdom of Heaven—it turns out that other people simply acting decently to one another, in community, are in fact the Kingdom of Heaven.

(I think Jesus did try to tell us that.)

In contrast, we in the lockdown states, the mandate states, barely knew how to approach one another; we'd lost two years of weaving our lives together.

The babies and toddlers of 2020 to 2022 in Florida still engage in peekaboo. I realized, when a Floridian toddler launched into the game with me, how much I missed that ancient interaction.

I happened to visit Houston after my Florida journey. And while the freedom of Texas had not been as absolute as the freedom of Florida, I saw the same relaxed pride and confidence among adults and the same expressiveness among little ones, that I had seen in Florida.

The babies and toddlers of Florida and Texas still issue crazy, heart-melting smiles at passing strangers, and wave at them or babble at them or try to tell them things, as human babies and toddlers evolved to do.

But this innate expressiveness became all but extinct among the babies and toddlers of 2020 to 2022 up in the Northeast, and in California, and in other lockdown, mandate states.

These Northeastern little ones of 2020 to 2022 stared with blank, impassive faces at adult faces that had only recently emerged from terrifying, disorienting masks.

The expressions of these poor children are more insect-like than human, and without that gorgeous interactivity, these babies and children of 2020 to 2022 lose much of the human charm with which they would otherwise be endowed. Their stony impassiveness is a devastating feedback loop. As they are not talking to or babbling to or smiling at adults, fewer adults talk to or smile at them.

Why do I raise all of this in relation to Thanksgiving 2022?

Because we must face the fact that adults in the parts of the country that locked down and endured mandates do not have this relaxed pride, so formerly typical of Americans, anymore, and their children too are now different—and perhaps always will be.

These populations, I saw so clearly as I went from Florida and Texas to the Northeast, now have something broken in them; in us.

I realized when I left Florida and Texas and landed in Boston and drove to New York, that what was blanketing the lockdown, mandate states was shame and fear.

Yes, even as late as November 2022.

There was a palpable blanket of shame and fear now over New York, over Massachusetts, because we all have been through a life-changing traumatic experience, and not just for a day or for a month but for two years.

We were all violated in front of one another.

We were all made helpless to save one another or ourselves.

Husbands could not protect their wives from being forcibly injected, if the wives had to keep their jobs.

Parents could not save their adult children from being forcibly injected, if the adult children wished to feed their own families.

Adult sons and daughters could not save their elderly parents from miserable isolation and from dying alone.

Wives could not save their husbands from being neglected in hospitals or even impaired or worse with remdesivir, a drug that had been assigned by the guidelines of compromised agencies such as NIH as the standard hospital protocol for treating COVID, but which caused kidney damage and death.[1] The WHO advised *against* prescribing remdesivir for COVID-19 patients.[2] A study published in *The Lancet* showed worse adverse events for those on remdesivir than in the control group, and the study had to be terminated because 12 percent of the participants taking the drug had adverse outcomes.[3]

I once knew a toddler who had to have her hair brushed, and there were tangles. She protested and bellowed and resisted, as a healthy child will. "You have to, darling," I said as soothingly as I could, as I brushed the tangles out as gently as I knew how. "Honey, you have to."

The minute she had the chance, a few days later, she sat me down on a stoop and pretended to pull tangles out of my hair. "Yer *hap* to," she told me furiously. "Yer *hap* to."

The desire to fight back, to avenge harm, is as innate in us as healthy animals.

But for two years we in lockdown states were stripped of our powers to defend ourselves or our loved ones; and everyone saw our powerlessness.

As any sexual assault survivor knows, as traumatic as the violation is, equally traumatic is the fact that most survivors were not able, whether they were overpowered or detained or threatened or simply froze, to resist or to fight back. Studies have shown that when a victim was not able to fight back, the attack leads to more serious and long-term PTSD compared with victims who were able to fight back (not to minimize their experiences). This is true for PTSD among veterans as well.

For the past two years, all of us in lockdown states were violated and traumatized, and very few of us were allowed, or allowed ourselves, to fight back.

I am a survivor of sexual assault in childhood. So I do not make this analogy lightly.

But there is so much of the same flavor, the same tenor, as that of the flavor and tenor of sexual assault, in the way that locked-down and mandated populations, men and women and children, were held against their will; forced inside; restrained, threatened, and intimidated; publicly shamed; and compelled to submit themselves to an implacable outside power that claimed and invaded and penetrated their bodies against their will.

So yes, sexual abuse traumatizes you for a lifetime, no matter how good your therapy is or how fortunate your circumstances or how safe your relationships are for the rest of your life.

By the same token, in the lockdown and mandate states, we are damaged and broken, with mass PTSD; and no matter what happens to us in the future, this damage and violation of us will always be part of who we are and part of what happened to us.

You always have messed-up trust-related skills, as a sexual assault survivor. This safe situation turns dangerous in the blink of an eye. How can you ever be safe again? This babysitter turns into a devil. This professor mutates into a monster. Where is true safety?

By the same token, the rest of us who lived in lockdown and mandate states, will always live with a shadow of fear.

The public demonstration of the helplessness of a hostage, or of a target of sexual abuse, is standard in warfare. I will always be haunted by the survivors of mass rape in Sierra Leone. Their assailants intentionally injured them vaginally and made the attacks a matter of public knowledge. The women were identified as having been damaged or "ruined." The shame inflicted on the victims was intentional, but the community, too, was targeted with shaming by the enemy, as the community was publicly revealed to the world as being too weak to protect its women and girls.

There is a reason that when an invading army wishes to break a population, it will force a father to watch the torture of a child or force a husband to witness the rape of a wife. This helpless shame breaks people.

So the blanket of shame and fear I felt in Massachusetts, in New York State, compared to its absence in Florida and Texas, will be part of the feeling, the atmosphere, in those states for decades; for the rest of our natural lives.

And again, what does this have to do with Thanksgiving?

We in New York State, in Massachusetts, all over the country that went along with COVID tyranny in 2020 to 2022, resumed shopping for, planning for, and preparing Thanksgiving dinner, in a deeply shameful context. Because we lost two Thanksgivings to what has now been revealed as a massive hoax.

And we all knew that we all knew it by now. Our gullibility, the wool that was pulled over our eyes, is now a public matter.

At the checkout counter in my local supermarket, people were trying hard to chat and joke casually about the upcoming holiday, as they used to pre-2020. "I have the pies and the ice cream, and there is enough food for an army, so I figure, if there is anything else they want, they can do without or get it themselves." "Yes, the older generation likes to take control of cooking the turkey, and I am fine with that." "Yes, it's so true, I always leave too much shopping for the last minute—" And so on.

As if everything were normal.

But—everything was not normal.

We were having Thanksgiving in 2022.

But it turns out we could all have had Thanksgiving together in 2021.

And we could even probably have had Thanksgiving—those of us who might have chosen to do so—in 2020.

We were lied to right . . . down . . . the line.

So we all lost at least two Thanksgivings.

There are children who are almost three years old now who have never had Thanksgiving at all.

A famous poem about springtime by A. E. Housman reads:

Loveliest of trees, the cherry now
Is hung with bloom along the bough
And stands about the woodland ride
Wearing white for Eastertide.

Now, of my threescore years and ten,
Twenty will not come again,
And take from seventy springs a score,
It only leaves me fifty more.

And since to look at things in bloom
Fifty springs are little room,
About the woodlands I will go
To see the cherry hung with snow.[4]

We don't have that many Easters, that many Christmases, in a human lifetime; that many Passovers, that many Thanksgivings.

How many Thanksgivings do you have left?

Twenty? Sixty?

Two?

One?

None of us knows.

But the Dr. Walenskys of the world, the Dr. Faucis, the presidents, the governors, who have no authority over you, decided without your consent that they knew better than you what was important in your life; and they decided to take away forever two of your Thanksgivings.

You will never get those back.

So, we try to pick up again, here in the Northeast, our rituals, with a sense of awkwardness and shame—shame that they were so easily stripped from us; shame that we were so duped; shame that we so publicly could not protect ourselves or our loved ones.

Men were unmanned. Women were un-womaned.

The Thanksgiving gatherings may even look different than they did pre-2020. Some families are broken right through. Some relationships will never heal.

All of us, outside of Florida, and Texas, and maybe South Dakota, the few nonlockdown, nonmandate states, are now victims. We never won't be.

For Thanksgiving, I want America back. But to make all of America, not just a few blessed states, free and confident, safe and relaxed once again, will take a generation.

And it can only happen for us as a nation trying to heal—just as this is true for any of us who try to heal as individuals—if we first face the agonizing fact that our bodies were, indeed, a battlefield, as feminists used to say; that we were indeed, as a nation, stripped, and shamed before everyone; held hostage, and plundered, and violated.

It can only happen for us if we seek out now not just abundance, but truth.

CHAPTER THIRTEEN

Twenty Will Not Come Again

On December 3, 2022, very early in the morning, I took a car from my cozy hotel in Boston, to the open commons in front of Yale's Old Campus. I got out of the car in nearly freezing weather.

Nothing was open. The early day was overcast. I had had no breakfast, and I needed coffee. The night before had been a late one for me, as I had made an evening business presentation. So, I was cranky, hungry, cold, and tired. I had nowhere to change or to brush my hair, so I did the best I could in the ladies' restroom of the New Haven Public Library.

I mention the discomfort of the morning because it seemed to be emblematic of the icy shoulder that my alma mater presented to me.

I—we—were there to protest the mandate by the university of "bivalent boosters" into the bodies of the students; this was required of them before they could—and in order that they might—return to campus after winter break.

Astonishingly, the faculty and staff—meaning, surely, the administrators too—were not thus mandated. (Harvard, too, has a similar mandate affecting students but not faculty.)

We who were there to protest were outcasts, reprobates. Yet all we were doing there was pleading for the safety of the young men and women in the campus just beyond us.

There were about three dozen people at the rally and then at the march; a small, committed, straggling group. Few parents of students were present; administrators, faculty—appeared to be entirely absent. A few dedicated health freedom activists, organized by TeamRealityCT, and we the speakers—stood vulnerably in a corner of the commons, shouting terrifying facts and urgent warnings into a crackly mic, into a heedless wind, expecting to be arrested.

As I awaited my turn at the mic, memories flooded in. They had been such happy ones, to start with. There was the Old Campus, just behind us; where I had been a joyful seventeen-year-old, racing across green lawns, meeting new friends. I recalled how my heart had soared at the beauty of the crenellated walls and the Romanesque arches. A California girl, I had never seen such buildings before in real life.

I recalled jumping into pickup games of Frisbee, or marveling at the turning of deciduous autumn leaves—a spectacle that I, who had grown up among evergreens, had never seen before. I'd been captivated at the sight of my first snowfall; at the delicate flakes drifting magically down, in the light of a streetlamp, outside the glowing stained-glass windows of Battell Chapel.

I had flashbacks of drinking in the heady atmosphere, as a freshman, as a sophomore, of a whole new culture: I had been astonished, as a raw child of the wild West Coast, as the daughter of a beat poet and a hippie anthropologist, at all the age-old rituals and precious mannerisms of the Ivy League East. Learning about Mory's, the legendary bar where generations of students have carved their names, and where more than a century of photographs of hopeful young men—and then, young men and young women—on sports teams, adorn the walls; about singing groups; about tailgate parties; about secret societies; about seersucker jackets and boating shoes; about preppies, and Andover and Exeter, and Locust Valley Lockjaw—a way of speaking that the kids of the ancestral fortunes used at that time—a bored drawl; about legacies and jocks; about how to make polite conversation with parents at the dean's garden parties. I remember realizing that the allure of an Ivy League education was not just what you learned—you could learn as well in any number of decent state schools—but rather it was that ticket to privilege, that Alice in

Wonderland–type access, that door to the sunlit garden; how it revealed to you—a metaworld, invisible to the less lucky; the cultivated network that would nurture and soothe you for your entire life; that world of sailboats and dinner jackets (not "tuxedos," I learned), and of turning to your right for the first course and to your left for the second. Far more than all that, though, I was high on being surrounded by what I saw as *smart people*; in an entire community that cared about being smart.

I was ecstatic at sitting in classrooms where the greatest minds of my day taught us about our intellectual heritage—Greek and Latin literary classics, Milton's *Paradise Lost*, the Romantic poets. I remembered learning about Galen—the father of Western medicine. About the Hippocratic oath. About the Geneva Conventions. About any number of human rights movements. About the Constitution.

The language of Yale University—whose motto was *"Lux et Veritas"*—"Light and Truth"—was the language of an institution devoted to sustaining and passing on the greatest values of the greatest civilization on earth. Once, I had sat there as a student in Battell Chapel and listened to then-President Bart Giamatti welcome us; he'd described what a liberal arts education was: its values of open inquiry and of freedom of speech. I'd watched the light pour through the arched windows and had felt, sitting among equally rapt students, the solemn thrill of the task we thus undertook: to protect and cherish civilization.

And I had believed it. I was so proud to have been part of that tradition.

So how stark was the irony, that now I was there to try to stop a barbarous betrayal of the student body by the very institution that claimed to speak up on behalf of civilization itself. How ironic that I was here to try to stop a crude act of foolishness, and of illogic and of sheer stupidity.

I was at the rally because I'd been informed by activist Joni McGary—not by the university's communications with its alumni, not by CNN or by the *New York Times*—that Yale University was, incredibly, mandating the "bivalent booster"—the one tested on eight mice—on its entire student population.

This demand was *in spite of* these students having been twice mRNA vaccinated. It was *in spite of* their having been already "boosted." It was *in spite of* any prior COVID-19 infection, or despite religious objections, physical problems, fears, or resistance.

My soul revolted.

I stood in the bitter cold on a low, makeshift wooden dais, speaking without notes, issuing what became a roar from the depth of a mother's heart, my own heart, about the danger to the young adults in the institution behind me, that was being posed—by the very institution itself.[1]

In my speech, I explained that 55,000 Pfizer documents, released via a lawsuit by Aaron Siri and his firm, had been reviewed by our volunteer group of 3,500 medical and scientific experts; that they had written, under the leadership of DailyClout COO, Amy Kelly, forty-eight reports. These experts have proven that 77 percent of the adverse events in the Pfizer documents are sustained by women, and that of those, 16 percent are, *in Pfizer's own words,* "reproductive disorders."[2]

In the Pfizer documents there are, as I cried out in my speech, twenty different names for ruining the menstrual cycles of women. You can bleed all month; or have two periods a month; or hemorrhage viciously; or have agonizing cramps. How could young women compete in scholarly terms, how could they be athletes, I asked, in the face of this certain suffering? And how was this knowing infliction of menstrual damage *not* discriminatory against women—and not thus a violation of Title IX, which requires an equitable learning environment?[3]

The Pfizer documents also confirm, I shouted to the crowd, as Dr. Chris Flowers has abundantly proven, that both Pfizer and the FDA knew, four months before there was any public announcement, that the mRNA vaccine had caused myocarditis in teenagers and young adults.[4] I warned the university that to force the students to submit to this injection would for certain cause infertility and / or horrific menstrual suffering in some of the young women, and that it would for sure cause heart damage in some of the young men.

I made the case, based on both federal and Connecticut state law, that this situation constituted human trafficking, which is defined under federal law as "the recruitment, harboring, transportation, provision, or obtaining of a person for labor or services, through the use of force, fraud, or coercion for the purpose of subjection to involuntary servitude, peonage, debt bondage, or slavery.[5]

A victim does not need to be physically transported from one location to another for the crime to fall within this definition."[6]

Connecticut human trafficking law definitions also apply directly to the situation of the beleaguered students at Yale, forced to provide the "service" of being lab rats or medical hostages.[7]

These are Class A felonies, punishable by twenty years in prison and a $20,000 fine.

I joined our sad little troop of moms and dads and activists after my speech was done. A young reporter from the *Yale Daily News* interviewed me; her face looked frozen, her eyes almost glazed, as she tried with pre-set questions to push me to define the activists at the rally as being politically motivated—that is, right-wing.

I told her that I had no idea how the other protesters voted. I felt sad that her editor had evidently insisted on her trying to get this nonsensical angle, prior to her even arriving at the demonstration.

I saw on her face the tension of a very young, very smart woman, who had just heard credible statements about damage to young women like her, and yet who was trying hard to do her job; but it was a job degraded already by a corrupted "news" organization.

The article was predictably defamatory (I'm not a "vaccine skeptic," or a conspiracy theorist) with an "expert," Dr. Hugh Taylor, trotted out to flat-out lie to students and faculty with the claim that there "has been no research" tying reproductive harm to the mRNA vaccines:

> Dr. Hugh Taylor '83—Chair of the Department of Obstetrics Gynecology and Reproductive Sciences at Yale School of Medicine, and Chief of Obstetrics and Gynecology at Yale-New Haven Hospital—told the News that there has been no research tying adverse effects in fertility to the Pfizer vaccine.
>
> "There's no risk to fertility or to a pregnancy," Taylor said. "But on the other hand, there's a tremendously increased risk of complications from the virus if you are pregnant when you get COVID. The risk of major complications in pregnancy and

even death significantly increase in pregnant women compared to others of the same age."[8]

This, even as I'd just *presented* the evidence—and even as the evidence elsewhere was also terrifyingly mounting. I tried later to contact the *Yale Daily News* for a retraction of the many falsehoods in their piece—but that incubator of journalism was no longer operating as the press is supposed to do in an open society. You could not call the editor. You could not even leave a message: the phone number connected weirdly to an internal phone message system that could take no messages. I felt so sad that young journalists were now being trained via a publication that was more like *Pravda* than like the *Yale Daily News* of the open-society past. What were they learning? To reproduce a party line.

A scary thread throughout the day was the suppression of free thought, and free speech, among students. Phoebe Liou, a University of Connecticut student, described how lonely and desolate she felt after she had decided not to get mRNA vaccinated, and how the universities dangled students' futures in front of them like a lure on a string. She described students being "switched off" of the CCP-style digital grid of their universities, if they are even late for weekly COVID tests. They are marked as "noncompliant."

I knew how fearful students were in the face of these mandates and in the face of this CCP-type surveillance and control on campus, because so many parents with kids in the Ivies had told me that their children had begged them not to speak out, not to call the dean, not to advocate for them or to protect them from these injections, in any way.

They feared reprisals, and they were right to do so.

The vibe on this once-vibrant campus was *keep your head down.*

As I pointed out in my speech, worse even than damage to the students' bodies, was the damage to their minds, as they bent their instincts for self-preservation to distort themselves to be "compliant" to the pimping of themselves, and to tyranny.

We finally marched across the campus, now truly trespassing. I hoped I would not be arrested, but I was resigned to that possibility. My heart—the heart of a mother—did not let me decline that risk.

That was the saddest part of the day of all. Cross Campus—the green heart of the university—once littered, in my day at least, with students lounging on the grass, reading poetry, debating, laughing, tussling, napping—was entirely empty.

The whole university center was eerily silent. Students and graduate students and even faculty crossed our paths as we marched, but they stole glances at us as if it was Poland in 1972. Furtive, interested, ashamed, hidden.

Ms Liou had described students living in fear, surrounded by bad information, so scared to be "out" on a university with their fears or their questions, so scared to be switched off, ejected, or penalized; and the campus felt indeed like a matrix of fear.

As we ended our march at a local pizzeria, and the organizers posted flyers on a bulletin board, an athlete came up to us. He reminded me of the athletes of my time there—a healthy, happy, robust young man, in that eternal striped polo shirt; smiling and eager and friendly. He had the clear eyes and ruddy skin of vigorous health and the broad shoulders of a rower.

He sought us out—us moms, us dads, us straggling, loving renegades—and asked what he could do to protect himself. He said that Yale's policies were forcing students not only to submit to the bivalent booster, but also to the flu vaccine. He asked about this with the sincerity of a truly very young man who really needed well-intentioned older adults to inform him and to help him, and we had so little real help to give him.

In his earnest, youthful questions there was the embodiment of this crazy paradox of this situation: this young man who may have been there on an athletic scholarship; a young athlete who cared for, cultivated, and took pride in his strength and in his body's capacities—was being forced to take something into his body that could harm him forever. For no reason.

And he probably knew it.

———

In trafficking cases, you follow the money. At the time of my speech, I had not yet looked at the money trail that would surely be behind such an egregious policy—but I was sure that I would find one. In every case I've seen of institutions coercing workers or students or congregants, the institution had taken vast sums of what were in effect bribes—money from the CARES

(Coronavirus Aid, Relief, and Economic Security) Act or from the Bill and Melinda Gates Foundation, with strings attached to push "COVID measures."

When I came home, later, my husband, the intelligence analyst, quickly found the money trail—from a site called TAGGS that tracks government grants, and from Yale's own documents.[9] The crime scene he found is indeed stunning.

Yale receives more from HHS than it does from tuition.

Yale has received $9 billion from HHS since 1998, and $1.7 *billion* since COVID began in 2020. Yale received $607 million from HHS for 2022 alone—versus the $475 million that the university received from tuition.

In other words, Yale needs HHS more than it needs its own students.

So Yale is trafficking the bodies of its students to please HHS and to keep that spigot open.[10]

Basically, Yale is a massive sponge for vaccine money. Department after department.

Yale received $3.4 million for "emergency measures" for COVID in regard to students. You can't tell what that was used for. Yale also got a $1,099,535 grant from the Bill and Melinda Gates Foundation for someone to study COVID-19 mortality by *looking* at burial sites in Karachi, Pakistan.[11] Follow the science!

And! Yale was the site of a Yale Institute for Global Health study that showed that richer countries have less vaccine hesitancy.[12] Ka-ching!

But! That's not all! Yale's School of Management received money for a study to overcome "vaccine hesitancy."[13]

There's more! Yale received funding for one of the original psychological studies that identified the main forms of emotional manipulation that were then adopted to drive the whole hellish neurosis-scape, the entire destruction of all of our social bonds, over the course of almost three years.

The study summary elaborates on these, as if there is nothing weird or wrong about an unethical experiment in manipulating people's reactions and perverting their alliances and their free will:

> *Personal freedom message: . . . how COVID-19 is limiting people's personal freedom and by working together to get enough people vaccinated society can preserve its personal freedom.*

> *Economic freedom message: . . . how COVID-19 is limiting
> people's economic freedom and by working together to get enough
> people vaccinated society can preserve its economic freedom.*
>
> *Self-interest message: . . . that COVID-19 presents a real
> danger to one's health, even if one is young and healthy. Getting
> vaccinated against COVID-19 is the best way to prevent oneself
> from getting sick.*

And on, and on, all the way to the "bravery" message, "which describes how firefighters, doctors, and front line medical workers are brave. Those who choose not to get vaccinated against COVID-19 are not brave."[14]

But! There's even more! Yale also received a thirty-five-million-dollar facility—from Pfizer, for Pfizer's benefit. To do what? It is a fifty-two *bed* facility—creepy as that sounds—for drug trials.[15]

Does this mean that humans in New Haven are receiving non-FDA approved experimental drugs, in beds, in a facility owned and operated by Pfizer? And Yale is the facilitator for this? Who *are* these test subjects—these people? What led them to "volunteer"? What *are* these substances? What happens if something goes wrong?

It is just one more example of massive price tags accompanying reckless human experimentation; just one more example of Yale now being aligned more fully with pharma and the COVID boondoggle, than with its alumni's values, or its core mission, or its stated traditions.

———

In New Haven, the activists' plans for the day had ended.

All done with our tasks, we had a lovely lunch at Mory's, the storied eating place for the university crowd, courtesy of an activist.

For a moment, in the comfortable interior, with the linens on the tables, the pictures on the wall of decades of young Yale athletes in their rows, proud of their young manhood—boys and young men in the 1880s, 1890s, 1900s, 1910s—with the jokey insider references to bulldogs and to the Whiffenpoofs and to campus rites—with the excellent salmon, the Welsh rarebit that remained on the menu from an earlier time—with the two glasses of Sancerre—I felt that warm embracing hug that is Yale's seduction; I remembered its promise of a lush, rich, cozy, tradition-bolstered, special world.

One that had meaning.

But then, as I got my coat and stepped out into the gray day, and saw the blameless young people who were simply there to get the educations for which they had worked so hard, for which their parents had slaved—young people who were standing under a hideous shadow not of their making—the mirage, for that was what it was, vanished.

Yale was a raddled old madam, after all.

Addicted to the money.

And buying and selling, with an icy heart, the bodies of her young.

CHAPTER FOURTEEN

How Lies Killed Books

Not long after I found my beloved Yale was trafficking the bodies of students, I stumbled into hipster Brooklyn—alongside of literary Manhattan—frozen in an amber of denial and silence.

There was a restored state of freedom that no one would discuss.

I'd wandered the cute little boîtes and trendy underground, hand-pulled-noodle, postmodern food courts, with mixed emotions.

There were the chic young moms with babies in strollers, both of them breathing freely in the chill air. There were slouching Millennials, with every demographic likelihood of having been masky and COVID-culty, now enjoying their freedom to assemble at will, to flirt and to window-shop, to stroll and to chat and to try on new sweaters in person at UNIQLO.

Many of these folks, no doubt, would have been repelled, from 2020 to the present, by people like my brothers and sisters in arms, and by me; as we struggled in the trenches of the liberty movement.

Some of them may have called us antivaxxers, extremists, insurrectionists; selfish, "Trumpers," or whatever other nonsense was the epithet of the day.

Some of them may have wanted to lock down *harder*, and lock us down harder.

My brothers and sisters in the freedom movement, though we lost employment, savings, status, and affiliations, fought every day—for these very folks; we fought for everyone; we fought so that some day, these young moms could indeed stroll with their babies, breathing fresh air; so that these slouching Millennials could one day indeed wander at will, not "locked down" still, not "mandated" any longer, and not living in fear of an internment camp.

It was bittersweet, seeing this demographic so chill, so relaxed, so back to "normal"—many of whom had been once so oblivious of, or so actively disrespectful of, the sacrifices we on the outside of society had waged *for* their very freedom.

Who knows where they would be now, if it were not for our combat on their behalf?

Still without their rights regained, like Canada? Still "mandated," like Canada? Still scared to speak, scared of having bank accounts frozen, scared of losing licenses, scared of being beaten in protests, forbidden to travel without dangerous injections—like Canada?

We are still not entirely free in the US, though we regained many of our freedoms. Not because the evildoers wanted to give them back, but because my brothers and sisters fought hard, strategically, bitterly, and furiously, for all of this liberty that I witnessed in front of me, on that almost-spring day on the crowded, tumultuous Fulton Avenue.

It was bittersweet to know that these people would never witness us, or acknowledge what we did for them and their children; let alone thank us; let alone apologize to people like me for the years in which they were just fine with folks like us being banished to the outer edges of society, to eat in the cold streets of New York like animals, or made jobless, or ostracized.

In addition to the dissonance of seeing people who had been perfectly okay with discriminating against the very people who had fought to return to them the liberties they now enjoyed, I suffered a sense of disorientation at realizing that there was a giant cognitive hole in the middle of contemporary culture.

The staffers at the Brooklyn branch of McNally Jackson Books, an independent bookstore that had for years been a stalwart outpost of free-thinking publishing, were still masked, against all reason. I walked in with some trepidation.

Peacefully, faces covered, three years and running, they stacked books on the shelves.

I was astonished, as I wandered the well-stocked aisles. Independent bookstores usually reflect the burning issues in a culture at that given time.

But—now—nothing.

It takes about two years to write a book and about a year to publish one. It was surely time for the important new books from public intellectuals, about the world-historical years through which we had just lived, to appear.

But—no.

In the center of an altar to literate culture, it was as if the years 2020 to 2022 simply did not exist and had never existed.

This can't be possible, I thought. This all—the "pandemic," lockdowns, denial of education for children, forced masking, forced vaccinations, mandates, a crashed economy—globally—as an aggregate, was of course the most important thing ever to have happened to us as a generation of intellectuals.

I kept on searching the stacks. Nothing.

I checked "The 10 Best Nonfiction Books of 2022" in *Time*.[1]

None had to do with the pandemic policies or the lockdowns or the mandated mRNA injections into billions of humans.

I surveyed the lanes lined with books, perplexed and saddened.

Surely the wonderful novelists of my generation, astute observers of the contemporary scene—Jennifer Egan, Rebecca Miller—would have written their Great American Novels about the mania that swept over the globe—the one that provided once-in-a-century fodder for fiction writers?

No—or at least, not yet.

Surely Malcolm Gladwell, author of *The Tipping Point: How Little Things Can Make a Big Difference*, the distinguished nonfiction observer of group dynamics, would have tracked how a psychotic delusion had intoxicated nations?

No, nothing.

Wouldn't Samantha Power, author of *"A Problem from Hell": America in the Age of Genocide*, have exposed the pandemic policies that sent millions of children into starvation unto death?

Nothing.

Of course Michael Eric Dyson, brilliant and brave commentator on race in America, author most recently of *Tears We Cannot Stop: A Sermon to White America*, would have written an excoriating exposé of how pandemic policies in the US drove brown and black children into even greater learning deficits and drained millions from small business owners of color?

No, nothing at all.

How about Susan Faludi, respected feminist author of *Backlash: The Undeclared War Against American Women*? Surely she would have addressed how decades of women's professional advancement were overturned by lockdown policies that drove women out of the workforce because someone had to watch the kids stranded at home?

No.

Undoubtedly Robert Reich, longtime champion of working people, author of *The System: Who Rigged It, How We Fix It*, would have analyzed the greatest wealth transfer in modern history?

Nothing there.

Certainly Michael Moore, author of *Downsize This! Random Threats from an Unarmed American*, who for decades amplified the voices of working men and women left behind in rustbelt America, would have likewise assailed the flow of wealth in the "pandemic" era from the locked-down, "distanced," forbidden-to-work working class, to tech CEOs and pharma shills and their oligarch friends?

Nothing to see.

I could go on and on.

From some of the other important public intellectuals whom I know or whom I have followed for decades—and I do not mean to shame anyone needlessly, so I won't name them—there were indeed some new books.

There were books on walks through the city.

There were books on "difficult conversations."

There were books on growing up with unusual parents.

There were books on how meaningful animals are, and how wondrous is their world.

Public intellectuals produced a lot of new books on eating more vegetables.

The bizarre thing about this moment in culture, is that the really important journalism, and the really important nonfiction books about the history, the racial and gender injustice, the economics, the public policy, of the pandemic years—are being written by nonwriters; people who are trained as doctors, medical researchers, lawyers, politicians, and activists.

And, for the most part, their books are not displayed *or even stocked* in bookstores like McNally Jackson.

So there is a massive void in the central thought process of our culture.

The courageous nonwriters have stepped in to tell the truth, because the famous writers, for the most part, can't.

Or won't. Or, for whatever reason, didn't.

This is because the public intellectuals are by necessity, for the most part, AWOL to the truth-telling demands of this time.

You cannot be a public intellectual whose work is alive if you have participated in manufacturing, or even accepting quietly, State-run lies.

The work of the cultural elite of every tyranny, from Nazi Germany to Stalin's USSR, reveals this fact.

For the artist, taking part in lies makes his or her creation of a vibrant cultural text impossible.

Nazi art is bad art. Socialist-realist Soviet fiction is bad fiction.

Journalism in a tyranny, that is written by State-approved scribes, is always going to be a mess of clichés and obsequiousness that no one wants to read, and that cannot stand the test of time. It vanishes like snow into the cauldron of the future—even as works by the hated, forbidden dissidents who *can and do* tell the truth—the Solzhenitsyns of the time, the Anne Franks—are like diamonds that cannot be crushed or lost to time.

It is only these that survive.

Because lies had entombed our whole culture beginning in early spring 2020, and because public intellectuals for the most part did not stand up to the lies at the time, and because many even participated in the lies (hello, Sam Harris); since horrible things happened to those of us who *did* stand up to the lies—most public intellectuals at this moment *cannot* address the really important events of the recent past.

And from conversations I had with people in liberal-elite publishing, media, education, and the arts—these public intellectuals are being enabled in their silence or distraction or collusion by a cultural nexus that wants them silent.

The consensus in media-elite land is that no one wants to talk about these issues at all.

"People just want to *move on*," I keep hearing, in my former haunts in Manhattan and Brooklyn.

Don't *talk* about it.

So this all led to a weird situation, culturally, indeed.

In the world of alt-media, of independent exiled dissidents, where I now live most of the time, were having the most riveting conversations of our lives. This was because we all know civilization itself, liberty itself, and maybe even the fate of humans, are at stake every day.

In the polite elite-media circles of Brooklyn and New York, people were—*not talking about any of it*.

They were not talking about the enslavement of humanity. They were not talking about young adults dropping dead.

They were talking about fermentation. They were talking about pets. They were talking, endlessly, like stalkers who cannot let it go, about how bad Donald Trump is, down to what he had for dinner at Mar-a-Lago.[2]

The *New York Times* these days has the most boring headlines I have read in my life, and it is for this reason: the truth of our time is toxic to the editors of that newspaper, because they *bathed* in the money of the lies.

"Adam Brody Feels All the Feels with Surfing, 'Avatar' and Cate Le Bon: The 'Shazam!' star revives himself with sprinkle doughnuts, Frank Black's 'Teenager of the Year' and daily naps."[3]

"How Many Friends Do You Really Need?"[4]

"With a Pocket of Shamrocks, Biden Celebrates St. Patrick's Day"[5]

In addition to these cruelly soporific headlines, the *New York Times* is down to running fully imaginary stories that the editors must believe someone somewhere will accept without howling skepticism: "New Data Links Pandemic's Origins to Raccoon Dogs at Wuhan Market."[6]

Then, of course, having committed that journalistic crime, the editors need to run this tragically hilarious follow-up story the next day: "What Are Raccoon Dogs?: The monogamous, hibernating canids, which are related to foxes, are sold for meat and fur."[7]

A formerly great newspaper had run through bats and civet cats, burning its credibility wholesale in a bonfire of flat-out State-mouthpiece deception and uncorrected assertions for three full years, and was now digging up the specter of raccoon dogs. It was explaining their mating habits to its readers—stop the presses!—even as elsewhere in untouchable-reality-land, Dr. Fauci furiously backpedaled, trying to avoid charges of crimes against humanity.

A formerly great city of public intellectuals, unable to address current reality, was thinking about raccoon dogs, and doughnuts, and shamrocks, as they were out taking their *New York Times*–approved walks or getting ready for their *New York Times*–sanctioned naps.

It was as if New York City and all its thought leaders were enchanted, ensorcelled, staring at one another, mouths open, unspeaking, inside of a conceptual snow globe, while all the rest of us ostracized dissidents were carrying on around this frozen spectacle, fighting a hand-to-hand-combat revolution.

I sighed, as I left the bookstore, and made my way through the freely moving hipster crowds.

We don't fight for freedom so that we can get credit.

We don't fight for truth because we want a byline.

We do both just because we can't help it.

We do both because our Founders fought to the death so that we ourselves would be free one day.

And we fight so that little children whom we will never live to see, will grow up free.

But it is painful to witness the beating heart of what had been a great culture, stunned and muted in denial, and unable to function intellectually.

I guess we just need to leave the sadly rotting carcass of the establishment culture of lies and denial behind.

I say that with sorrow. I will miss the bookstores, universities, newspapers that I once revered.

I guess we have to follow the voices of the truth-tellers of the moment, to other, surprising, beleaguered campfires.

I guess we need to pitch our tents in new fields, outside the walls of the crumbling, breached, and decadent city.

CHAPTER FIFTEEN

Rock of Ages

I lit candles for the first night of Hanukkah—December 2022—with my Irish Catholic husband standing nearby. He proudly mentioned the *shamash*, the guardian candle that lights all the others. "I've been doing research," he said; and I took that as a gift.

(We had been alone during Hanukkah and Christmas of 2021, of course, after President Biden had told our loved ones that we could kill them with a hug.)

My aunt in California, who is a rabbi, lit candles of her own, and we joined her via Zoom; seeing her lovely face in the candlelight, I was happy to notice the resemblance with, and to remember, my formidable, departed grandma, Dr. Fay Goleman.

My grandmother had been tiny; and yet she had been a force of nature: a professor of sociology, far before her time; a defender of civil rights; an advocate for the rights of immigrant women, of farm workers, in her community. Her fierce belief in civil liberties and her disdain for bullies are always with me; her spirit is present in me—yes, I feel it; it keeps me from ever letting the flag of her principles—our principles—droop in the dust.

Grandma Fay was watching.

My grandmother's face is traceable now in the faces of the women on that side of my family: the lovely hooded eyes; the high cheekbones; the sensitive bow mouths, like the mouths of starlets of the 1920s; the beautiful teeth.

There have been at least five generations of these beauties: from the winding streets of Odessa to America: Chicago to San Francisco, San Francisco to Sebastopol. My cousin is the latest iteration of the beauty that descends from my great-grandmother: the cupid-like lips, the merry brown eyes, the high cheekbones—unmistakable; how our lineage lives from the past into the present.

But it was not just the lovely women of part of my family—the part of my family that is still is communication with me—that celebrated the first night of Hanukkah with us. My Greek Orthodox stepson had celebrated with us, earlier, too.

Our celebration was unorthodox: we'd had a nonkosher feast of blue crabs, easy-peel shrimp, and garlic- and lemon-soaked mussels, all dumped out on paper sheets on tabletops in a little family-owned hole-in-the-wall restaurant in Somerville, Massachusets.

The restaurant was called The Happy Crab.

"Not happy anymore," remarked Brian, as he broke one open with the nutcrackers that were provided for just that purpose.

I came home after this feast, to light the first candle, and to sing "Rock of Ages," the song my family used to sing on this night, when my dad was alive and my brother and I were small:

> *Rock of Ages let our song,*
> *Praise thy saving power;*
> *Thou amidst the raging foes,*
> *Wast our sheltering tower.*
>
> *Furiously they assailed us,*
> *But Thine arm availed us*
> *And Thy word*
>
> *Broke their sword,*
> *When our own strength failed us.*
> *And Thy word*
>
> *Broke their sword,*
> *When our own strength failed us."*[1]

True love, I think, leads you to open your arms to every important memory of your beloved's, and to say, I don't really get it, perhaps, but I will cherish this with you.

My husband's mother, a nurse, made Cornish game hens for their Christmas every year; coated in bacon, basted in white wine. My husband makes these as well, to remember her; to remember his own now-deceased father, who worked 364 days a year—but not on Christmas Day—managing his own donut shop.

I, a Jewish lady who does not understand Christmas or Cornish game hens, open my arms to these memories of my husband's, because—because love.

Cornish game hens! Christmas! They are—it is—delicious.

When I prepare Christmases for my husband, he enjoys them, because I have no idea what to do. On Christmas Day, half-jokingly, I call myself "Mindy, Santa's Jewish helper." I decorate a brightly lit little tree, and adorn our home with candy canes, and ply Brian with butter cookies, and encourage his naps—formerly with our elderly dog, the sadly departed Mushroom, and now with our new puppy, because— what do I know?

My image of Christmas is from movies and from Hallmark cards. I don't understand what is supposed to happen after the presents are all opened. I don't get the rhythms or cadences of it, at all.

For my own part, before Christmas arrives, I set up the menorah, I dig out my deceased father's recipe for latkes—a recipe that descended in turn from my father's mother, Rose—"Raisa"—now also deceased; a woman who was born in a humble wooden house in Sighet, Romania, in the early twentieth century, in a world that no longer exists. The whole world she knew, before she came to this country, was an Orthodox Jewish one. She kept a holy Shabbat every Friday night and Saturday of her life.

"Latkes!" says my husband—whose surname is one of the oldest in Ireland. He opens his arms to the prospect of oily potato pancakes. Because—because love.

Isn't this all we can do? Witness—and embrace one another?

Isn't that all it really means, to have a Season of Lights?

Maybe no one alone is right. Maybe no one alone has the whole story. Maybe the whole story is too big for any one narrator to grasp it.

The Maccabees, witnessing their miracle, do not have the only miracle in the world. In our Hanukkah story, the beleaguered Jewish rebels who took up arms against a tyrannical Seleucid world power entered the devastated Holy of Holies, and found oil remaining for the sacred lamp. The oil that was only enough for one night, burned, implausibly, for eight days.

God showed up for us and helped us in our direst need; so says our foundational story.

And:

A star appeared over Bethlehem. A baby was born in a manger.

That baby would be a Light of Lights, Wonderful Counselor, King of Kings.

A virgin would hold and nurse him.

Three kings journeyed to honor him: bringing gold, frankincense, and myrrh. The animals bowed their heads in homage.

God showed up for these people and healed them in their direst need—says their foundational story.

Why can't it—all be true?

Why can't God find us—everywhere?

In every land? In every story?

Why do labels matter at all?

Maybe the labels are not the point. Maybe God is not at all interested in labels.

Who cares whose miracle wins?

Maybe all the miracles win.

Maybe love is the only real miracle; and all the stories simply manifest this river of love.

Wondrous lights in a ruined temple; divine child in a manger; holy night, or nights; isn't it all, in essence, the same miracle?

Humans embrace one another, and thus honor their Lord.

Isn't that the only miracle, after all?

The way love weaves through us and through generations, from Sighet to Chicago to San Francisco to Sebastopol; the way love says: How amazing! I am here for you!

Rock of Ages

Cornish game hens! Easy-peel shrimp! Latkes!

Isn't that the Hanukkah miracle, the Christmas miracle?

Isn't the light in the ruined temple—everyone's light; and isn't the baby born to save us all, the salvation of everyone?

Doesn't God talk to us in every single language He knows?

CHAPTER SIXTEEN

Have the Ancient Gods Returned?

I reached a tipping point in early 2023.

As I wrote earlier, I had looked at the events of the past two and a half years using all my critical thinking skills, all my knowledge of Western and global history and politics; and I could *not* explain the years of 2020 to the present.

I could not explain them in ordinary material, political, or historical terms at all.

This was not how human history ordinarily operated.

When ordinary would-be-tyrants try to take over societies, there is always some flaw, some human impulse undoing the headlong rush toward a negative goal. There are always factions, or rogue lieutenants, in ordinary human history; there is always a miscalculation, or a blunder, or a security breach; or differences of opinion at the top. Benito Mussolini's power was impaired in his entry to the Second World War by his being forced to share the role of military commander with King Victor Immanuel.[1] Adolf Hitler miscalculated his ability to master the Russian weather—right down to overlooking how badly his soldiers' stylish but flimsy uniforms would stand up to extreme cold.[2] Before he could mount a counterrevolution against Stalinism, Leon Trotsky was assassinated in Coyoacán, Mexico City.[3]

But none of that fracturing or mismanagement of normal history took place in the global rush to lockdowns, the rollout of COVID hysteria, of

mandates, masking, of global child abuse, of legacy media lying interna-
tionally at scale and all lying in one direction with thousands of "trusted
messengers" parroting a single script, and of forced or coerced mRNA
injections into at least half of the humans on planet earth.

So, as you know, I reluctantly concluded that human agency alone
could not coordinate a highly complicated set of lies about a virus and
propagate the lies in perfect uniformity around an entire globe, in hundreds of languages and dialects. Human beings, using their own resources
alone, could not have turned hospitals overnight from having been
places in which hundreds of staff members were collectively devoted to
the care of the infirm, the prolongation of human life, the cherishing of
newborns, the helping of mothers to care for little ones, the support of
the disabled—into killing factories in which the elderly were prescribed
"run-death-is-near" (remdesivir) at scale.

Also, look at the speed of change. Institutions turned overnight into
negative mirror images of themselves, with demonic policies replacing
what had been at least on the surface, angelic ones. Human history change
is not that lightning fast.

The perception of the rollout, the unanimity of a mass delusion, cannot be explained fully by psychology; not even as a "mass formation," as
described by Belgian professor and clinical psychologist Mattias Desmet.[4]

There have been other mass hysterias before in history, from "blood
libel"—the belief widespread in medieval Europe that Jews were sacrificing Christian children to make matzah[5]—to the flare-up of hysteria
around witches in Salem, Massachusetts, in 1692,[6] to the "irrational
exuberance" of Tulipmania, also in the seventeenth century, in the
Netherlands, detailed by Scottish journalist Charles MacKay in his classic account of group madness, *Extraordinary Popular Delusions and the
Madness of Crowds*.[7]

But all these examples of mass frenzy had dissidents, critics, and
skeptics at the time; none of these lasted for years as an uninterrupted,
dominant, delusional paradigm.

What we lived through from 2020 to 2022 was so sophisticated, so
massive, so evil, and executed in such inhumane unison, that it could not
be accounted for without venturing into metaphysics.

I shared earlier that I started to believe in God in more literal terms than I had before, because this evil was so impressive; so it must be directed at something at least as powerful that was all good.

I knew that "Satan" was, at least for me, an insufficient explanation for the evil I saw. One reason that I felt that "Satan" was an insufficient name for what we were facing, as I've explained, is that I am Jewish, and we don't have the same tradition of "Satan" that Christian Western culture takes for granted.

In Jewish tradition, this entity's role is not that of the rather majestic adversary of God who appears fully fledged in the Christian tradition—a character who was developed subsequent to, as some scholars point out, the influence of Zoroastrianism on Judaism, and then on Christianity, in the years leading up to and after Jesus's life and death.

In the Old Testament, in contrast, *ha-satan*—"the Accuser"—makes a number of appearances; but *ha-satan* is an opponent, rather than being the majestic villain of the New Testament and of Dante's and Milton's characterizations.

The way in which the Hebrew *ha-satan* differs from the Christian Satan is important, as Old-Testament scholar Chad Bird explains:

> *In Old Testament Hebrew, the noun* satan *(which occurs twenty-seven times) and the verb* satan *(which occurs six times) are often used in a general way. If I "satan" someone, I oppose them, accuse them, or slander them. David uses it this way in the psalms, "Those who render me evil for good accuse [שׂטן (satan)] me because I follow after good" (Psalms 38:21). If I act as a "satan" to someone, therefore, I am their adversary or accuser, as the messenger of the Lord stood in the way of Balaam "as his adversary [שׂטן (satan)]" (Numbers 22:22) or as Solomon told Hiram that he had no "adversary [שׂטן (satan)]" who opposed him (1 Kings 5:4).*
>
> *Thus, in Hebrew, the noun and verb שׂטן (satan) can have the non-technical meaning of "stand opposed to someone as an adversary." In the case of Balaam, even the Lord's messenger was a "satan" to him, that is, a God-sent opponent. That is the first point to keep in mind: unlike in English, where "Satan" always refers to a malevolent being, in Hebrew* satan *can have a generic, non-technical meaning."[8]*

Because, as I explained earlier, the Jewish tradition of Satan is more impressionistic than the character who appeared later under Christian narratives, I felt that "Satan" was not sufficient to explain fully the inexplicable, immediate mirror-imaging of what our society had been—from ordered at least on the presumption of morality, to being ordered around death and cruelty. But I did not at that time have a better concept with which to work.

Then I heard of a pastor named Jonathan Cahn, who had written a book titled *The Return of the Gods*.[9]

The title resonated.

Though I don't agree with everything in his book, Pastor Cahn's central argument—that we have turned away from the Judeo-Christian God and thus we opened a door into our civilization for the negative spirits of "the Gods" to repossess us—feels right.

Jonathan Cahn is a Messianic Jewish minister. He is the son of a Holocaust refugee. Formerly a secular atheist, Cahn had a near-death experience as a young man that led him to accept Jesus—or, as he refers to this presence by the original Hebrew name, Yeshua—as his Lord and Savior. Pastor Cahn has a ministry based in Wayne, New Jersey, which brings together Jews and Gentiles.

In *The Return of the Gods*, his improbable, and yet somehow hauntingly plausible thesis is that ancient dark and metaphysically organized forces, the gods of antiquity, have "returned" to our presumably advanced, secular post-Christian civilization.

Pastor Cahn's central theme is that, because we have turned away from our covenant with Yahweh—especially we in America, and we in the West, and especially since the 1960s—therefore, the ancient gods—or rather, ancient pagan energies that had been vanquished by monotheism and exiled to the margins of civilization and human activity—have seen an "open door," and thus a ready home to reoccupy, in us.

He argues that they have indeed done so.

Pastor Cahn makes the case that the ancient gods were initially, in essence, put on the defensive, as the Hebrew Bible (Old Testament) recounts: first by Yahweh, and by the introduction of monotheism and the revelation of the Ten Commandments; and then, that they were vanquished altogether and sent into outer darkness, by the arrival of the being whom he sees as the Messiah, Yeshua.

One might right away resist such a phrasing; what do you mean, "the gods"? But Cahn is both careful and accurate in his translations and his tracing of four millennia of religious history through a set of phrases.

Cahn points out that the Hebrew Bible refers to what in Hebrew is rendered *shedim* or "negative spirits" (in modern Hebrew, this word means "ghosts".). Cahn points out that these spirits, powers, or principalities were worshipped in the pagan world in many guises—from the fertility god Baal; to the sexuality goddess Astarte (also known as Ashtaroth or Asherah); to the destructive idol Moloch (or Malek). He rightly points out that the ancient world was everywhere consecrated to these dark or lower entities, and that worshippers went to the point of sacrificing their own children to propitiate these forces. He correctly reflects the central narrative of the tribes of Israel as alternately embracing Yahweh and his Ten Commandments and ethical covenant, and finding it all too taxing, and thus falling away to whore after these pagan gods. He notes that the gods of the Old Testament world descended in updated guise into Greco-Roman life, taking on new names: Zeus, Diana, and so on.

He notes that the Septuagint, the early Greek translation of the Hebrew Bible, rendered *shedim* as *daimones*. This word is rendered also as "spirit personifications"; we receive this word in English today as "demons."[10]

Having traced the lineage of pagan worship and pagan forces, Cahn makes the case that they were never overcome by the West's embrace of Christianity; but rather that they were pushed to the margins of Western civilization; weakened by our covenant with Yahweh, or with Jesus, depending on whom we are.

He argues that these negative but potentially powerful forces have been dormant for two millennia by virtue of the Western Judeo-Christian covenant. And that they have now taken this opportunity, of our turning away from God, and they have returned.

We, thus, are the house that has been cleaned—by the covenant with the Judeo-Christian commitment. But we subsequently abandoned the house, he maintains, and left it vulnerable; open, for negative energies to re-enter.

Though it is unfashionable now to talk about our Judeo-Christian founding and heritage in the West, it should not be. This legacy is simply an historical fact. I do not think one needs to be dismissive of or insulting to Buddhism or Islam (which is also part of the Judeo-Christian lineage, but that's another story) or Jainism or Shintoism, to acknowledge the fact that the West's civilization for the past two millennia has been a Judeo-Christian one, and that our Founders in this nation, though rightly establishing religious freedom, believed that they were consecrating a nation in alignment with the will of God as they understood Him.

Cahn cites Puritan minister Jonathan Winthrop in warning that America's state of being blessed by God will last only as long as we hold up our end of the covenant.[11]

While it would be easy to dismiss Pastor Cahn's theory as wacky and fanatical, I have reluctantly come to believe that his central premise may be right.

In the Old Testament, it is not *ha-satan* who is the most fearsome, treacherous, and dangerous of figures. It is, rather, the gods who are the seductive abominations—that is to say, the ancient, pre-Yahweh, pre-Mosaic, pre-Christian gods: our old adversaries in the Hebrew Bible—Yahweh's adversaries: Baal, Moloch, and Astarte.

Those are the gods that traduced, lured, hounded, bedeviled, and seduced my people—again and again. Those are the gods about whom this extraordinary innovation in the human story—the monotheistic God of all—continually, specifically warns us; warns the Children of Israel.

Those are the gods to whose sacrifice the Children of Israel constantly stray, disappointing and enraging our Creator. Those are the gods, with their child sacrifice and their graven images, against whom our father Abraham rebelled and taught his descendants to rebel. Those are the gods whose acceptance of child sacrifice—a real thing, a barbaric, culture-wide practice that continued for centuries in the tribes and civilizations surrounding the Children of Israel—was supplanted by animal sacrifice; this was an evolution in human civilization that is represented by the story of Abraham's near-sacrifice of his son Isaac, when the child on the altar is replaced miraculously by a ram provided, at the last moment, by the Lord God.

The sheer amoral power of Baal, the destructive force of Moloch, the unrestrained seductiveness and sexual licentiousness of Astarte—those are the primal forces that do indeed seem to me to have "returned."

Or at least the energies that they represent—moral power-over; death-worship; antagonism to the sexual orderliness of the intact family and faithful relationships—seem to have "returned," without restraint, since 2020.

There may well indeed be negative forces reappearing or emerging into daylight from out of their less visible domains, whom we, after two millennia of Judeo-Christianity, have literally forgotten, at least in Western civilization, how to identify. It may well be that these negative forces are highly complex, extraordinarily powerful, and stunningly well organized.

It may indeed be the case that they have swept themselves back into our "house" in the West and emerged visibly in the past two years.

I do believe that they were able to do so because we dropped our own end of upholding a basic covenant with God.

After having gone back to the Old Testament, it is clear to me that Yahweh warned us that this could happen—that we could easily lose his protection and break the covenant.

He warned us, indeed, over and over, in the Hebrew Bible, of this risk.

I was taught in Hebrew school that we as Jews are forever God's "chosen people."

But God does not say that consistently in the Old Testament, at all.

There are many times a "covenant" is mentioned in the Hebrew Bible. But when Yahweh explains what He wants from His children in Exodus, He is clear that certain conduct is expected from us in order for us to receive His blessing.[12]

So He does not say that we are automatically set under His protection forever; rather He says, again and again, that *if* we, the Children of Israel, act justly, love mercy, visit the sick, and protect the widows and orphans, *then* we will be "His people" and we will have His covenant—His blessing and protection.

He also warns, directly Himself and also through His many prophets—that we can lose His protection by dropping our end of the covenant; a covenant that goes, as all contracts or agreements do, two ways.

And God is very clear, at least in the Old Testament; He says in certain places: you left the paths of righteousness, so now I withdraw my protection from you.

I always thought that many Jews, and indeed the education I had in Hebrew school, alarmingly misread what Yahweh so clearly stated. I was taught that being "chosen" as God's people was a static, lucky status. All you had to do was to be born Jewish—better yet, to be born Jewish, marry a Jewish spouse, raise Jewish children, light Shabbat candles, go to synagogue on the High Holy Days, and visit the State of Israel. I was also taught that God bestowed the Land of Israel to the Jewish people unconditionally.

We were not taught in Hebrew school what the Hebrew Bible really says—that we could indeed *lose* God's favor and be "un-chosen" again.

What God tells us, again and again, throughout the Old Testament, is that He asks for a living, actual, organic relationship with us, the Children of Israel, in which we show our commitment to Him and our devotion to Him as "His people"—through how we treat Him every day; meaning, through how we treat those around us, as He asked us to, in His name.

That is what He calls "His covenant." That is what He means by "my people."

Though He promised Noah an "everlasting covenant" after the flood,[13] that does not mean we get to do whatever we desire to do here on Earth. He never said He wouldn't ever, under any circumstances, give up on humanity as we are, in our current context on this planet. He promised, rather, He would not ever again do away with wicked humanity by water.

He always, rightly, made clear to us that, in a living partnership with Him, we are supposed to show our love and our recognition of the privilege of being wedded to His path—through our zealous, difficult, freely chosen, unending actions.

Feed the hungry. Every day. Visit those in prison. Care for the orphans. Protect the widows. Do justly.

So—the truth of God's requests of us, Jews, in the Hebrew Bible, is not "once Chosen, always Chosen."

The covenant is not defined as carte blanche for us to abuse our relationship with our Creator.

Again and again, as chronicled in the Hebrew Bible, we showed God that we were not up to that daily walk with Him that He requested of us. It's hard; it's draining. The ancient gods around us in the days of the prophets were so very seductive. They were so much easier—sacrifice a bullock; pour some oil; pay a priest. Visit a temple prostitute.

The ancient gods did not demand daily acts of justice, mercy, charity, and sexual self-restraint, as Yahweh, so morally demanding by the standards of the ancient world, did.

If God's courtship of the Children of Israel in the Old Testament were a romance novel or a film—which it really is, if read properly—the well-meaning best friend would counsel the Lord of Israel: Give them up. Walk away.

They are just not that into you.

God never said, once I choose you as "my people"—then you can do whatever you want. He does not want a codependent or an abusive relationship.

He wants a real marriage.

Today, we are in grave danger if we, as Jews, think that by honoring our ethnic heritage or even our religious traditions, even if we keep kosher and light the Shabbat candles, that we are doing what Yahweh really asked of us.

And the same could be said, and I say this with equal respect, of many Christian churches, books, and media messages. I am in dialogue with devout Christians of many denominations, with whom I have shared these anxieties, who also feel that we are in a time of similar moral danger for their own coreligionists, and for similar reasons.

Too few in either community, we agree, seem to understand how dangerous to a nation, to a civilization, abandoning God can be.[14]

I feel that many Jews and many Christians are at risk right now of unduly positive thinking—of thinking that everything is okay; that we will all automatically be redeemed—when it manifestly *isn't* okay.[15]

Because Jewish history is longer than Christian history (not a value judgment, just a statement of fact), we have more experience of God's having indeed withdrawn His protection and left us to the fate about which He warned us.

But even Christian history does not have a promise that God can never withdraw. Though these darker or more wrathful warnings seem less often taught from many pulpits these days than they used to be taught in our

Puritan past, Jesus Himself warned His followers about the dire consequences of amoral behavior—the serious dangers of being "whited sepulchers"—of neglecting or hurting the poor—or of bringing children to harm.[16]

My point being that our forefathers for both faith traditions, Jewish and Christian, understood that a covenant—involving God's blessing and protection—required action from *both* the Lord and from His people, to be in effect.

It was not an eternal hall pass.

We in this generation have forgotten this.

But I think it *is* possible that for 4,000 years—and then for 2,000 more— God's covenant *has* in fact largely protected the West, and that we have had His blessing for so long that we have taken it for granted; and that in the last few years, we have released our hold of God's covenant—and that God has simply, as He warned us in the Old Testament that He could— withdrawn, and left us to our own devices—so we can see for ourselves how we will do when we depend on humans alone. In the absence of God's covenant and protection in the West, great evil is flourishing.

Pastor Cahn's premise resonated with me, because the energies that I have felt flooding into our world, feel primally recognizable to me as a Jew—ancestrally recognizable.

These dark forces now freed into the world around us, feel like the way the world must have felt before Moses ascended Mount Sinai; before a baby was born in a manger.

They feel again like the premonotheistic past; like the world the Hebrews confronted, when the Word of God was first revealed to them.

It feels again like the ancient world that continually tempted the Hebrews away from the hard, rigorous, daily, demanding practice of morality and of adherence to the Ten Commandments. It feels again like the ancient world felt, being as it was under Baal's, Moloch's, and Astarte's dark, inexorable, complex, and antihuman rule.

That is to say: it was—and now it is—a world in which humans did not, do not matter. It was—and it now is—a world in which children can be slaughtered by their parents, or by the authorities. It was—and it now is—a world in which slavery had and now has no moral valence. Lust and greed were—and now are again—everything. God was not then fully present—and now I argue, as Pastor Cahn argues, God has withdrawn.

The commitment to Judeo-Christian norms and values, which have been the hallmark of the West for two millennia—even when we fell far short of them—has fallen apart altogether.

The great genius of America was not that it was consecrated to a *specific* religion—the genius of our nation included *freedom* of religion—but our distinction was that we were founded as a City on a Hill; spiritually, we were consecrated, via our ultimate organizational manifestation of human freedom, with its basis in free will—to God.

If we withdraw our role in that covenant, perhaps Pastor Cahn is right, and pagan entities—long held at bay in the West—are empowered, and rush back in.

And so, decency, human rights, human values, all of which we thought were innate secular Western values—turn out to be values that cannot be protected enduringly without the blessing of what has been in the West a Judeo-Christian God. They are all being cleared out of our society, and almost no one—certainly very few people who are not people of faith—is standing in the breach as this takes place.

Now look at our political leaders, our national structures in the West. They went overnight from ethically oriented, at least overtly, to purely nihilistic organizations. Before 2020, Judeo-Christian norms had not entirely left the West, even though explicit religious language was no longer invoked in its public spaces.

What I mean is that until 2020, Biblical belief systems structured our institutions even though we no longer explicitly invoked God.

The Bible is all around us in the West—or it had been—even though we think we are living in a postmodern reality. We have been blind to its influence, for the most part.

The idea that you should seek peace with your neighbors with whom you disagree, rather than trying to harm them or their children; the notion that a court should deliver impartial justice rather than hand over goods to the more powerful litigant; the idea that the poor and orphaned in a community should be cared for, rather than enslaved or left to starve; these were not the norms of the pagan world.

These are, rather, Biblical beliefs, even though the explicit Judeo-Christian religiosity has been removed from public discourse.

Our institutions in the West, thus, have been like vessels made with the "lost wax" process; they have kept the shape of Biblical concepts and beliefs even though Biblical language in public is now against the law, or has fallen away from being a cultural norm.

But we don't leave babies to starve—at least we didn't kill living babies before 2020—for a reason; our courts at least ostensibly—at least until recently—don't allow cheating or theft in our society for a reason; we don't abandon the elderly to the modern equivalent of wild animals—for a reason; and the reasons derive straight from the Ten Commandments; and from both the Old and New Testaments.

Though secular, in the West, until 2020, our institutions had retained a Biblical, not a pagan, shape.

Congresses, parliaments, and nonprofits were organized along what were basically Judeo-Christian ethical frameworks. Respect for human rights, the equal value of all, the cherishing of life, the seeking of a peaceful society—while our institutions were far from perfect, these were our institutional values, in the West, at least overtly, until 2020.

All of that changed seemingly overnight.

Pastor Cahn notes that Jesus identified Satan alongside the *daimones*. Pastor Cahn refers to these ancient gods and powers, as well as the more modern Satan, together, as the "anti-God" forces.

I do feel that this is what we are terrifyingly grappling with. Since 2020, the world, I feel, has been bathed, infused, bombarded even, with intensely powerful energies that are totally unfamilar to us in this generation but that may derive from a pre-Christian, pre-solidly Jewish time, a time when early Judaism was struggling with the seductive and oppressive entities that always sought to lure the Children of Israel away from the monotheistic truth, the One God.

The ancient *shedim* are the only "principalities and powers" I can imagine that can manifest a national, and now a global, network of policy advocates, social workers, graphic designers, and members of parliament who are all on board with an escalating euthanasia death cult.[17] The ancient *daimones* are the only entities I can imagine powerful enough in just two years and a bit, to destroy families, to ruin sexuality and fertility, to make a mockery of human rights, to celebrate the end of critical thinking, to march us all in lockstep to worship of technocrats and technocracy; medical cultism and an orgiastic cult of self- and other-annihilation.

All of Western Europe was once consecrated to Jesus, Mary, and saints—or to the church; almost every chapel, town, village, crossroad; Santander, Mont Saint Michel, Greyfriars. Much of America, too: Santa Barbara, San Francisco, San Mateo, Santa Catalina. Did that consecration do more than establish place-names?

Did it help keep us safe?

Are we now seeing the costly and intentional process of global elites reconsecrating our America, our West, to negative entities that are—despite the dominant narrative since the twentieth century began—in fact, *real*?

As the poet Charles Baudelaire pointed out, "The greatest trick the Devil ever pulled was convincing the world he didn't exist."

The only thing that feels intuitive to me is that these pagan forces may indeed once again have gained a foothold on our planet.

What feels intuitive to me is that God is at the limit of His patience with us.

And He has said,

Okay, you want to do it yourself?

Do it yourself.

And He let us go.

And that this—the absence of the protection of our God—the ascendancy of a realm on earth of us doing it all ourselves; regarding ourselves; worshipping ourselves; whoring after only human works; releasing ourselves from all lawful constraints; embracing all lusts and obedience to nondivine authorities; rejecting mercy; celebrating all narcissisms; treating children like animals whom we own; treating the family like a battlefield; treating the churches and synagogues as marketing platforms.

This is, indeed, what the realms of pagan darkness—or of "principalities and powers"—look like.

This may, indeed,

be what Hell itself looks like.

CHAPTER SEVENTEEN

A Fall

One Thursday afternoon, in mid-January 2023, in the quiet neighborhood near Salem, Massachusetts, where my husband has a little place where we hang out when we spend time with my wonderful stepson, I foolishly decided to go for a run with our new puppy.

After we had mourned Mushroom for six months, we realized we could not manage without another little dog, and we found a new creature to bring furry mischief into our home, in the guise of little Loki.

Loki is now ten months old. He is a "Shi-Poo"—a shih tzu–poodle mix, an adorable combination.

Loki is very different from the much-mourned Mushroom. Where the late Mushroom was, certainly in his elder years, a judgmental, eccentric Oscar Wilde character, Loki is all a young Jimmy Stewart; wide-eyed innocence, good intentions, purity of heart.

Brian keeps up a narration of the excited, tolerant inner monologue of Loki, just as he did with an equally funny, finicky, and censorious inner monologue for Mushroom. Where Mushroom would gaze at us with relentless hostility until we broke down psychologically and yielded any delicious human food in our possession, Loki's voice is something like: "I see you guys are having steak tips! I'm having puppy chow! But that's cool! I love you!!"

Loki has long hind legs like a rabbit, and he runs like a rabbit—with joy in motion. I began to run with him—as who could fail to want to share in that delight? And I made the mistake of using a long extensible leash, as he loved to cavort about with all that length. Had I done more research, I would have known that that was a recipe for an accident.

I was racing with him on the uneven sidewalks of the town, a few blocks from Brian's little flat. The next moment, I realized that I was on my back on the icy sidewalk, in an agony unlike anything I had ever experienced in my life, and probably screaming.

Worse still, I could see that Loki was about 100 feet further away from me on the sidewalk, with the leash, fallen out of my hapless grasp, trailing near him. He was looking back at me in confused concern.

But I was unable to get up, and I realized with horror that I could not move my left arm or hand at all. Loki could easily wander away and be lost or hit by a car.

I started shouting, "Help me! Please help me!" I put all my will into those screams, and I prayed someone would respond before I passed out, or before I went into shock, which would mean that my puppy would be in terrible danger.

Amazingly, I soon felt someone kneel by me. A woman had come out of her nearby home, having heard my screams. She sought to calm me, as someone else called 911.

"Please get my puppy," I begged. Miraculously, another woman appeared, from another house—I believe from across the street. I heard two voices then gently luring Loki back toward where I lay, and then my heart was in my throat until one woman was able to seize his leash handle securely.

"Please tell my husband what happened," I managed to say between groans, and I gave that woman our address. Her wife also, I believe, called 911 on my behalf.

Amazingly, this neighbor took Loki three blocks away, accurately located our address, knocked on our door, gave Loki safely to Brian, and let him know that I had fallen. Amazingly, too, another neighbor, an older man, appeared out of nowhere, while all of this was happening, a look of concern on his face, bearing a pillow and blanket.

The neighbors deliberated about not using the pillow, as they decided that they should not move me. Meanwhile I felt myself start to sink into shock—I felt my heart rate slowing, and I grew colder and began to tremble. I felt that sense of, "My body and mind can't take this pain any longer; I am about to lose consciousness."

Then the four neighbors, working together, put the blanket gently over me. The sidewalk was frozen, and my body temperature kept dropping; keeping me warm, I am sure, prevented me from going into shock or hypothermia, and their decision not to move my head also helped me avoid further injury.

The first woman who had come out to help me, knelt beside me and asked about my dog's breed. She kept chatting with me. This could not have been pleasant for her, as I was still inarticulate—howling and groaning.

I realized, even in my increasing confusion and agony, that she was making small talk with me in order to keep me from passing out.

My husband arrived, and the ambulance arrived as well, and the EMTs wonderfully took over, loaded me excruciatingly onto a stretcher, and whisked me into the most painful ride of my life. They cut off my winter coat, so that there were feathers everywhere in the ambulance interior.

By now I was screaming unreservedly.

"We are in Massachusetts, so there are going to be potholes," one of the EMTs explained, and indeed I shrieked aloud with every jolt—he was not kidding. But they got me quickly and efficiently to the ER, where, after I underwent agonizing X-rays and MRIs, Brian and I were told by a cheery ER doc that I had broken my shoulder.

But I was so lucky. I had not lost consciousness. I had not gone into shock. I had not been left on the wintry sidewalk, my vital signs steadily dropping till someone finally reacted, perhaps too late.

What I mean to say is that four strangers came out at once into the freezing street at the sound of a human voice in distress. Four strangers stayed at the uncomfortable, no doubt upsetting scene, prioritizing a stranger's and a little pup's visible risks over whatever else they had been doing at that moment, and over their own cozy comfort; strangers patiently lured, then secured, and thus saved the life of my little dog. A stranger patiently brought him home, and let my husband know I was hurt. A stranger had held my good hand and talked to me of random subjects, in freezing temperatures, for quite a long time, so that I would not pass out. A stranger had brought me a pillow and a blanket of his own and put the blanket down for me on the icy, gritty sidewalk.

The decency of these people—who themselves may not have even known one another—created an instinctive choreography of goodness, which was lifesaving.

Then, once my dog and I were safe, these strangers melted away, back into their lives, asking nothing of the moment—not even my thanks. I don't even know their names.

These four strangers may indeed have saved my life, or at least kept me from a much more serious injury. And they certainly saved the life of my little dog.

Five days later I walked—very carefully, and without Loki—and now wearing a sling supporting my shattered left shoulder—around the corner, to see where it all had taken place. There was the ridge in the uneven sidewalk that I had not noticed as I had been running. There was the place I'd fallen.

I looked around—these kind people must live nearby, but I literally don't know where to find them to thank them.

Our little community showed that it was emotionally and morally healthy. In a healthy community, *humans save each other.*

These people had in each one of them a moral compass and a sense of selfless compassion that led them to act together with such a beautiful, positive outcome.

That is the society, the community, that sense of unity, we all used to have—at least as an ideal.

Human communities' ability to save one another, to save the community itself, out of values of internalized decency and compassion, is a resilient, effective, powerful, unstoppable thing.

That is why when others wish to take power from us, they create policies to keep us apart, unknown to, and in fear of, one another.

That, of course, was the damage that lockdowns sought to do—to dissolve the communities that allow us to save one another.

I don't mean to politicize a great blessing I received at the hands of my neighbors, but I can't help considering that if, God forbid, this had happened to us during lockdown—or during some time of global messaging about our fellow humans being untouchable, or somehow dangerous to others—I might have lost consciousness, or frozen to death, and Loki too surely would have been lost.

And that risk is true for anyone in times and places that treat some humans as "others"; a person of color injured or fainting in the wrong neighborhood in the Jim Crow era; someone suspected of being HIV-positive, if injured or losing consciousness, during the bad old days when we were asked to shun those with AIDS.

The poet William Butler Yeats's beautiful lines from "Easter, 1916" reveal the risk to us of losing compassion:

> *Too long a sacrifice*
> *Can make a stone of the heart.*
> *O when may it suffice?*
> *That is Heaven's part. Our part*
> *To murmur name upon name.*[1]

My neighbors did their human part; they seamlessly together manifested the ancient human miracle of compassion; they saved one of their own, saved indeed two sentient beings, purely out of kindness.

If we are to survive all of this, we must defy any pronouncements that seek to make "a stone of the heart."

CHAPTER EIGHTEEN

Dear Conservatives,
I Apologize

I realized I needed to write a formal letter of apology. From me. To conservatives and to those who "put America first" everywhere.

It's tempting to sweep this confrontation with my own gullibility under the rug—to "move on" without ever acknowledging that I was duped, and that as a result I made mistakes in judgment, and that these mistakes, multiplied by the tens of thousands and millions on the part of people just like me, hurt millions of other people like you all, in existential ways.

But that erasure of personal and public history would be wrong.

I owe them a full-throated apology.

I believed a farrago of lies. And, as a result of these lies, and my credulity—and the credulity of people similarly situated to me—many conservatives' reputations have been tarnished, on false bases.

The proximate cause of this letter of apology is the airing, in March 2023, of excerpts from tens of thousands of hours of security camera footage from the United States Capitol taken on January 6, 2021. The footage was released by House Speaker Kevin McCarthy (R-CA) to Fox News commentator Tucker Carlson.[1]

While "fact-checkers" state that it is "misinformation" to claim that Congresswoman Nancy Pelosi was in charge of Capitol Police on that day,[2] the fact is that the USCP is under the oversight of Congress, according to—the United States Capitol Police.[3]

This would be the same Congress that convened the January 6 Committee subsequently, and that used millions of dollars in taxpayer money to turn that horrible day, and that tragic event, into a message point that would be used to tar a former President as a would-be terrorist, and to smear all Republicans, by association, as "insurrectionists," or as insurrectionists' sympathizers and fellow-travelers.

There is no way to unsee Officer Brian Sicknick, claimed by some Democrats in leadership and by most of the legacy media to have been killed by rioters at the Capitol that day, alive in at least one section of the newly released video. The USCP medical examiner states that this Officer died of "natural causes," but also that he died "in the line of duty."[4] Whatever the truth of this confusing conclusion, and with all respect for and condolences to Officer Sicknick's family, the circumstances of his death *do* matter to the public, as without his death having been caused *by* the events of January 6, the breach of the capitol, serious though it was, cannot be described as a "deadly insurrection." Sadly, though the contrary was what was reported, Officer Sicknick died two days after January 6, from suffering two strokes.[5]

There is no way for anyone thoughtful, even if he or she is a lifelong Democrat, not to notice that Senator Chuck Schumer did not say to the world that the footage that Mr. Carlson aired was not real. Rather, he warned that it was "shameful" for Fox to allow us to see it. The *Guardian* characterized Mr. Carlson's and Fox News's sin, weirdly, as "over use" of January 6 footage.[6] Isn't the press supposed to want full transparency for all public-interest events? How can you "over use" real footage of events of national relevance?

Senate minority leader Mitch McConnell did not say the video on Fox News was fake or doctored. He said, rather, that it was "a mistake" to depart from the views of the events held by the chief of the Capitol Police.[7] This is a statement from McConnell about orthodoxy—not a statement about a specific truth or untruth.

I don't agree with Mr. Carlson's interpretation of the videos as depicting "mostly peaceful chaos."[8] I do think it is a mistake to downplay how serious it is when a legislative institution suffers a security breach of any kind, however that came to be.

But you don't have to agree with Mr. Carlson's interpretation of the videos to believe, as I do, that airing the footage is valuable journalism.

Remember: by law all Capitol footage belongs to us—it is a public record, and all public records literally belong to the American people. "In a democracy, records belong to the people," explains the National Archives.[9]

You don't have to agree with Carlson's interpretation of the videos, to notice the hypocrisy by the Left. My acquaintance and personal hero Daniel Ellsberg was rightly lionized by the Left for having illegally leaked the Pentagon Papers.[10] The *New York Times* was rightly applauded for having run this leaked material in 1971. I do not see how Mr. Carlson's airing of video material of national significance that the current government would prefer to keep hidden, or Fox News's support for its disclosure to the public, is any different from that famous case of disclosure of inside information of public importance.

You don't have to agree with Mr. Carlson's interpretation of the videos to conclude that the Democrats in leadership, for their own part, have cherry-picked, hyped, spun, and in some ways appear to have lied about, aspects of January 6, turning what was a tragedy for the nation into a politicized talking point aimed at discrediting half of our electorate.

From the start, there have been things about the dominant, Democrats' and legacy media's, narrative of January 6, that seemed off, or contradictory, to me. (That does not mean I agree with the interpretation of these events in general on the right. Bear with me.)

There is no way to un-hear the interview that Mr. Carlson did with former Capitol police office Tarik Johnson, who said that he received no guidance when he called his superiors, terrified, as the Capitol was breached, to ask for direction.[11]

That situation is anomalous.

There is *always* a security chain of command in the Capitol, at the Rayburn Building, at the White House of course, and so on, which is part of a rock-solid "security plan."[12]

There are usually, indeed, multiple snipers standing on the steps of the Capitol, facing outward. I made note of this when I was researching and writing *The End of America*. There is *never* improvisation, or any confusion in security practices or in what is expected of "the security plan," involving "principals" such as Members of Congress, or staff at the White House. I know this as a former political consultant and former White House spouse.

The reason for a tightly scripted chain of command and an absolutely ironclad security plan in these buildings, is so that security crises such as the events of January 6 *can never happen.*

The fact that so much confusion in security practice took place on January 6, is hard to understand.

There is no way to not see that among the violent and terrifying scenes of that day, all clearly illegal, there were also scenes of officers with the United States Capitol Police, as the footage aired by Mr. Carlson showed, accompanying one protester who would become iconic, the "QAnon Shaman," Jacob Chansley—and escorting him peaceably through the hallways of our nation's legislative center.[13]

I was oddly unsurprised to see the "QAnon Shaman" being ushered through the hallways by Capitol Police; he was ready for the cameras in full makeup, horned fur hat, his tattooed chest bare (on a freezing day), and adorned in other highly cinematic regalia. I don't know what Mr. Chansley thought he was doing there that day, but so many subsequent legacy media images of the event put him so dramatically front and center—and the barbaric nature of his appearance was so illustrative of exactly the message that Democrats in leadership wished to send about the event—that I am not surprised to see that his path to the center of events was not blocked but was apparently facilitated by Capitol Police.

A point I have made over and over since 9/11 is that many events in history are both real and hyped. Many actors in historic events have their agendas but are also at times used by other people with their own agendas, in ways of which the former are unaware. Terrorists and terrorism in the Bush era constitute an example. This issue was both real and hyped.

"Patriots" or "insurgents" (depending on who you are) entering the Capitol can be part of a real event that is also exploited or manipulated by others. We don't know yet if this is the case in relation to the events of January 6, or to what extent it may be the case. That is where a real investigation must come in.

But as someone who has studied history, and the theatrics of history, for decades, I was not surprised to see, on Mr. Carlson's security camera footage, the person who was to become the most memorable face of the "insurrection" (or the riot, or the Capitol breach)—escorted to the beating heart of the action, where his image could be memorialized by a battery of cameras forever.

There are other aspects of the January 6 breach that from the start seemed anomalous to me. I study the relationship in history of buildings such as the White House and the Capitol to the US public; I follow the way in which the public is either welcomed into or barred from these structures.

Civic violence is always wrong, and interfering with elections unlawfully is always wrong. I restate this so that my points here will not be taken out of context.

However the story of January 6, as it was told and retold via the Democrats in leadership, is a departure from our history (and from our Constitution) in that it drummed into the awareness of the nation the message that the American public is categorically forbidden to enter the Capitol, and that the Capitol is the province of legislators alone.

This is false.

———

The media furor around January 6 erased from memory the fact that the White House itself and the Capitol too—including its interior—have always been open to US citizens and foreign visitors. These are public buildings.

The US government website, Visitthecapital.gov, explains that anyone can watch Congress in session; tickets to the gallery are available from one's Representative.[14] You can also enter the Capitol, show ID, and visit the Exhibition Hall. Passes to the gallery are issued to foreign visitors right when they walk in.[15]

The right to mass peacefully at the Capitol and at other public buildings, and indeed to enter the Capitol to observe the legislators at work, is part of our inheritance as citizens. This use of our First Amendment right to assemble has a long history.

The Gallery—the upper balcony that surrounds the legislative action—was constructed in 1857 *in order* to allow the public to watch their legislators and to listen to debates. Even before they had a vote, women had access to a "Ladies' Gallery." After Reconstruction, African American citizens also joined observers in the gallery.[16]

In 1876 and 1877, massive, raucous public crowds thronged the Gallery to observe the outcome of the contested election between Rutherford B. Hayes and Samuel J. Tilden. A painting (shown on the website of the Constitution Center) depicts crowds almost spilling out of the observer's gallery, as they watched the 1876 Electoral Commission deliberate on who would have won the Presidential election.[17]

The Capitol is not a sealed space exclusively for legislators, but it is one that is supposed to, and indeed was constructed to, welcome and host the public, in an orderly way.[18]

Our leaders should not be encouraging us to forget this.

Indeed, inaugurations themselves have been open public events in which the US citizenry simply entered the building for the celebration; this tradition lasted from President Jefferson's inauguration, in 1801, to 1885.

Things got very chaotic indeed in 1829. The editors of History.com described the scene:

> *On March 4, 1829, Andrew Jackson upholds an inaugural tradition begun by Thomas Jefferson and hosts an open house at the White House.*
>
> *After Jackson's swearing-in ceremony and address to Congress, the new president returned to the White House to meet and greet a flock of politicians, celebrities and citizens. Very shortly, the crowd swelled to more than 20,000, turning the usually dignified White House into a boisterous mob scene. Some guests stood on furniture in muddy shoes while others rummaged through rooms looking for the president—breaking dishes, crystal and grinding food into the carpet along the way. . . .*
>
> *The White House open-house tradition continued until several assassination attempts heightened security concerns. The trend ended in 1885 when Grover Cleveland opted instead to host a parade, which he viewed in safety from a grandstand set up in front of the White House."[19]*

And inaugurations were not the only occasions in which US citizens approached or entered their public buildings in Washington.

The Bonus Army, which massed in the summer of 1932, during the Depression, to claim the financial "bonus" promised to veterans who had served in World War I, was made up of thousands of angry citizens assembling peaceably at the Capitol. When I was an undergraduate, we were taught that the Bonus Army sat on the steps of the Capitol and lobbied the legislators who were entering and leaving the building. I remember, from my history textbook, images of crowds seated on the Capitol steps in 1932. Historian Paul Dickson described the events of that day:

> More than 25,000 veterans and their families traveled to Washington, DC, to petition Congress and President Herbert Hoover to award them their bonus immediately. Fortunately for the marchers, Pelham Glassford, the local police chief and a veteran of the war himself, made accommodations for this influx, including the creation of an enormous camp in the Anacostia Flats. . . . Glassford understood that Americans had an inherent right to assemble in Washington and petition the government for the "redress of grievances" without fear of punishment or reprisals. . . . On June 15, the House of Representatives passed the new bonus bill by a vote of 211 to 176. Two days later, some 8,000 veterans massed in front of the Capitol as the Senate prepared to vote, while another 10,000 assembled before the raised Anacostia drawbridge.[20]

The dominant narrative from the Democratic leadership around January 6 often implies that it is an act of violence or of "insurrection" simply to march en masse peacefully, let alone angrily, as the Bonus Army did, to the Capitol. But we should be wary of a history rewritten so as to criminalize peaceful, Constitutionally protected assembly at "The People's House."

The violence that did take place on January 6, and its subsequent use as a talking point by the Democrats' leadership, threatens us with its being used to justify the closing off of our public buildings from US citizens altogether.

This would be convenient for tyrants of any party.

Leaving aside the release of the additional, complicating January 6 footage and how it may or may not change our view of US history—I must say that I am sorry for believing the dominant legacy-media "narrative" pretty completely from the time it was rolled out, without asking questions.

Those who violently entered the Capitol or who engaged in violence inside of it, must of course be held fully accountable. (As must violent protesters of every political stripe anywhere.)

But in addition, anyone in leadership who misrepresented to the public the events of that day so as to distort the complexity of its actual history—must also be held accountable.

January 6 has become, as the DNC intended it to become, after the fact, a "third rail"; a shorthand used to dismiss or criminalize an entire population and political point of view.

Peaceful Republicans and conservatives as a whole have been demonized by the story told by Democrats in leadership of what happened that day.

As a result, half of the country has been tarred by association, and is now in many quarters presumed to consist of chaotic berserkers, anti-democratic rabble, and violent upstarts, whose sole goal is the murder of our democracy.

Republicans, conservatives, I am sorry.

I also believed wholesale so much else that has since turned out not to be as I was told it was by NPR, MSNBC, and the *New York Times*.

I believed that stories about Hunter Biden's laptop were Russian propaganda. Dozens of former intel officials said so. Johns Hopkins University said so.[21]

"Trump specifically cited a 'laptop' that contained emails allegedly belonging to Hunter Biden," said "CNN Fact-Check," with plenty of double quote marks.[22]

I believed this all—until it was debunked.

I believed that President Trump's campaign colluded with Russia—until that assertion was dropped.[23]

I believed that President Trump was a Russian asset, because the legacy media I read, said so.[24]

I believed that President Trump instigated the riot at the Capitol—because I did not know that his admonition to his supporters to assemble "peacefully and patriotically" had been deleted from all of the news coverage that I read or heard.[25]

I believed in the entire Steele dossier, until I didn't, because it all fell apart.[26]

Because of lies such as these in legacy media—lies which I and millions of others believed—half of our nation's electorate was smeared and delegitimized, and I myself was misled.

It damages our nation when legacy media put words in the mouths of Presidents and former Presidents and call them traitors or criminals without evidence.

It damages our country when we cannot tell truth from lies. This is exactly what tyrants seek—an electorate that cannot know what truth is, and what is falsehood.

Through lies, half of the electorate was denied a fair run for its preferred candidate.

Again, I hate violence. I do believe our nation's capital must be treated as a sacred space.

I don't like President Trump. (Do I not? Who knows? I have been lied to about him so much for so long, I can't tell whether my instinctive aversion is simply the habituated residue of years of being on the receiving end of lies.)

But I like the liars who are our current gatekeepers even less.

The gatekeepers who lie to the public about the most consequential events of our time—and who thus damaged our nation, distorted our history, and deprived half of our citizenry of their right to speak, champion, and choose, without being tarred as would-be violent traitors—deserve our disgust.

I am sorry the nation was damaged by so much untruth issued by those with whom I identified at the time.

I am sorry my former "tribe" remains furious at a journalist for engaging in—journalism.

I am sorry I believed so much nonsense.

Though it is no doubt too little, too late—

Conservatives, Republicans, MAGA:

I am so sorry.

CHAPTER NINETEEN

Red Sparkly Shoes

So we'd witnessed charming, well-educated, "civilized" people all around us—especially from what my husband calls (as others do) "the laptop class"—reveal, during lockdowns and medical tyranny, a side that was nakedly sadistic.

Then, as our stunned society slowly tried to set itself upright from having wallowed for nearly three years in an irrational, animalistic seizure of hatred and cruelty—as it struggles to settle its hat and to brush the dust and mire of the gutter off its suit, and to straighten its necktie—few indeed from that group want to glance back at the Lord of the Flies–type scenes of savagery that these "civilized" people cheered on.

But we who were targeted know what happened and cannot forget it. We click, sometimes ruminatively, on compilations in social media of "respectable" politicians, comedians, talk show hosts, and "thought leaders," avidly stating that they wished we would just die, that we should be denied medical care, that we should be locked indoors forever, lose our jobs, and so on.

We—the targeted—must reckon with the traumatizing fact that we were on the receiving end of cruelty that the perpetrators seemed really to enjoy.

Remember all of those affluent ladies (so often affluent ladies)—total strangers—who gestured wildly at you to pull your mask up over your nose? What was their energy like? Almost eager, almost erotic, right?

They *liked* it. They liked the power.

Remember the tone of the society hostess who told you that you can't come to a private event at a major philanthropist's penthouse—because "he is being *careful*"? Was there a bit of a thrill, a sensual savoring, for the hostess, of the words that excluded you, and that included all of them?

Remember the stories of disabled children who came home from schools, weeping, with their masks tied to their faces by their special education teachers? Remember the tone of the elementary school principals who told anguished parents that there was nothing that they could do about the forced masking, or about kids being socially exiled in full view of the class for shamingly structured weekly testing? Remember the Ivy League deans who told distraught parents that there was nothing they could do about mandated mRNA injections that had been tested on only eight mice? Recall the hospital administrators who told miserable adult children that they could not sneak ivermectin to their elders, or even hug them?

They were sorry, but there was nothing they could do. Remember that?

"We are just *following CDC guidelines*," all of these gatekeepers parroted, not noticing, or choosing not to notice, the famous phrase, from about eighty-five years ago, that this recalls.

What was the frenzy of 2020 to 2022 but Sigmund Freud's and Wilhelm Reich's repressive hysteria?

Early-twentieth-century psychologists, notably Wilhelm Reich in *The Mass Psychology of Fascism*, presciently published in 1933, believed that when people deny themselves pleasure and meaning, they become ripe for the attractions of sadism and the lures of totalitarianism.[1] Reich believed that the repression of German interwar culture resulted in that population's attraction to Nazism.

Even earlier than Reich, in 1920, Sigmund Freud formulated the "Pleasure Principle." Freud suggested that in pleasure and joy there is a release of tension, and that hysteria and other neuroses manifest when these instinctive impulses to joy and pleasure are blocked.[2]

While controversy swirled around Mattias Desmet's 2022 book *The Psychology of Totalitarianism*, and its core proposal of "mass formation" as an explanation for the mania of the recent lockdown past, his thesis is far from new, as he himself plaintively had to argue.[3] Indeed, Desmet's is an updating of directly antecedent work from Reich, which he cites, and even more centrally from Hannah Arendt's classic 1951 book, *The Origins of Totalitarianism*, which he also cites.[4]

Though many readers today think Desmet's thesis is novel and controversial, it truly isn't; it is far from novel for sociologists, social commentators, and psychologists to speculate about what psychological dynamics cause paroxysms of totalitarian or fascistic behavior in populations behaving hysterically as a mass. They've been doing so for a couple of centuries.

Desmet largely bypasses the aspects of Reich's work that center on the suppression of pleasure for a more mechanistic focus on general thought control.

But could these theories of suppressed pleasure and the hysterical reactiveness that can arise from it—theories from the past—help usefully to explain the mania of the early 2020s?

Many progressive urban elites, especially, while expressing themselves on social media, seemed to *like* being "locked down"; seemed to boast about how isolated they were, in the depths of our mass incarceration; seemed even to enjoy being scared of "the virus"—seemed to like having something larger than themselves, larger than their $12 green juices and their pilates workouts at Equinox Luxury Fitness Club, larger than their swiping right on dating apps, larger than the "Culture" section of the *New York Times*, on which to focus, and to which to yield their passions.

They were hungry for a cause, for a way to be part of the collective "greater good," for a methodology to demonstrate their self-sacrifice; and so the "rules" handed down one after another by what friends of mine are now calling "our overlords," seemed to stimulate, fulfill, and gratify that longing for greater meaning, that desire to yield to authority and to lose one's troublesome, bored, neurotic self in the collective "altruistic" hive mind.

Their lust for obedience had in it an element of pleasure; an erotic of submission as captured in the only half-joking phrase on a meme, "Lock me down harder, Daddy."

The past three years, this social lust for submission, coinciding with a lust for domination and control; this embrace by certain elites of the performing of cruelty and of imposing cruelty (injections, more and more of them; the masks, the isolation) on oneself—recall of course the Sylvia

Plath poem, "Daddy," in which Plath makes the case that "every woman adores a Fascist."[5]

But in this case those adoring the fascist were of both genders, and the brute was the worshipped State.

What could have contributed to this neurosis, this perverse dynamic of dominance and submission, this desire of millions to lose their individuality, their willingness to sacrifice, in what should have been obvious ways, the wellbeing of their children, and their acceptance, at Milgram- and Zimbardo-experiment-speed,[6] of more and more levels of dystopian sadism in their own and in others' lives, in the years from 2020 to (at least) 2023?

What contributed to turning the culture of liberal elites, in cities especially, into a fertile soil for breeding acts of public cruelty?

Coming from that world, and having lived in it for decades—and now living in a totally different world, a world that we may call "the Rest of America"—I suspect that one contributing factor to this sadism / sadomasochism of the elites is what Freud and Reich both suggested could be dangerous: that is, the systematic denial of pleasure, spirituality, fun, and meaning in the lives of the "laptop class."

The world of liberal elites is one of workaholism, in which family life is often downgraded as a priority, and in which spiritual life has little focus on it at all; it is also made joyless by constant self-surveillance and self-denial.

It is a world full of opaque rules, and the rules constantly shift; some of the rules are about virtue signaling, so you don't get kicked out of your tight, judgmental, privileged little society; but many of the rules are about maintaining a class status that feels, to members of this group, as if it is constantly in danger.

Only by one's knowing the secret codes of the elite—how one is supposed to talk, dress, decorate one's home, entertain—can one signal to others that one is a member of the in-group and that one knows its rigid signifiers.

The code serves to keep everyone else out, even as it reinforces the status of the insiders. But the code, along with the workaholism, contributes to the self-denying atmosphere—the sense of deprivation in relation to spontaneity and fun.

I once sat in a La-Z-Boy recliner, and I loved it; so, secretly, I always longed for a recliner. But you can't *have* a recliner if you are in the world of liberal elites. Don't ask why, you just can't. "Those people"—the people who support "Don't Say Gay," who love Trump, those "out there" who are benighted, the "deplorables"—*they* have recliners.

So *you* can't. Your friends will smirk.

(It is only now that I am in that "other" world, the Rest of America, that I have learned that if you are worried that your friends will smirk, then they are not really your friends.)

I loved the feel of wall-to-wall carpeting, when I encountered it in old-fashioned hotel rooms. But you can't *have* wall-to-wall carpeting in the elite world. It's tacky. You have to have bare, polished wooden floors, with hand-made rugs from some Central Asian location. Whether you like that or not.

In the elite world, there are certain *crackers* you can't put out, for heaven's sake, when guests are expected. It has to be Carr's table water crackers. Why? Who knows?

That's the *rule*.

I do not come from money. I don't come from that world. I was raised barely middle class; my father was a professor at a state university. My mom was a graduate student.

When I got to Yale (which was only possible for me via a scholarship), I was humbled to discover that the Oxford button-down shirts I had bought at Sears, and had felt so proud of having selected—to prepare to fit in, as I had expected, to my new life on the glamorous East Coast—were completely unwearable.

Why?

Because they were not *all cotton.*

They were an unspeakable, unmanageable, polyester-cotton *blend.*

How did the unacceptable nature of my poor shirts, with their taboo admixture of fabrics, even get communicated to me? Who knows.

In the world of elites and their prep-school children, a lifted eyebrow, a barely hidden glance between two better-informed friends—friends who were roommates at Andover, of course—can do it in a heartbeat.

But once you have been on the receiving end of elites' smug displeasure and censoriousness, you don't forget it.

I internalized their codes, over time, for survival at first. But eventually their codes became my atmosphere, my world. I forgot how little they really mattered.

I knew that I was bored as a member of the world of "liberal elites," but I did not know the remedy, because that was the only world I eventually knew. I knew that I wanted to take a Valium (not that I did) when I was a young mother in Washington, D.C., during the Clinton years, because all—*all*—conversation among the senate aides, speechwriters, chiefs of staff, TV pundits, *Washington Post* journalists, lobbyists, and so on, was about work—or else about the gigantic, costly extensions that they were building on their homes.

No art, no emotion, no spirit, no God, no philosophy, no deep questions, and little real sharing.

Later I was bored, bored, as a liberal journalist in New York City, though I was going to the most celebrated gatherings in town; to Literary Lions' galas at the public library; to the trendy screenings; to the most written-up events. I was a regular on the formerly golden publicist Peggy Siegal's B list; hooray for me.

I was *bored* talking to the star writers at the *Nation*, at the *Wall Street Journal*, at the *Atlantic*, because—after you got the news of the day, it was so limited a world of discourse and so dry a cultural context. Politics, work, work, status, work, status—and maybe, as an aside, competitive conversations about how their kids were doing better than other kids with Ivy League waitlists; that was the fare of our conversations, week after week, dinner after dinner, gala after gala.

When I was first dating Brian, we were going to a Peggy Siegal screening in the Hamptons. I explained that the dress expectation for men there would be khakis, a white or blue open-necked Oxford shirt, a navy blue blazer, and brown loafers; it was a *uniform*. I thought I was making him comfortable by explaining this code related to privilege.

Brian wears black Punisher T-shirts and black jeans and combat boots and heavy silver chain bracelets.

He looked at me with pity—pity that my life, my society, was so circumscribed.

It was not until I was ejected from the world of liberal elites and welcomed by the Rest of America that I realized that there is a massive community of people who accept others based on their character, no matter what they are wearing; who don't look around the interiors of their friends' homes, or assess their canapés, with icy judgment.

I have been learning that in "The Rest of America," people have other things going on in their lives than just or primarily their work or their status; and that they are allowed, and allow themselves, to incorporate meaning, adventure, and even fun into their lives.

So in contrast to a subculture of hardworking super-achievers who, as adults, have no fun—I am amazed to find that the world I inhabit now allows for joy, fun, and meaning.

And I think that the joy and the sources of meaning kept this half of the country from devolving into animal rage and cruelty.

When I was single, I was invited on a date by a local contractor. He took me hunting. I sat beside him at the foot of a tree, at dawn, in a field, watching the world of animals wake up, and listening to the meadow itself thrum with life and then start to sing. The cool mists burned away before my eyes as the sun rose. The man later shot a wild turkey and cleaned it and presented it to me as a gift. I could not cook it—it was very tough—and the date never turned into a relationship; but I recall sitting there in wonder at where I found myself, with the whole world coming alive before our eyes, and thinking, *This is fun*.

I remember hanging out with my friend in the modest country neighborhood where we live now. She and her husband had put a pool table in their garage and had built a bar, and had a dartboard on the wall, and had brought some old couches out to the garage; we and our neighbors would all hang around, listening to country music and drinking Jim Beam, and Coors, and playing pool, and making each other laugh, as warm summer breezes swirled around us, the garage door open to the view of green hills, and to the sight and sound of children playing in the street.

And I thought: This is *fun*.

When Brian first took me on an ATV and we sped around our property, and he revved it to jump the wheels up over hillocks along our little river, I thought: *Damn*, this is so much fun.

But in my former life, one was not allowed to like hunting or pool tables in the garage, or ATVs. They are all on the naughty list.

In the past, elites have always hoarded pleasure; look at the rob-ber-baron era. Look at Versailles. It is historically anomalous that today's American elites are so grim and gray and abstemious. Some-times I wonder if the same enemy that is degrading various aspects of our culture, has also sought to weaken our elites by fostering this culture of anemic self-denial.

In contrast, though, the people I know now, in the Rest of America, have a great deal of art, music, beauty, family as a priority, community, and faith in their lives. I don't mean to generalize or romanticize, and I am sure there are many exceptions, but speaking broadly, the people I used to know, for all of their money and privilege, had relatively dry, lonely, empty lives, compared with what seems often to me to be the richness of lives, the permission to have joy and fun and adventure, in the Rest of America.

Church, friends, family, hunting, shooting, patriotism, music, celebra-tions—there is so much, I have learned, that makes many of those outside of liberal urban-elite circles feel that they are part of something larger; there is so much more joy and adventure and meaning culturally *allowed* outside the purviews of the "laptop class"—so perhaps as a result of this, if Freud and Reich are right, the Rest of America is less susceptible to the lure of collectivist cruelty.

A few months ago I was speaking to the East Valley Republican Wom-en's Club in southern California. I was full of vestigial trepidation, as I had been propagandized for most of my life to believe that "Republican women" are Puritanical, blinkered, Church Lady–caricatures.

Of course, when I met them, I encountered a group of sophisticated, delightful, powerful, elegant, and perceptive community leaders. I liked them all and was pleased and honored to be taken into their midst.

I was staying at a casino/resort, where the ladies' luncheon was being held. I realized I had packed only shoes fit for East Coast weather. I did not have sandals for my down time; we were in the desert, and it was hot.

I looked in the shop in the casino, and saw that only a pair of glittering red-and-gold-beaded sandals were available—and I kind of loved them!

But with my lifelong training in the world of liberal elites, I instinc-tively thought: I can't possibly buy and wear those shoes.

They were sparkly and red. They were too much fun. It was unthinkable.

But then I went into the luncheon. There was a beautiful woman onstage, a singer, with long black hair, and perfect makeup; and at midday, she was wearing a blazing red, floor-length gown, with cutout shoulders. She looked stunning. The lighting on her glowed as she sang the national anthem.

We all stood and sang with her. I got chills.

We remained standing and recited the Pledge of Allegiance. Again, this was something that never would have happened in my former world. But a shiver went through me at the awesome sight of so many solemn faces, of the room full of hundreds of people, hands on hearts, all swearing their loyalty to "One nation, under God, indivisible, with liberty and justice for all."

Lastly a female minister gave an invocation. She asked for blessings for the gathering, committed its efforts to the service of God, and expressed heartfelt gratitude for the chance for old and new friends to be in fellowship together. ("Fellowship" was a term about whose nuances I am just learning.)

The luncheon had many subsequent high points; but what I felt above all was that people in this community had meaning in their lives. They had friends, faith, they were prioritizing family life; there was music, beauty, idealism.

There is no way to know this for sure, and history shows as many right-wing tyrants as left-wing ones. But the emotional richness I saw and the acceptance I felt at gatherings such as that—and that I feel in my country community now, and when sojourning among the many conservatives, Libertarians, and others I meet these days in the Rest of America—compared with the poverty of spirit, self-denial, and censoriousness on the elite Left out of which I have been exiled—is striking.

Are the early-twentieth-century philosophers and psychologists correct? Does emotional repression prime people for fascism?

Whatever the answer, I am glad to be free of that shadow world.

I bought the shoes, and I wore them, and I had a lovely time; and I joined my new friends in the sun.

CHAPTER TWENTY

The Last Taboo

I was talking to Ora Nadrich, the gifted author of books about spirituality. We were mulling over the disturbing state of the world. Given that she is at home in the more mystical realms, I let down my guard.

"I feel," I blurted out, "as if in the last few years, the physical world has almost melted away, and that the institutions we thought were permanent have visibly collapsed; and now what has emerged into obvious, palpable form are primarily positive and negative energies."

I try never to share these kinds of observations with anyone but close friends, and only with those who I know are open to such discussions.

I thought she would look at me as if I had two heads.

But Ora said something like, "Exactly."

We delved into how we both sensed that the world itself—not just history, not just human behavior—but the planet; the dimension in which we found ourselves; time and space, and our relationship to them—felt to us as if they had somehow *changed* in the last three years or so; leaving us—us humans—uprooted; trying to make a home again, in a place that was now unfamiliar and new; a place that was shifting; one that was hard to navigate or to understand.

Ora embraces the change and is ready for a new world. Many people in the spirituality community feel that the previous world (pre-2020) was deeply corrupt anyway—the corruption was just better disguised and better dressed—and that it is bracing to see at last the unmediated nakedness of all that was wrong, so that change can come about quickly in the old world passing away and the building of the new.

I wish I had her courage.

But I am uneasy. I feel as if my whole life I have lived on dry land and now I have somehow stepped onto a lurching boat, and I do not yet know our destination. Yet others seem not to see these massive changes at all.

When I read in Ora's book *Time to Awaken* that she believed we as humans on the planet were living in parallel realities, this had the shock of verisimilitude for me, though it was a pretty startling notion.[1]

As Ora explained, we shouldn't be concerned with those whose perception does not contain the "invisible"—that which they cannot see. As it is now, we have come to know that there are those who "see" what is going on, and those who don't.

Ora describes that we are living in a parallel universe, so perhaps there are the "seers of the invisible" and those who cannot see what is not visible to them because they can only live in the visible realm, and even in that realm, there is so much they still do not see.

How else could some millions or billions of people see so clearly the abyss of lies, coercion, and tyranny of the past three years, and the other millions or billions saw nothing but the snooze-worthy status quo?

How is it that we keep speaking directly *past* one another? We do seem to be in different realities.

Or if not two dimensions, what if humanity is now divided into two modes of perception, which is—even trippier—essentially the same as our inhabiting two worlds?

And even beyond that alarmingly intriguing hypothetical, there is the possibility of a major metaphysical shift overall, of some still-to-be-understood kind.

I think it is really possible that the world has indeed changed and shifted in some mysterious way, such that we are blinking into new awareness in a time in which more than ever before, "we wrestle not against flesh and blood, but against principalities, against powers, against the rulers of the darkness of this world, against spiritual wickedness in high places."[2]

I think we need to break the taboo, in our educated, Western discourse, against talking about metaphysical energies, both positive and malevolent.

I believe the world has indeed changed—recently—in such a way that the taboo against such discussions is disempowering to us.

The idea that the world in which humans find themselves changes energetically—that there are palpably different "ages" that bring with them different qualities—is familiar to all great civilizations except our own, post-Enlightenment, mechanistic, Newtonian culture.

The Vedic world believes that time brought humans, about 5,000 years ago, into Kali Yuga; that we are in the middle of "the era of the demon"— of vice and darkness, of conflict and hypocrisy.[3] Astrologers, whose art derives from Mesopotamia, India, and China, believe that we entered the Age of Pisces about 2,000 years ago, and that in the next few hundred years (there is debate about just when) we are due to enter a golden age, the Age of Aquarius.[4] The Aztecs, for their part, believed that there were four ages of creation, each lit by a different sun.[5]

The bottom line is that other civilizations have seen this planet and its environs and humans themselves in relation to their planet and era, as being always in a state of existential flux. It is only our post-Copernican worldview here in the West that, anomalously among cultures, insists that we inhabit a stable, measurable planet.

But might physical reality itself be subject, as most other cultures have always believed, to era-level change?

Our Western modern culture insists that only phenomena that we can see and explain are real, and that human perception must be contiguous and must universally be the same.

But what if that is not true?

I've always been intrigued—as have many scholars of the Greek—with Homer's description in *The Odyssey* of a "wine-dark sea": "And now have I put in here, as thou seest, with ship and crew, while sailing over the wine-dark sea to men of strange speech."[6] Scholars have wondered if the ancient Greeks actually did not perceive color the way we do.[7]

Could people have actually *seen* differently than we do, in former times?

Cognitive scientists are confirming that this different color palette could be a real thing, and caused by differences in language practices: they are finding that if a culture does not have language to describe a thing, the brain does not perceive it as clearly, or sometimes not at all. In "Effects of Language on Visual Perception," Gary Lupyan, Rasha Rahman, Lera Boroditsky, and Andy Clark find that:

> *Effects of language on perception can be observed both in higher-level processes such as recognition and in lower-level processes such as discrimination and detection. A consistent finding is that language causes us to perceive in a more categorical way. [emphasis mine] Rather than being fringe or exotic, as they are sometimes portrayed, we discuss how effects of language on perception naturally arise from the interactive and predictive nature of perception.*[8]

So—could humans have gained different ways of seeing over time, through the development of new languages involving new layers of distinction? The cognitive sciences conclude that this is certainly possible.

Cognitive scientists, and now also quantum physicists, are confirming what mystics from many traditions have long understood: that there is more to reality than flat material being-ness. Kabbala, for instance, one mystical tradition, sees sparks of the Divine as being hidden within all earthly matter. Even though Hollywood has appropriated a weird distortion of it, and the name, it is, if properly understood, in its traditional form, an established part of the Jewish people's faith history; not "occult," but rather a rich discourse of practical mysticism. The Zohar, the foundation of Kabbalism, is a set of medieval commentaries on the Torah. Kabbalists believe that Yahweh is on a continuum closely involved with humans and earth and that the Divine (as well as its oppositional force) can be exposed *within* humans and within material reality. The Zohar sees evil as separation from the Divine: and, "[a]ccording to the *Zohar*, evil is like the bark of a tree of emanation: it is a husk or shell in which lower dimensions of existing things are encased."[9]

These insights about good and evil inhabiting our material world are shared in similar terms by other mystical traditions, including Christianity's and Islam's.[10] Here, for instance, is Saint Theresa of Avila, who also was able physically to perceive both divine and hostile forces: "I used unexpectedly to experience a consciousness of the presence of God, of such a kind that I could not doubt that he was within, or that I was wholly engulfed in him."[11]

On a related note, could modern, secularly trained humans have *lost* certain abilities to perceive the world and the divine or malevolent powers manifested within it, as certain ways of describing reality, including certain words and concepts, have been abandoned, or have atrophied?

What if we have lost our abilities to discern energetic changes and to adapt to them? What if we have lost sophistication in sensing and reacting to—many things that were palpable to our forebears in many nations?

What if we have, through disuse and the abandonment of language for it, lost our ability to see—the spirits of animals and trees and water, which ability is universal in preindustrial societies? What if we lost our ability to see and to hear the voice of God—which ability also was commonplace in earlier times, and around the world? What if we have lost our ability to detect and react to what can only be called beneficent and malevolent energies and entities?

Just as every other culture except ours believes in cycles of time with different attributes, every other culture but ours has a highly developed discourse of positive and negative energies and entities here with us on the planet. We, though, in the modern West, are not supposed to name, and therefore are not supposed to perceive, any of this.

These positive entities, found in all other cultures, can be called angels, guides, archangels, or divine beings. The positive energies from higher positive realms are called blessings, or states of holiness; the positive energies can be found in a location—like a shrine—or maintained in a talisman or amulet, like a *mezuzah* or a Hand of Fatima, or conveyed to a person, as in a baptism, or with relics or holy water.

Negative entities and negative energies, in every other culture but ours, are described with just as complex a discourse and have just as elaborate an iconography; devils, or Djinns, rebellious spirits in Islam; banshees in Ireland; or "hungry ghosts" in Japan. Places can be possessed by negative entities. People can be possessed. In India, today, negative vibrations are taken for granted as being so real that there are advice columns about them in daily newspapers.[12]

We, though, in the modern West, were taught that the coming of monotheism wiped out all notion of negative entities from our Western civilization, or made them tame and manageable.

But the Hebrew Bible actually shows that this process was a dynamic battle.

The Old Testament, as I am learning by reading the Geneva Bible and Chabad.org's Hebrew, does not describe the pagan gods, the "graven images" that Yahweh assailed, as being useless or lifeless or inert, though that was how they were mis-described to me in the versions of these stories that I was mis-taught in Hebrew school.

No, the Hebrew text (and the Geneva Bible) describe them rather as transmitting real powers of their own, but also as transmitting powers that are *bad and dangerous*.[13]

The Hebrew Bible's text makes stunningly clear (though later mistranslations into English do not so simply) the premise that right action aligns people with a moral universe, and that engaging in acts of righteousness is a kind of technology that elicits blessings and abundance from heaven; and that crime, violence, sexual immorality, and hatred put humans at cross-purposes with divine laws, and that it is this—and not the pettiness of a punitive, irrational God—that inevitably draws crisis, chaos, and annihilation—the effects of a curse—onto these individuals and communities.

Why this preamble? Because I think it is time to break the taboo against talking about energies, positive and negative, in this world. Why? Because I think that these forces' emergence into the light of day—the battle between existential, cosmic good and evil, the dueling between forces that extend beyond the mechanistic, beyond the material, beyond the political—is the battle of our time.

We had better learn to resee these energies; to rename them; if we are to survive.

This metaphysical battle is now the defining *Weltanschauung*—worldspirit—of our time. The term, made famous by the German philosopher Martin Heidegger, is literally "world-intuition" or "being-in-the-world," according to the *Cambridge Heidegger Lexicon*. "Heidegger understands worldview existentially—that is, as a modality of Being in the World, in which a particular stance (*Haltung*) or way of having a hold on the world predominates."[14] Heidegger too, shamanistically, warned that human perception affects "reality," and coined the term *welten* or "worlding": the making of a world.

But *Weltanschauung*, too, was mistranslated into modern English, mechanistically and reductively—as so much formerly potent language related to metaphysics has been—as "worldview."

The world-spirit now is overtaken by the struggle between good and evil. Nothing stands in between.

You *can't* stand in between any more.

Everything else now on the planet is secondary to this battle; everything else is a symptom, a byproduct and manifestation, of this metaphysical world-conflict.

Most people I know have had experiences about which they never speak in public; these involve either majestic and beautiful and inexplicable—or scary and negative and inexplicable—forces or energies, that our Western mechanistic worldview does not accept as being real.

As a result, most people are scared to discuss these experiences, lest they be dismissed as flaky or fanatical or mentally ill.

I've been afraid to discuss these matters.

But I must face this last taboo.

I feel I must explore this question of "energies" on this planet, both positive and negative; explore questions about how to recognize both good and evil forces; and investigate how we can become alert to and aware of these flavors and gradations of unseen reality once again, so as to keep ourselves spiritually safe and strong and on the right path, in a time of grave spiritual danger.

I am, as I often insist, a devoted rationalist. I believe in the scientific method. I believe in facts and I cherish the verifiable.

I know that there are real dangers in opening the door to discussion of that which cannot be proven by two objective witnesses; dangers of fanaticism, of hysteria, of group hallucinations. All you have to do is look at history, from the Inquisition to the Salem witch trials, to see how assertions about the unseen, about good or evil forces and the metaphysical, have been perverted into savagery or collective lunacy.

That said, I do believe that the world in which we could manage quite well enough by *never* talking about metaphysical energies—blessings or curses, angelic or demonic forces—has died away.

I feel it gone, in all of its dumb, familiar, reassuring solidity. I miss its stolid, lumpen thickness, its cozy materiality, its prosaic predictability.

In this old world being destroyed and this new world being born, I believe we will need to start telling the truth about the energies we feel and that we encounter.

I believe we need our prophets and our shamans back; our guides; our Josephs, our dreamers; our poets and our interpreters.

We need our spiritual practices, and thus our spiritual discernment, back.

We need to remember what it means to see and name the invisible color "blue"—all the levels of meaning and being that we have been told are not really there—if we are safely to forge this tossing, mighty sea.

I sought my entire career to secure a reputation as a serious, academically trained intellectual in the post-Enlightenment tradition. I did largely achieve that.

However, that came with a cost.

For this tradition—especially now, since World War Two—is a thoroughly mechanistic one. If you are a "serious person," in the discourse of the West, today, you cannot possibly believe in anything that cannot be objectively measured—and measured, to take that one step further, with the physical instruments that currently exist. If you believe in anything beyond the purely mechanistic, materialist Newtonian universe, you are a rube, a fantasist, credulous, ignorant, deceived.

So—like many people—I have taken care to censor rigidly the fact that all my life, I have also had experiences that were dramatic, and that made deep impressions upon me—but that went beyond what the physical universe could contain or explain.

I have recently come close to death (a story which I'll soon relate), and am, as a friend put it, "playing with House money." Meaning that I have a second chance at life, and I have nothing left to lose.

So I am putting a match to my reputation once again, by sharing my conviction, and attesting to my lived experience, that the world is awash with "energies," both good and evil, and that these affect humans—and probably animals, and the planet itself—in profound and important ways.

Ever since I was first conscious, I was aware that I perceived some things differently than did many of those around me. In kindergarten, I realized (without, of course, having the word for this) that I had synesthesia—the condition in which one sense spills over into another; people with this form of perception hear colors, or taste sound, or in other ways activate different senses at the same time.[15] In my case, I so vividly saw numbers as colors—"1" as yellow, "2" as green, "3" as red, "4" as brown, "5" (my least favorite number) as black, "6" as light blue, and so on—that I was astonished to discover that this way of seeing the colors of numbers, was not experienced by everyone in my class. That was the first time I felt ashamed and embarrassed when I realized that my perception made me different from the peers with whom I wished so much to fit in.

Somehow I managed to suppress this "odd" way of seeing numbers—a suppression which also, sadly, later made it quite difficult for me to enjoy numbers (or, as a result, to do math).

Though I managed to censor my synesthesia, my awareness as a child that perception was fluid, and that currents of all kinds were continually flowing around us all—and that the physical world was illuminated and glowing and magical, but also that it contained dark and scary forces—could not be suppressed.

Luckily I was born into a family of eccentrics, and of people who believed in and respected the creative fire. My father knew the literature of the mystical poets and of the Transcendentalists very well. He knew that the way I saw the world was not that unusual, and that plenty of reasonable people—from Walt Whitman to Henry David Thoreau to Emily Dickinson—had similar sensibilities. My dad knew his William Blake, so he was fine with his weirdo daughter's tendency to see "a World in a Grain of Sand / And a Heaven in a Wild Flower."[16] My mother, when I was a child, was a folklorist. Nothing I shared, as a child, was too weird for my folks.

The world of intellectuals has not always been as divorced as it is today from mystical perception. In the nineteenth century, for example, intellectuals *pursued* mysticism: indeed, there was a word for it: the perception of, or the artistic capture of, "the Sublime." Instead of mocking those who were aware of the larger currents animating the physical world, many nineteenth-century aesthetes, and certainly our own Transcendentalists, actively pursued awareness of the Sublime; they read poems and looked at paintings to hone their sensibilities in that direction. It was understood then that anyone could perceive the Sublime, and that doing so ennobled the observer.

Here is Walt Whitman in *Leaves of Grass*:

> *What do you think has become of the young and old men?*
> *And what do you think has become of the women and children?*
>
> *They are alive and well somewhere;*
> *The smallest sprout shows there is really no death,*
> *And if ever there was it led forward life, and does not wait at the*
> *   end to arrest it,*
> *And ceas'd the moment life appear'd.*
>
> *All goes onward and outward, nothing collapses,*
> *And to die is different from what any one supposed, and luckier.*
>
> *Has any one supposed it lucky to be born?*
> *I hasten to inform him or her it is just as lucky to die, and I know it.*
>
> *I pass death with the dying and birth with the new-wash'd babe,*
> *   and am not contain'd between my hat and boots . . .*
>
> *I am the mate and companion of people, all just as immortal and*
> *   fathomless as myself,*
> *(They do not know how immortal, but I know.)*[17]

By the time I was coming of age, though, those days were gone. I grew up in a jet age, a Jetsons age. The Transcendentalist poets were passé.

My family, when I was a child, accepted me, but the larger world would be a problem.

If you could not measure it, it did not exist.

———

When I was nine, I invited a little friend to see the "magical place" that I knew was hidden like a gem in a corner of a sedate garden. It was a garden that dated to the beginning of the twentieth century; there were stone garden walls rising up to the magical place, and they were covered with moss; there was a little concrete bench set into the wall, at an angle outward into the street, crafted in that 1910 style. Parts of the ancient garden were overgrown—an elegant, elderly lady lived in the lovely old house and rarely emerged, but when she did, she was as beautiful as her forgotten garden.

This little grotto was a miniature land of dreams.

If you stood on the bench and looked into the corner of the garden, which was raised up, you could see nasturtiums made of tongues like fire—with apricot and russet, lemon-yellow and radiant orange petals; all of them were streaked with deep red at the hearts, and all bore tiny cups of honey.

You could see pale-blue bluebells too, bending their necks like dancers. The nasturtiums and the bluebells were like two companies of ballerinas, clothed in different costumes. There were shafts of sunlight somehow *within* that circle of nasturtiums and bluebells. And all of this treasure was contained somehow within *another* circle, one made up of dark green—of wet, tangled, protective grasses, that overshadowed and enclosed the secret place.

The magical place looked like a ballroom for fairy dances.

The glow of its magic was palpable to me.

My little friend asked her mom if she could go see it; and her mom—who as I recall was something really glamorous and cool and slightly intimidating, like a flight attendant—was excited, in spite of herself as an adult, to see this magical place of which I spoke.

So the mom drove her daughter over. And they got out of the car. And I showed the grotto to them.

And there was silence.

And more silence.

Neither of them had any idea what I was talking about.

After a beat, I could feel that my friend was confused, and that she was a bit sorry for me. There was nothing to see!

The mom turned away with a brisk motion. "Come on, let's get home." She was terse and annoyed. There was nothing there.

And to my amazement, I looked at the magical place and—there was indeed nothing there!

The magic had fled at the denial of perception.

What had happened? It was nothing now, it was utterly banal, it was just a tangle of grasses, a dim mess of foliage.

I was—again—horribly humiliated and embarrassed. No one saw what I saw! I was *such* a weirdo.

I was never invited over to play with that child again, and she never came over again to my house.

So yet again, I tried to put away my troublesome perception.

———

Many experiences in my life as an adult followed this theme—that the world is animated with energies, for good and evil, and embroidered all over with magic; and I sustained these experiences but did not discuss them. I also learned that lots of people suppress similar experiences along these lines.

Once in a while I would tell a story about a metaphysical experience— one that really had happened to me—and then everyone else—lawyers, editors, journalists, scientists—would rush to share their own stories of the metaphysical. So I learned that lots of us are *not talking* about import- ant experiences, from which we could all surely learn important lessons.

And when I ask these folks *why* they don't talk more publicly about their experiences, I get the same responses that I recognize in my own inhibitions: no one wants to be seen as hallucinating, or not credible, or unbalanced. Two-thirds of people, according to Yougov.com, say that they have had a paranormal experience.[18] About half of Americans, according to Pew Research, say that they have had a mystical or meta- physical experience.[19]

That is a lot of Americans who are, understandably, keeping quiet.

———

We are awash with energies, good and evil, beyond those for which post- war science has names.

Some of these energy fields are beautiful and miraculous. Perhaps they are even healing.

When I went to visit the grave of the "Lubavitcher Rebbe"—Rabbi Menachem Mendel Schneerson, one of the most revered holy men of the twentieth century—I was directed to the *Ohel*, or "tent," a gathering-place in Queens, built adjacent to the Rebbe's gravesite. This is a destination where people from all walks of life gather to pray at this saintly person's final resting place.[20]

"The Rebbe keenly understood that our every action is part of a bigger picture," explains Chabad.org.

> *Every good deed we do brings humanity closer to the ultimate goal, the era of cosmic perfection and universal awareness of G-d, known in Judaism as the time of Moshiach. The Rebbe spoke tirelessly about this time, demonstrating how the world is heading closer and closer to this special era and how every person can actualize it by increasing in acts of goodness and kindness.[21]*

I was early to my appointment. So I walked for many blocks around my destination. And the further away from the gravesite I wandered— block after block, into the peaceful Queens suburbs—the fainter grew the aura or force field of holiness.

But as the time of my appointment drew closer, and I walked *toward* the *Ohel*—the closer I drew to the sacred location—the more intensely one could feel the magnetism of great holiness. It was like a giant ziggurat of sacred energies, ascending to a peak over the quiet cemetery in Queens; and gently sloping off into all directions, like a mountain of emotional gold.

At the gravesite itself, the vibration of sanctity was so palpable I felt as if I were in the presence of an aspect of the Divine.

So many places are vortices of sacred energy.

When I visited the Scottish island of Iona, I was an ill-informed, day-tripping tourist. I had done no research on the island; and this visit was before cellphones or the internet. To my amazement, the moment my feet touched Iona's earth, I wandered the island in a state of joy and exaltation; in a daze of glory. Was that what heaven felt like?

I did not realize—until I boarded the tourist bus again, and the bus driver explained—that Iona was a sacred island. It always had been, back to pre-Christian times, and right up to the present. The sacred presence on the island had been described and testified to, over and over, for centuries. It was believed in the traditions related to the place, that Christ had visited Iona—and would reappear again on that sacred island.[22]

Some people react like that, explained the bus driver—most people; most wander around in a state of exaltation and joy.

And some people simply cannot take it, he said; the energies burn them; and they need to get off the island as quickly as possible.

———

Some of the energies out there are simply alarming.

The leadership institute I cofounded long ago in the Hudson Valley was housed in a fine old building on 300 acres of land. I recall that the real estate broker would not get out of the car when she first showed the building to me.

She sent me in alone.

Once my colleagues and I bought it, we realized it was truly haunted.

Kitchen cabinet doors would swing open of their own accord. There was a spot in the library that was always icy cold. Lights would flicker off and on, and doors would bang shut in empty rooms. Retreatants would have troubled dreams.

It got so bad that we expected the presence in the house—everyone agreed that it was a masculine one—to act up at certain times during retreats. When we lit the Shabbat candles, the candles would flicker. Or one candle would be snuffed out.

At one point, two serious witnesses—neither prone to exaggeration—described a Shabbat candlestick dematerializing. It simply *disappeared*.

By now, we had learned that the long-ago owner of the home had been murdered (in the library), by his tenant, who had lived in a smaller home on the property.

The house subsequently had had so much supernatural activity, that, in the 1940s, there had been an actual old-school exorcism. This exorcism had been matter-of-factly reported in the local newspaper.

I was at a loss. The paranormal activity was taking a toll on everyone. I described this disturbing situation to my then-therapist, a spiritually oriented gentleman. He suggested that the being in the house seemed to be trying to get our attention when we lit the Shabbat candles.

He suggested that we say the Kaddish next time we lit the candles— the Jewish prayer for the dead.

We did. We said Kaddish.

The house filled with peace.

The unsettled presence seemed right away to have moved on—and nothing ever bothered anyone in that house again.

————

Other energy fields, I have no doubt, are just pure evil.

I visited Guantanamo, in the first six months of President Barack Obama's administration. I could feel the presence of what one might call Satan; or of some other magisterial, high-level administrator of evil.

I felt that presence. Not in the service men and women assigned to that post, not in the housing for reporters; not in the cynical mock-up of the courtroom on the site; not in the prison yard—where I could see the men who had been penned up for years without charge or trial, and I could hear their roar of distress and outrage.

Rather, I could feel the presence of Satan—or some other adjudicator of evil on earth—standing *right* behind the "doctors" and the "nurse" and the "psychiatrist," in the pristine "medical facility," where "difficult" prisoners were housed. That facility was part of the creepy tour that the US government had arranged for reporters who were covering the prison.

These "healers" in the medical bay were showing me rather proudly how they forced tubes down the throats of the recalcitrant prisoners who went on hunger strikes. They showed me—as if this selection were a treat—the range of *flavors* of liquid nutrition—chocolate, strawberry, vanilla—that they pumped into the unwilling bodies of striking prisoners.

A prisoner who had been on hunger strike, and who was being force-fed, died of starvation while I was at the facility.

I could almost *smell* the evil of the force field that surrounded those "doctors" and "nurses" at that scene. There was something huge, and awful, and terrifying, and intelligent, and dark—just behind them; inhabiting them; all around them.

We are in a time of extraordinary change—the nature of reality itself is changing, as you now know I believe—and if we are to survive this time and indeed if we are to evolve safely to wherever we are supposed to arrive next, we need to talk honestly about good and evil energies; about healing and killing energies; and about sacred and profane energies.

This discussion is not even as metaphysical as it sounds. Brian, my husband, who very early in his military career worked in "SIGINT," or "Signals Intelligence," points out that everything has a vibrational signature or frequency—and that mapping those signals is how many technologies work that scan a field to gather intel through the interception of those signals.

So many technologies use various energy fields that we scarcely notice how weird they would have seemed in an era before their mechanisms were understood. Is it so weird to grapple with energies?

Sonograms send sound energies into our bodies to give our doctors intelligence. Ultrasounds also use sound waves.

Given all this, is it surprising that we "vibe" with some people and that our energy fields "clash" with others? Is it surprising that people who are happily married have heart rates that align when they sit side by side? Is it surprising that stories about relatives who know at distances of thousands of miles that something bad has happened to their loved ones, are as commonplace as stories of finding bargains at a mall?

We live in a mysterious world. Mechanics do not explain the totality of it.

We are held together human to human, by energies of love that are as strong as death. Our lives are held in the palm of the Divine, like leaves on the surface of water.

Who knows all that is around us and that animates us?

Our ancestors dealt with these mysteries by inviting and seeking and invoking blessings, and by assiduously avoiding curses.

Every culture except our own has amulets, phylacteries, prayer shawls, talismans, Yad Fatimas, invocations, prayers for protection.

Every culture except our own seeks the blessing of positive energies, and respects the miraculous nature of positive powers.

Every culture except our own fears and dreads curses and maledictions; is wary of the workings and powers of negative energies; and seeks divine protection from them.

Is our denial of powerful energies—especially in a time of great pressure and great change—a form of cultural suicide?

Are we super-enlightened?

Or just really incredibly dumb?

It is time for us, too, urgently to relearn some ancient wisdom.

CHAPTER TWENTY-ONE

Not Dead Yet

As chance would have it, as I was finishing this book, I was struck with appendicitis. I checked into a peaceful little local hospital, on the advice of my wonderful friend and gifted healer, Dr. Henry Ealy. That was not a horrible experience.

But then I sustained an infection after my surgery, and was rushed to a terrifying major urban hospital, where I came very close to death. I am now home from the second hospital—the "Vortex Hospital," as I think of it, a hospital of near-no-return—and am pleased to report that I am:

Not Dead Yet.

I suffered in ways I won't trouble you by describing, but suffice to say that my stay at the Vortex Hospital involved the final three of what had been five days with no food or water, as I had lain, hooked up to an IV, with an acute abdominal infection, post-appendectomy.

I watched my vitals being taken again and again and saw that over time my blood oxygen levels had started sinking into the 80s; I could not get them back up into the safe 90s range, no matter how hard I inhaled and exhaled. I knew that when blood oxygen levels drop too low, people are intubated, and I knew that meant that the lungs could get damaged irrevocably. The internal infection raged on.

The morning of what was supposed to have been the day on which my procedure was to have taken place—one to treat the severe abdominal infection—we sustained a four-and-a-half-hour power outage ("Unprecedented," the staff said wonderingly), leaving the massive brand-new hospital facility in unnerving darkness, even as the small, cozy, 1970s-era original building, right next door, trundled along with all its lights on.

By the end of my Day Five with no food or water, the staff at the Vortex Hospital told me that, due to the power outage, the procedure for which I had been transferred to that facility was being delayed further and further into the future.

"Maybe tomorrow," said the RN vaguely. "Maybe the day after."

When I expressed panic that that would mean seven days or more without food or water, the RN said, with no emotion, "People can live for seven days without food or water."

The unsaid observation was: "Then, they can't."

And then she "reassured me": "If you don't get seen after Day Seven we'll just put you on a feeding tube." This terrified me. Finally she said, flatly: "Your vitals are stable."

After this exchange, I truly panicked. I knew that while my vitals might look fine, I could feel that I was losing the ability to keep fighting for my life. I felt the subsiding of my will to fight, as clearly as if I were watching water swirling around an emptying drain.

I was exhausted, and had stopped caring about outcomes. I just wanted the suffering to end, in whichever way it might. In conventional nursing, I am sure that that collapse of my will to live would have been visible to a caring observer, no matter what my "vitals" had to say. But the machinery of data-based management ground on.

When I could fight no longer, I thought weakly of my loved ones; and realized that even though I no longer cared if I survived or not, they would care if this was indeed the end of my life.

So I asked God to please save my life. I also told God that if He spared my life I would write all the things I was currently scared to write—I knew He knew exactly what those things were—and then I collapsed into a feverish dream.

I found myself coming to consciousness free of pain, and feeling light and small. For good reason: I was myself, but I was now a nine-year-old version of myself, and I was all spirit. It felt good and very simple—as if I was made of light and energy. I was on a beach, and my dad (who has passed away) was there with me.

The beach was incredibly peaceful. But there were some unusual things about it. It faded into mist in both distances, so that all I could see clearly was the stretch where my father and I were present together. And it was "pearly." So much so that I almost laughed. "Really?" The waves were edged with a bioluminescent quality, even though, as I watched a single wave break near my foot, the water itself was extraordinarily clear. The mist was edged with a silvery and lavender glow.

Then there was my dad—whom I felt completely unsurprised to see, just as he seemed to take seeing me there very much in stride. His age and mine in that scene were not in accordance with our earthly time-lines. He was not the forty-plus father of my actual childhood in the 1960s; here on this beach he looked about thirty-five. He was dressed the way old photos show him to have dressed in the late 1950s, before I was born—before the crazy 1960s.

Here, he wore a pale moss-green fisherman's sweater, and chinos with the ankles rolled up. His feet were bare. ("Mom, did Dad have a moss-green fisherman's sweater, and did he wear chinos, in the 1950s?" Mom: "Yes.")

He looked extremely well; his hair was fully black, not streaked with gray as it had been from my earliest memory of him. My father had had very distinctive feet, with high arches, in life; those were indeed his elegant feet on the sand. His hands were dry and warm, in life; he put his right hand gently on my hair and yes, that was his hand.

Then we had a calm, serious, direct talk. It did not matter that I was nine and he was thirty-five, or that I was alive—somewhere—and that he was dead. It seemed as if that talk was the purpose of this encounter.

After my father's death, I had learned about certain aspects of his life that had confused me, and that had led me to struggle with my memory of him. These questions had become a barrier to my properly mourning him, and certainly they had kept me from feeling his presence. But in this chat we were having—thoughtful, father to daughter, transparent, not sentimental—I got to ask him every question that had haunted me, and he answered them one by one, and the answers set my mind entirely at ease. As that conversation unfolded, and he was accountable to me in my questions, I felt the spiritual connection I had had with him, which had been blocked, reopen like a channel; and all the love that he felt for me—and that I felt for him—sluiced through to connect us once more, undeniable, as it was intended to do, death or no death.

At one point, I asked him what God had thought about a certain issue. My dad replied, in the context of explaining that God was more forgiving than humans—"God is different from you and me." That was another moment in which I enjoyed evidence that this really was my dad; that is just the kind of thing he would have said; he was an English literature professor; and that is a witty paraphrase of a famous F. Scott Fitzgerald quote.

After all the questions had been answered, I asked, neutrally curious, if I was staying there. He gestured toward a broad silvery stream, like a runnel on an estuary, that cut off the wet sand on that strand of beach from some other place; and indicated that no, I was now to cross back over that shimmering divide.

There wasn't a leave-taking or anything else dramatic—I simply found myself again at length lying on my bed of pain, the infection raging still.

By this time Brian had done his wonderful Brian thing, of making things happen when they are not happening, by saying certain things, in a certain way, and leaving certain things unsaid. I don't know how he does it, but I thank the US Army for its training of him in this arcane but useful art. For the second time, he saved my life. After he made a call, the orders came from above, and I was rushed at last into the room where my lifesaving procedure took place.

I will skip over those details.

Then, after a night of recovery—after seven days without food or water—I was ordered a breakfast—half a pound of dehydrated egg "skillet," a quarter-pound of home fries, sausages the size of doorstops, a bowl of instant oatmeal—that contained 1010 calories and 65 grams of fat. I looked at it in aversion and sipped some juice.

And then, I was free to go.

———

I did not have any street clothes with me, but the minute the RN said I could leave, I asked for some scrubs, and just kept my hospital gown on; and we fled, before they could all change their minds.

The sunlight outside was dazzling. I wanted to kiss the earth, and every human being I saw. I loved the mulch. I loved the Hondas. I loved the security guard.

The red tiger lilies in front of the parking garage looked to me like the most beautiful flowers I'd seen in my life—trumpets of rusty glory.

The instant I was seated on a concrete bench outside the hospital, breathing, I began to feel better—which made me realize that for two and a half weeks, medical staff, all of whom were of course vaccinated with mRNA injections, had been "shedding" on me continually, by leaning over me and breathing into my face while taking vitals, or by constantly handling me.

This situation had been bad enough in the small local hospital, where at least my window opened a crack. But at the massive Vortex Hospital to which I had been transferred, the windows—overlooking a spectacular vista—*did not open at all.*

(We know that "shedding" is real because it is in the Pfizer documents, and that Pfizer defines "exposure" to the mRNA vaccine as transmission through skin contact and inhalation.[1] And we know that spike proteins cause systemic inflammation—which, sadly, is the *opposite* of the condition one needs in order to heal from an infection.[2] Who knows to what extent it was the exhaled spike proteins themselves, in a completely sealed facility that housed thousands of vaccinated people, that had been helping to kill me? The pharmaceutical industry has managed the greatest of ironies—it has managed to turn hospitals' staff, whose jobs are to help patients heal, into physical vectors of a biologically destructive agent that creates a shared environment thoroughly *antithetical* to healing.)

Being able to breathe at last, without inhaling each time the effluent of an entire ward of constantly recirculating spike proteins and other toxins, immediately made me feel as if I could surely find a way to recover.

The day I was liberated from the hospital was our nation's birthday. Independence Day. Our forefathers and foremothers risked their lives, and many died, in order to create a blessed society grounded in sacred values of freedom and justice.

In its lived reality it was not perfect because they and we and history, as remembered by us, are all human, and thus not perfect. But the values on which they founded it, are indeed perfect, and sacred, and eternal. No one yet had done so beautifully in establishing a human society according to the Divine Plan of freedom and justice.

For three years, evildoers sought to murder our Republic.

But looking back over recent history, and out over this land, we see: our victory is that we are not yet in a state of defeat; on this Independence Day of 2023, our Republic is Not Dead Yet.

The fight to save our Republic, waged over the last three years, did indeed wear me down, and did indeed, just now, as an aggregate, nearly kill me.

But I too am—you got it—Not Dead Yet.

I think of that passage from the Jewish Haggadah Ve'hi She'amda:

And this is that (promise)
which sustained our fathers and us.

That it is not one (enemy) alone
that stood up against us to destroy us.

But that in each generation there are those
standing up against us to destroy us.

But the Holy One Blessed Be He
saves us from their hand.[3]

I thanked God on that Independence Day for second chances. I would try to make the most of my restored second chance at life.

Thanked God, too, on that day that "the enemy" did not yet succeed, three years in of trying, at murdering our Republic.

Not.

Dead.

Yet.

CHAPTER TWENTY-TWO

Soup

I was supine on the couch, recovering from my very near brush with the Void. I'd given myself, with my doctor's blessing, permission to be in a state of "rest"—that retro condition—without guilt, for a while at least; which seems at once naughty and luxurious.

Brian made me chicken soup, as Dr. Ealy has prescribed pretty much just smoothies, soups, and fermented foods for me, till I am stronger.

I noticed some chunky white strips floating in the soup, like thick little rafts. "What is that, honey?"

"Pork fat. It will give it flavor."

"You know this is supposed to be Jewish chicken soup, right?" I asked, smiling.

"You have to respect my Irishness," he declared.

I did, and the soup was delicious: "restorative," as we say, half-joking, in our household. I felt the life force burn a little brighter in me as I blew on my spoon, and took it all in.

Chicken soup has a very allegorical presence in our history. A Jewish chicken soup I made long ago, it is not an overstatement to say, turned our relationship from that nervous status of "dating" onto the steady path to marriage.

Nine years ago, Brian and I had been courting for about six months. I was still incredibly jumpy about him, part delighted and part terrified. Half of me believed that he had been sent by some intelligence agency to infiltrate my life and my social network.

What was he doing hanging around me so consistently, I wondered? He was much younger than I, very handsome, sort of scary, extremely comfortable with a range of weapons, and strangely highly trained in many arcane white and black arts.

He was not like anyone I knew. He had hacker friends. He had spy friends, and mercenary friends, and special operator friends. And he was friends too, oddly, with a couple of governors, a couple of ambassadors, and some high-level businessmen; as well as being friends with riffraff of all kinds.

Surely he couldn't be making the long train journey every week from Washington to New York to see me, just for my sake—just for me, an exhausted single mom, from a completely different milieu?

What was his *real* agenda?

Friends were continually warning me about just this scenario—of subversion via seduction. A friend sent me news stories about a detective in the UK who infiltrated a group of environmental activists by seducing a female member—he lived with her for *months* before she realized that the relationship was a setup. Other friends of mine would pepper Brian with probing questions when he accompanied me to parties. He patiently answered them, barely rolling his eyes.

I would ask him about my fears directly.

"How do I know you haven't been sent here by the CIA, or by Mossad, to kill me?"

He'd answer with a mocking scenario that always made me laugh in spite of myself.

"Well, if I have, I'm doing a terrible job, and I'll probably get fired: 'Agent Seamus here.' 'What's going on? Why isn't she dead yet? It's been months!' 'Well, I was going to knock it out last week, but we had that thing at the town hall. Then I was going to take care of it last Wednesday, but we can't miss *Dancing with the Stars*. I was going to do it this morning, but Starbucks didn't open till 8:00 am, and you know I can't function without that first cup of coffee . . .'"

So, slowly, I let my guard down. I got used to the imponderable world of Brian O'Shea. I got used to finding three different passports on the shelf where he kept his toiletries. I got used to being put on FaceTime to say hello to some wizened, sectarian warlord who had been tossing back vodka shots for some reason with Brian, as he was for some reason in Tbilisi. I got used to hearing that Brian had been detained at a local airport because he had forgotten that there were hollow-point bullets in his carry-on backpack ("Not my fault! I was packing so quickly, I forgot to check the bag.") I learned to accept that when we stepped outside of a dance club in eastern Sarajevo, where we had traveled for a speaking engagement of his, he froze and turned white at the sound of a car back-firing. He did not go into detail about his reaction.

I got used to weird moments: we were in the elegant, seventeenth-century, oak-paneled drawing room in the home of the master of my then-college at Oxford; and we were introduced to a visiting ambassador. Brian and the official looked at each other with simultaneous white-hot rage, leaving the master and me standing by in a befuddled silence. A long-ago operation had gone awry, it seemed, in a way that left each of these men infuriated at the other.

There were other strange experiences that were becoming familiar to me. I went to a party in a massive, mostly empty mansion in the Virginia woods. Russians, Serbs, Frenchmen, Argentinians—everyone seemed to be a "tech CEO," but had little interest in or conversation about technology. One fellow had tiny skulls embroidered as a pattern on his expensive, tailored shirt. I found out later these were gray arms dealers.

I got used to the barbeques in backyards in the suburbs in D.C. full of young men who were working in the embassies of certain European countries, and young women from those same countries who were all working as "au pairs," but who all—the young men and the young women both—talked with intense, in-depth knowledge about geopolitics. I got used to meeting "couples" who seemed completely ill-matched, with zero chemistry between them, who indeed seemed hardly to know each other.

I got used to the fact that one of Brian's colleagues was a gigantic young former Spanish army sniper, whose identity had been revealed by terrorists years before in a troubled part of Spain. Hence his presence in Old Town, Alexandria, working for Brian. I got used to the fact that "Paolo" was now also a part-time baker. Indeed, he was the *second* sniper-baker to whom Brian introduced me. (Paolo's specialty was macaroons, whereas the first sniper-baker focused upon miniature cupcakes.)

I was scared of Paolo, for the same reasons I was scared of Brian; until Paolo showed up at the door, when I was looking after Brian; tall and immensely muscled and pleasant-looking, with an open, innocent face, and bearing a small, perfectly decorated pink paper box.

"I am not here to kill you," he said solemnly, having been told of my fears. "I have brought you macaroons."

Who were all of these people? What was happening in this world?

Slowly it dawned on me.

There is a world of people with clearances, people in the "intelligence community," people who are associated with embassies, or who are military or ex-military, or people who make their way for various reasons in the margins of that world. I had had no idea. This underworld/mirror world lies, in D.C. and Alexandria, beneath, or alongside, the overt world that I knew. Before I met Brian, I had spent years in D.C. surrounded by people *without* clearances: journalists, policy wonks, White House functionaries. We thought we were everything. But I came to realize that there is a whole shadow-ecosystem: some helping the nation, getting no public credit, and some, their adversaries, trying to subvert or surveil the nation, getting no public blame.

I had no idea of the dimensions of the complex alternative/subterranean world that is the shadow side of the public drama of personalities, roles, and relationships that appears to lead the nation, and to set the national discussion, in the glaring light of day.

———

So I did not understand then much about who this man really was; but I could not help the fact that I was falling irrevocably and helplessly in love with him.

I was at that dangerous, vulnerable point in a relationship in which "dating" had not yet turned into something more committed. At that point, Brian told me that he was very ill with the flu. He could not come up to see me. He seemed surprised and pleased that I offered, if he wished, to come down to see him.

I got myself from Penn Station to Union Station, and from there to the townhouse where he lived in Alexandria. A key had been left for me, and I let myself in.

The townhouse itself was an absolute mystery to me. Just as Brian was like no one I had ever encountered before, this dwelling was like nothing I had ever seen. What was it? What did it mean?

It was a very expensive, small eighteenth-century townhouse, made of pale yellow brick, in Alexandria's historic district. Inside, the costly exterior was confusingly contradicted by aggressively middlebrow decor. The interior looked as if it had been staged by a window dresser at Raymour & Flanigan. In short, it did not look like the house of any real people who really lived there.

The walls were taupe—that awful taupe that was so popular in suburbs about ten years ago. There were white wooden motto signs made of cursive letters, placed on white wooden shelves, that said such things as "Smile." Other signs read, "It's five o'clock somewhere." The leather sectional couch was generic, the wrought-iron dining chairs and the round glass dining table were generic, the artificial plants were generic. There were photographs of one of the house's inhabitants (for there were several, as Brian had explained to me) in white wooden frames in odd places—on the living room wall, for instance, rather than on a bedside table upstairs.

The kitchen had instructions on a printed sheet of paper that was affixed to the inside of an upper cabinet. The instructions seemed to be for people who were entirely unfamiliar with the house, and the neighborhood; even with the dog, who was a big, disoriented-seeming golden retriever who was ever-present.

The name of the dog, in the printed instructions, was *different* than the name by which the inhabitants of the house called the dog.

Who *was* this dog?

There were no toiletries in the upper bathroom cabinets. Weird! All three of the people who lived in the house kept their toiletries in kits in their bedrooms.

None of it added up.

Brian had once told me about safe houses. Was *this* a safe house?

Wherever I was, I had to make peace with it. I looked in on Brian in his upstairs bedroom; he was in a deep, flushed, flu-driven sleep, and looking very ill indeed.

I texted my mom: "What was Dad's Jewish chicken soup recipe?"
She texted back:

Simmer a whole chicken, a good one. Put two carrots, two celery stalks, an onion, and a parsnip, in the water. Add tons of crushed garlic. Simmer. Skim the froth. Remove the carcass, shred the meat, put it back in the broth. Simmer. At the end of a couple of hours, add fresh dill, fresh parsley, and a squeeze of lemon.

So I did that. And eventually Brian came slowly downstairs, took a bowl of soup, and slowly returned to life. "Jewish penicillin," it's called for a reason. He drank that soup and he drank it.

We sat on the weird nondescript couch, and he introduced me to reruns of *Seinfeld*. "I can't believe you haven't watched *Seinfeld*," he said, between sips of soup. He later told me that he was amazed that I had come all the way down to D.C. and made soup for him. No one had ever done anything quite like that for him, he said.

For my part, I blessed my dad's recipe. For by then I had turned over, in my courtship of this man, every single card at my disposal. Brian at that point knew what I looked like; he knew how I dressed; he knew what my conversation was like, what my apartment was like, who my friends were.

This was the very last card I had.

He did not know I was a nurturer.

It was not just Brian who was restored, as if by magic, by this iconic soup.

One of the housemates, a chain-smoking, shell-shocked military woman who had overseen the notorious prison in a legendary conflict area, also crept down the stairs as the house filled with fragrance.

She asked humbly if she could have some soup. Of course!

She had her first bowl, and then her second; and she seemed less haunted, and more comforted—even peaceful—with every spoonful.

Everyone needs someone to look after him or her.

Lastly her boyfriend appeared. He was "Force Recon," explained Brian. Those sent to accomplish the most terrifying deeds. Here was another military giant—a pale-haired young man with a superhero physique, and completely blank eyes.

These people were, I had been trained to believe, the worst of the worst. "Killers." "Torturers."

But as we all sat on the back deck, and the house inhabitants drank their soup, and then slowly began chatting more openly with me, I realized—eventually—that they were just human beings; indeed, damaged human beings. These two were just a fairly young man and woman, who had been sent by our leaders, men far above their heads, to oversee horrible things, or to accomplish horrible things. They would carry the tasks they had completed, as burdens, for their entire lives.

Brian's world may have shifted that weekend, because soon after that, we were going steady.

My world shifted too, though, that weekend. People whom I was trained to hate and fear, I was able to look at a second time, and, through the steam of that magical soup, to see them with compassion.

I brought Brian back to health with my dad's Jewish chicken soup.

Almost nine years later, he brought me back to life with his Irish iteration.

How amazing it is when we can keep one another alive.

How extraordinary it is when we can feed one another.

What a revelation it is when we can see one another—not as monsters; but simply as living beings, who are always hungry—for nurture, for understanding, and for love.

Epilogue

August, 2023. It had been a summer of painful healing, in many ways. For me and for the country.

Slowly, men and women returned to workplaces, to bars, to restaurants; eventually these seemed to be in full force again.

Some communities, though, never recovered. I went to a church service in a modest neighborhood in Brooklyn, New York; there were only six parishioners, all elderly, in the pews. The deacon explained that the community had never recovered from being habituated to worship on Zoom.

When it was time for the traditional "kiss of peace," the community "passed the peace." What was that, I wondered? This turned out to be a practice left over from guidance received from the State, during the pandemic.

The parishioners turned and waved their arms at one another, like people on shore waving at a distant ship bearing loved ones away.

I thought of all the elderly who live alone, and for whom the hugs and kisses of times past, at church on Sunday, would have been the only human touch of their week.

Now that was gone.

So much was gone.

––––––––

Elsewhere, things seemed to have gone "back to normal." A young relative and I went to dinner on a lovely summer night in Hudson, New York. We chose a Thai restaurant. It had a spacious, festive outdoor seating area, decorated with lights and planters and Buddhist prayer flags. There was a soundtrack of Grateful Dead music.

Epilogue

Diners had brought their dogs, so dogs of all shapes, sizes, and breeds sat peacefully at their families' feet, smiling, bowls of water nearby.

Puffy clouds drifted overhead as the late afternoon turned into a blue evening, deepening with the beat of the music, and a sense of camaraderie descended over us all.

"See?" said my young relative. "Everything is back to normal."

I bit my tongue, smiled, and said nothing.

I did not say, We nearly killed ourselves fighting to get this back for you and your generation. I did not say, Half of these people would have left me to eat in the street like an animal, six months ago, instead of here among them, if the mandates had told them to go along with that.

I nodded my head in silence.

In thirty-three states, my organization DailyClout helped to pass our "Five Freedoms" bill: No mask mandates; open schools now; no vaccine mandates; freedom of assembly; end emergency law.

That and other fights had helped to keep the US free, relative to other nations, by summer of 2023. This, that is, compared to the ruination in Canada, Australia and New Zealand, where formerly robust democracies had become vassal states in many ways. In Australia, as you recall, protesting citizens had been fired on by rubber bullets, and in New Zealand, police had used sound cannons against protesters.[1] When I did podcasts to those countries, the brave and resistant citizens looked drained and haunted. Canada was a charnel house; the protesting truckers had had their bank accounts frozen in 2022.[2] Until October 2022, Canadians living in the US were not able to cross the border to see their families if they were unvaccinated.[3]

The so-recently free, open society, just north of us, was unrecognizable.

At the end of August 2023, after we had released seventy-nine reports detailing this greatest crime against humanity in recorded history, Pfizer's manufacturing demand had collapsed. The company's quarterly report attributed the drop in demand to noncompliance. The Moderna papers began to be released via court order; we found that Moderna too, like Pfizer, knew that they were destroying (and studying the destruction of) female mammals' reproduction. It had always been a false choice—"Team Pfizer" and "Team Moderna"—and the results were now in.

As I noted earlier, in Sweden, live births were down 8.3 percent.[4] Maternal deaths were up 40 percent, and two independent midwives as well as fetal-maternal medicine specialist Dr. James Thorp attributed the dangers now facing women in childbirth to the impaired placentas of many vaccinated women. The placentas were falling apart during childbirth, they all testified separately, terribly raising the risks to moms as well as babies. Multiple studies confirmed the story we had broken—that vaccinated women's cycles were disrupted, and that there was mRNA and other vaccine material in vaccinated mothers' breast milk. Breast feeding was down, from 34 percent of all new moms and babies to 14 percent. Dr. Thorp, along with the two independent midwives whom I mentioned, also warned that babies were now being born with fetal malformations, chromosomal malformations, and many other problems.[5]

The very sick passed away.

Excess deaths were up 11 percent in Britain in 2022.[6] The United States' excess deaths were up a stunning 1,273,971 since 2020. The United Kingdom, 216,749. Italy, 240,705.[7]

Edward Dowd reported on disabilities in the US workforce and made the case, using government and insurance data, that the numbers of people who described themselves as disabled had risen by 10 percent since the rollout of the mRNA vaccine. He found that millennials aged 25 to 44 had an 84 percent increase in excess mortality.[8]

And yet—and yet. In spite of all of this trauma, we began to heal, as if we were new tentative growth after a massive wildfire.

Then, in August 2023, a new "variant," Eris—which is the name for the Greek goddess of discord and strife—was introduced to the world's press.[9] And a "booster" that allegedly protected against this new "variant" was also promoted in the press. This happened, though the FDA advisory panel had recommended in June of 2023 that upcoming mRNA boosters be approved in advance—even as this "variant" was yet unknown. In other words, the press campaign for the "new variant" came out after the product had been created, but before it was FDA-approved—and after a global drop in demand had been sustained by the mRNA vaccine manufacturers, for two quarters.[10] "Overall, Moderna's second-quarter sales crashed

93 percent to $344 million . . . Moderna noted lower demand for its COVID vaccine, the company's only commercial product."[11]

Why pass up revenue of billions?

Morris Brown College in Atlanta, Georgia, reintroduced masks, social distancing and quarantines.[12] Rutgers University brought back indoor masking for the Fall semester, and incoming students must abide by a COVID-19 vaccine mandate, according to the school website. The mandate says there will be no exceptions.[13]

So, after a deceptive lull, a chill wind rose up again against humanity.

As the stories in the media proliferated, preparing us all for more repression ahead, this time with all the core elements of the oppressor's toolkit debunked in terms of "the science," I thought of the 1965 experiment on "learned helplessness," in which psychologist Martin Seligman shocked one group of dogs in a context in which they learned to escape, then gave the second group of dogs shocks in a context of no escape. This caused the second group of dogs to give up. The animals seemed to conclude that no action on their part would affect their environment. Humans learn to be helpless as well, if bad things happen to them that they cannot avert.[14]

As we braced for this new fight, one as stupid and pointless, if not more so, as the old fights, I considered how sick of it all I was.

We were now back in Salem, Massachusetts, visiting again. I took an afternoon and went on a long walk. I ended up at a casual outdoor music festival that was held in a handful of tents that extended alongside the storied harbor. It was a warm, bright afternoon. Historic ships were anchored near the dock.

Under a white canvas tent, a band played songs from my youth. A handful of listeners sat on folding chairs. A number of older people were there, and some were dancing.

There were almost no people in their twenties or thirties or forties. Who knows where they were? Maybe the habit of joining together for music and dancing, of participating "irl" (in real life), had been extinguished in them, just as the "kiss of peace" had been extinguished in the churchgoers in Brooklyn.

Was this practice too, this human behavior that creates meaning and community—that separates us from animals—dead, at least for some of us?

One grandmother sat on a folding chair, holding a six-month-old boy on her lap.

She danced a little, while seated, holding her grandson's hands. She beat their hands together gently to the music.

The wind from the harbor mounted up and blew. The flaps of the canvas tent rattled.

A revered physician in the freedom movement, who had issued early warnings about what humanity faced via medical tyranny, had said, before he died in 2022, that he believed that these years would prove to be a test for humanity from God.

Were we indeed hurtling, as if in a storm, helplessly ourselves, and with no help from anywhere else, into an abyss of destruction?

Or was there still somehow a loving, unseen hand on the tiller?

There would be storms ahead.

The little boy's eyes were wide open as he listened to the music.

The wind shook the canvas harder, like an angry intruder.

But the child listened, transfixed, to the drums; to the guitar.

He listened to the soaring human voice.

ACKNOWLEDGMENTS

I am grateful to Margo Baldwin, the intrepid publisher of Chelsea Green Publishing. *Facing the Beast* is my third book with this press, which has championed free speech in a censorious time. I am honored to be published by a house that publishes many of the most important dissident voices of our era.

Thank you to the wonderful editorial team at Chelsea Green: Brianne Goodspeed, an ideal editor; Rebecca Springer, talented managing editor; and Sean Maher and his colleagues, a wonderful PR team.

Thank you to my literary agent, Jane Dystel, along with Miriam Goderich and colleagues at Dystel, Goderich & Bourret, for their skilled representation.

A.J. Rice and his team at Publius PR are stellar press advisors.

Thank you to Steve Bannon, Cameron Wallace, Captain Maureen Bannon, Grace Chong, and the team at WarRoom. The work of the WarRoom/DailyClout Pfizer Documents Investigations Team would never have reached millions of listeners if these men and women had not supported this project by getting the message out. I cannot thank enough the generous, committed, and courageous "WarRoom posse." Thank you of course to the WarRoom/DailyClout research volunteers for their work on behalf of humanity.

Jamie Glazov at FrontPageMag.com, Jeffrey Tucker at Brownstone.org, Lew Rockwell at LewRockwell.com, Brent Hamachek at HumanEvents. com, and others republished many of these essays after I ran them on my Substack, *Outspoken*. Tucker Carlson has been consistently supportive. I am grateful to all of these for amplifying my work.

Steve Berger, Wendy Ractliffe, Jenin Younes, Dr. Paul Alexander and family, Jan Jekielek and Cindy Drukier, Dr. Peter McCullough, Dr.

Acknowledgments

Harvey Risch and Sharon Risch, Dr. Howard Tenenbaum, Reggie Little-john, Frank Gaffney, Jeff and Ora Nadrich, Dr. Chris Flowers, Dr. Robert Chandler, Josh Stylman, and others shared important insights, and valued friendship, during the writing of these essays. I thank them for making me less afraid, via their own examples of courage and integrity.

My team at DailyClout—COO and WarRoom/DailyClout Pfizer Documents Research Analysis project director Amy Kelly, Kate Melgoza, and the rest of the DailyClout crew—worked inexpressibly hard to bring forth some of the most relevant reporting and editorials of our moment. Ms Kelly and Ms Melgoza also held the fort while I wrote and edited this book, and Ms Kelly gave me essential information about the Pfizer documents reports. I hope what Ms Kelly has done in convening and overseeing the Pfizer Documents research volunteers is remembered, as it should be, by history.

My mother, Deborah Goleman Wolf, is always my best reader and interlocutor.

Thank you to my extraordinary children and stepchildren.

A special thank you to Brian O'Shea, my husband, who saved my life twice; who kept us secure during the writing of this book; whose own research continually enlightens me; and who explained to me what war is—that a war can last for years without being lost, and that a real soldier never yields the fight.

NOTES

Introduction

1. Allie Malloy and Maegan Vasquez, "Biden Warns of Winter of 'Severe Illness and Death' for Unvaccinated Due to Omicron," *CNN*, December 16, 2021, https://www .cnn.com/2021/12/16/politics/joe-biden-warning-winter/index.html.

2. *Missouri v. Biden*, 2023, https://ago.mo.gov/docs/default-source/press-releases /missouri-v-biden-ruling.pdf; Associated Press, "Injunction Filed by Missouri, Louisiana Attorneys General Blocks Biden Administration from Working with Social Media Firms about 'Protected Speech.'" July 4, 2023, https://www.ky3.com/2023/07/04 /injunction-filed-by-missouri-louisiana-attorney-generals-blocks-biden-administration -working-with-social-media-firms-about-protected-speech.

3. Naomi Wolf, "The Pain of Listening to Twitter Censorship Testimony," *Outspoken*, February 9, 2023, https://naomiwolf.substack.com/p/the-pain-of-listening-to-twitter.

4. America First Legal, "AFL Lawsuit Reveals Damning CDC Documents Proving Government Collusion with Big Tech to Censor Free Speech and Promote Biden Administration Propaganda," July 27, 2022, https://aflegal.org/afl-lawsuit-reveals -damning-cdc-documents-proving-government-collusion-with-big-tech-to-censor-free -speech-and-promote-biden-administration-propaganda.

5. WarRoom/DailyClout Pfizer Documents Analysis Reports, "Read the Latest Pfizer Reports," *DailyClout*, https://dailyclout.io/category/pfizer-reports.

6. Genesis 50:20 (New American Standard Bible).

7. Victor Klemperer, *I Will Bear Witness 1933–1941: A Diary of the Nazi Years* (New York: Modern Library, 1999).

8. Jared S. Hopkins, "Pfizer's Covid Boost Crashes to Earth," *Wall Street Journal*, August 6, 2023, https://www.wsj.com/articles/pfizers-covid-boost-crashes-to-earth-51e1d0; Derek Saul, "Covid Vaccine Makers' Stock Crashes to Multiyear Lows Monday as Sales Keep Sliding," *Forbes.com*, August 7, 2023 https://www.forbes.com/sites/dereksaul/2023/08 /07/covid-vaccine-makers-stocks-crash-to-multiyear-lows-monday-as-sales-keep-sliding.

9. Ethan Huff, "Dr. Mercola Files Lawsuit against JP Morgan Chase for De-banking Mercola Market Employees," *Natural News*, August 23, 2023, https://www.naturalnews .com/2023-08-23-mercola-lawsuit-jpmorgan-chase-debanking-employees.html.

Chapter 1: A Lost Small Town

1. "Preventing Transmission Never Required for COVID Vaccines' Initial Approval; Pfizer Vax Did Reduce Transmission of Early Variants," *Reuters Fact-Check*, October 14, 2022,

https://www.reuters.com/article/factcheck-pfizer-vaccine-transmission/fact-check
-preventing-transmission-never-required-for-covid-vaccines-initial-approval-pfizer-vax
-did-reduce-transmission-of-early-variants-idUSL1N31F20E.
2. Emily Oster, "Let's Declare a Pandemic Amnesty," *Atlantic*, October 31, 2022, https://
www.theatlantic.com/ideas/archive/2022/10/covid-response-forgiveness/671879.
3. Naomi Wolf, "The Covenant of Death," *Outspoken*, August 26, 2023, https://
naomiwolf.substack.com/p/the-covenant-of-death.

Chapter 2: Opening Boxes from 2019

1. "Most Students Set to Study Online Under New National Lockdown" (press release),
Oxford City Council, January 12, 2021. https://www.oxford.gov.uk/news/article
/1686/most_students_set_to_study_online_under_new_national_lockdown.
2. Daily Caller News Foundation, "CDC Regularly Called the Shots on Facebook's
COVID-19 Censorship Decisions, Docs Show," *Maine Wire*, January 19, 2023, https://
www.themainewire.com/2023/01/cdc-regularly-called-the-shots-on-facebooks
-covid-19-censorship-decisions-docs-show.
3. New Civil Liberties Alliance, "*Missouri, et al., v. Joseph Biden Jr., et al*," August 7, 2023,
https://nclalegal.org/missouri-et-al-v-joseph-r-biden-jr-et-al.

Chapter 4: Principalities and Powers

1. John Ley, "Pfizer COVID-19 Vaccine Delivers Less Long-Term Protection from
Hospitalization After Four Months," *Clark County Today*, September 21, 2021, https://
www.clarkcountytoday.com/news/pfizer-covid-19-vaccine-delivers-less-long-term
-protection-from-hospitalization-after-four-months.
2. Matthew Gertz (@MattGertz), Twitter post, September 27, 2021, 4:53 p.m., https://twitter.
com/mattgertz/status/1442593185700716544?s=61&t=VbG0UmH0NSve2JqKI2ulEg.
3. Roni Caryn Rabin, "Women's Periods May Be Late After Coronavirus Vaccination,
Study Suggests," *New York Times*, https://www.nytimes.com/2022/01/06/health
/covid-vaccine-menstrual-cycles.html.
4. Connor Boyd, "Nearly 4,000 Women Report Menstrual Problems Including Heavy
Bleeding and Delayed Periods after Getting Their COVID Vaccine—But Watchdog
Insists There's No Proof Jabs Are to Blame," June 22, 2021, *Daily Mail.com*, https://
www.dailymail.co.uk/news/article-9708213/Nearly-4-000-women-report-period
-problems-getting-covid-vaccine.html; Mansur Shaheen, "The Truth about 'Pfertility':
COVID Vaccines Can Disrupt Menstrual Cycles but Do Not Appear to Damage
Fertility Because Birth Rates Went Up during Pandemic," February 3, 2023, *Daily
Mail.com*, https://www.dailymail.co.uk/health/article-11710119/the-truth-pfertility
-covid-vaccines-disrupt-menstrual-cycles.html.
5. "Pregnancy & Childbirth," *Our Bodies, Ourselves Today*, https://www.ourbodies
ourselves.org/subject-area/pregnancy-and-childbirth.
6. Heidi Murkoff, *Eating Well When You're Expecting* (New York: Workman Publishing
Company, 2005).
7. Heidi Murkoff, "COVID-19 Q&A with Heidi Murkoff and Dr. Rochelle Walensky," https://
www.whattoexpectproject.org/covid-19-qa-with-heidi-murkoff-and-dr-rochelle-walensky.

8. William Saunders, "Kagan Must Explain Abortion Stance," *Politico*, June 28, 2010, https://www.politico.com/story/2010/06/kagan-must-explain-abortion-stance-039096.

9. Ed Pilkington, "Sotomayor Decries Abortion Ruling but Court's Conservatives Show Their Muscle," *Guardian*, December 10, 2021, https://www.theguardian.com/us-news/2021/dec/10/supreme-court-abortion-ruling-texas-ban.

10. Ephesians 6:12 (King James Version).

Chapter 5: Thinking Like a Tyrant

1. Hannah Arendt, *Eichmann in Jerusalem: A Report on the Banality of Evil* (New York: The Viking Press, 1964), xiv.

2. "New York City Mayor Eric Adams Allows Noncitizen Voting Bill to Become Law," NBCnews.com, January 9, 2022, https://www.nbcnews.com/politics/politics-news/new-york-city-mayor-eric-adams-allows-noncitizen-voting-bill-n1287225.

3. Saul McLeod, "Stanley Milgram Shock Experiment: Summary, Results & Ethics," *Simply Psychology*, updated July 20, 2023, https://www.simplypsychology.org/milgram.html.

Chapter 6: The Subtlety of Monsters

1. The Holocaust Explained, "Creation of Extermination Camps, 1941–1942," The Wiener Holocaust Library, https://www.theholocaustexplained.org/how-and-why/how/creation-of-extermination-camps.

2. Auschwitz-Birkenau Memorial and Museum, "Josef Mengele," http://www.auschwitz.org/en/history/medical-experiments/josef-mengele.

3. Amos Elon, *The Pity of It All: A History of the Jews in Germany, 1743–1933* (New York: Picador, 2002), 388.

4. Elon, *The Pity of It All*, 389.

5. Elon, *The Pity of It All*, 391.

6. Elon, *The Pity of It All*, 391.

7. Elon, *The Pity of It All*, 391.

8. Jim Garamone, "Service Members Must Be Vaccinated or Face Consequences, DOD Official Says," *U.S. Department of Defense News*, December 21, 2021, https://www.defense.gov/News/News-Stories/Article/Article/2881481/service-members-must-be-vaccinated-or-face-consequences-dod-official-says.

9. Emily Schultheis and Geir Moulson, "Austrian Parliament Approves Vaccine Mandate for Adults," *AP News*, January 20, 2022, https://apnews.com/article/austrian-parliament-covid-vaccine-mandate-8539164285f87443a8b80a213d2dacc0.

10. Anne Steele, "Spotify Takes Down Neil Young's Music After His Joe Rogan Ultimatum," *Wall Street Journal*, January 26, 2022, https://www.wsj.com/articles/neil-youngs-music-is-being-taken-down-by-spotify-after-ultimatum-over-joe-rogan-11643230104.

11. Robert Hart, "Parler Sues Amazon Again in Wake of Deplatforming," *Forbes*, March 3, 2021, https://www.forbes.com/sites/roberthart/2021/03/03/parler-sues-amazon-again-in-wake-of-deplatforming.

12. Washington State Legislature, "Procedures for Isolation or Quarantine," Washington Department of Health, Communicable and Certain Other Diseases, Section 246-100-040, https://app.leg.wa.gov/wac/default.aspx?cite=246-100-040.

13. "Coronavirus (COVID-19) Update: FDA Revokes Emergency Use Authorization for Monoclonal Antibody Bamlanivimab" (press release), U.S. Food and Drug Administration, April 16, 2021, https://www.fda.gov/news-events/press-announcements /coronavirus-covid-19-update-fda-revokes-emergency-use-authorization-monoclonal -antibody-bamlanivimab.

14. Katherine Times-Union, "Lawsuit to Allow Ivermectin to Be Administered to Jacksonville Man Moves to 1st District Court," *Florida Times-Union*, January 14, 2022, https://www.jacksonville.com/story/news/2022/01/14/mayo-clinic-lawsuit-to -allow-ivermectin-as-a-treatment-moves-out-of-duval/9120594002.

15. Michael A. Grodin, Erin L. Miller, and Jonathan I. Kelly, "The Nazi Physicians as Leaders in Eugenics and 'Euthanasia': Lessons for Today," *American Journal of Public Health* 108, no. 1 (January 2018): 53–57, https://doi.org/10.2105/AJPH.2017.304120.

Chapter 7: White Feathers

1. "Dr. Naomi Wolf and Courageous ER Physician Dr. Patrick Phillips on 'Lockdown' Public Health Policies" (video), *DailyClout*, https://www.youtube.com/watch?v=hoeAo00KdLI.

2. Jay Bhattacharya on *Tucker Carlson Tonight*, March 1, 2022, https://www.foxnews.com /transcript/tucker-this-may-be-the-single-thing-that-unites-this-country.

3. "Edward Dowd Explains Bombshell 'Fraud' Charge re Pfizer Hiding Deaths Data" (video), *DailyClout*, https://rumble.com/vwfu7j-edward-dowd-explains-bombshell -fraud-charge-re-pfizer-hiding-deaths-data.html.

4. Audre Lorde, "The Transformation of Silence into Language and Action," paper delivered at the Modern Language Association's "Lesbian and Literature Panel," Chicago, Illinois, December 28, 1977. First published in *Sinister Wisdom* 6 (1978) and *The Cancer Journals* (San Francisco: Spinsters, Ink, 1980).

Chapter 8: Rethinking the Second Amendment

1. U.S. Constitution, Second Amendment.

2. Thomas Paine, *The Writings of Thomas Paine, Volume 1*, collected and edited by Moncure Daniel Conway (New York: G.P. Putnam's Sons, 1894).

3. Jane Austen, *Pride and Prejudice* (London: Penguin Books, 2003).

4. "Amendment 178: Moved by Lord Lester of Herne Hill," Parliament.uk, July 9, 2009, https://publications.parliament.uk/pa/ld200809/ldhansrd/text/90709-0013.htm.

5. Clare Feikert-Ahalt, "Sedition in England: The Abolition of a Law from a Bygone Era," *Library of Congress Blogs*, October 2, 2012, https://blogs.loc.gov/law/2012/10 /sedition-in-england-the-abolition-of-a-law-from-a-bygone-era.

6. Chris Day, "'Wicked and seditious writings'—Thomas Paine, Rights of Man and Treason," The National Archives (UK), April 5, 2023, https://blog.nationalarchives .gov.uk/thomas-paine-and-treason.

7. Thomas Paine, *The Trial of Thomas Paine, for a Libel, Contained in the Second Part of Rights of Man, Before Lord Kenyon, and a Special Jury, at Guildhall, December 18, 1792, with the Speeches of the Attorney General and Mr. Erskine, at Large* (London: C & G Kearsley, 1792), https://www.baumanrarebooks.com/rare-books/paine-thomas/trial-of -thomas-paine-for-a-libel/111286.aspx.

Notes

8. Phillip S. Foner, "Thomas Paine: British-American Author," *Britannica*, https://www.britannica.com/biography/Thomas-Paine.

9. Joseph R. Biden Jr., "Notice on the Continuation of the National Emergency Concerning the Coronavirus Disease 2019 (COVID-19) Pandemic," White House Briefing Room, February 18, 2022, https://www.whitehouse.gov/briefing-room/presidential-actions/2022/02/18/notice-on-the-continuation-of-the-national-emergency-concerning-the-coronavirus-disease-2019-covid-19-pandemic-2.

10. Joseph R. Biden Jr., "Notice on the Continuation of the National Emergency with Respect to the Stabilization of Iraq," White House Briefing Room, May 9, 2022, https://www.whitehouse.gov/briefing-room/presidential-actions/2022/05/09/notice-on-the-continuation-of-the-national-emergency-with-respect-to-the-stabilization-of-iraq-2.

11. Joseph R. Biden Jr., "Notice on the Continuation of the National Emergency with Respect to the Western Balkans," White House Briefing Room, June 20, 2023, https://www.whitehouse.gov/briefing-room/presdential-actions/2023/06/20/notice-on-the-continuation-of-the-national-emergency-with-respect-to-the-western-balkans-3.

12. New York State, "Governor Cuomo Announces New York Ending COVID-19 State Disaster Emergency on June 24" (press release), June 23 2021, https://www.governor.ny.gov/news/governor-cuomo-announces-new-york-ending-covid-19-state-disaster-emergency-june-24.

13. New York State Executive Order No. 211: "Declaration of a State Wide Disaster Emergency Due to Gun Violence," July 6, 2021, https://www.governor.ny.gov/news/no-211-declaration-state-wide-disaster-emergency-due-gun-violence.

14. New York State Executive Order No. 3.20: "Continuing the Declaration of Disaster Emergency," May 16, 2023, https://www.governor.ny.gov/executive-order/no-320-continuing-declaration-disaster-emergency.

15. New York State Executive Order No. 3.23: "Continuing the Declaration of Disaster Emergency," August 13, 2023, https://www.governor.ny.gov/executive-order/no-323-continuing-declaration-disaster-emergency.

16. Samuel Osborne, "COVID-19: Australian Riot Police Fire Rubber Bullets at Anti-Lockdown Protesters in Melbourne," *Sky News*, September 22, 2021, https://news.sky.com/story/covid-19-australian-riot-police-fire-rubber-bullets-at-anti-lockdown-protesters-in-melbourne-12414439.

17. Zack Beauchamp, "Australia Confiscated 650,000 Guns. Murders and Suicides Plummeted," *Vox*, May 25, 2022, https://www.vox.com/2015/8/27/9212725/australia-buyback.

18. Kat Lonsdorf, "New Zealanders Hand in More Than 50,000 Weapons as the Country's Buyback Program Ends," National Public Radio, December 21, 2019, https://www.npr.org/2019/12/21/790466492/new-zealanders-hand-in-more-than-50-000-weapons-as-the-countrys-buyback-program.

19. Chen Guangcheng, "Warning: Chinese Authoritarianism Is Hazardous to Your Health," *Washington Post*, February 6, 2020, https://www.washingtonpost.com/opinions/2020/02/06/warning-chinese-authoritarianism-is-hazardous-your-health.

20. WION, "Residents Scream from Windows, Horrifying Videos Emerge from Shanghai," April 12, 2022, https://www.youtube.com/watch?v=5LouYOdroKs.

21. Li Yuan, "Has Shanghai Been Xinjianged?" *New York Times*, May 6, 2022, https://www.nytimes.com/2022/05/06/business/shanghai-xinjiang-china-covid-zero.html.

22. Emma Farge, "WHO Pandemic Treaty: What Is It and How Will It Save Lives in the Future?," *Reuters* via the World Economic Forum, May 26, 2023, https://www.weforum.org/agenda/2023/05/who-pandemic-treaty-what-how-work.

23. Natacha Larnaud, "Bill Gates Warned of a Deadly Pandemic for Years—And Said We Wouldn't Be Ready to Handle It," *CBS News*, March 19, 2020, https://www.cbsnews.com/news/coronavirus-bill-gates-epidemic-warning-readiness.

24. Matt McGregor, "Intelligence Analyst Sounds Alarm on CCP's Influence Over WHO Through 'One Health' Ideologies," *The Epoch Times*, June 13, 2023, https://www.theepochtimes.com/us/in-depth-intelligence-analyst-sounds-alarm-on-ccps-influence-over-who-through-one-health-ideologies-5323462.

Chapter 9: The Next Thing

1. "Women's Rights in Afghanistan," Medica Mondiale, https://medicamondiale.org/en/where-we-empower-women/Afghanistan; The Center for Preventative Action, "Instability in Afghanistan," Global Conflict Tracker, accessed June 22, 2023, https://www.cfr.org/global-conflict-tracker/conflict/war-afghanistan.

2. Matthew 5:45 (King James Version).

3. Amos 5:24 (King James Version).

4. Matthew 10:34 (King James Version).

Chapter 10: The Pfizer Documents

1. "In accordance with the Parties' agreed production schedule detailed in the Joint Status Report, the Court ORDERS that: 1. The Food and Drug Administration's ('FDA') rolling productions will each be due on the first business day of each month, instead of once every thirty days. 2. The FDA will produce 10,000 pages for the first two productions, which will be due on or before March 1 and April 1, 2022. 3. The FDA will produce 80,000 pages on or before May 2, June 1, and July 1, 2022; 70,000 pages on or before August 1, 2022; and then 55,000 pages on or before the first business day of each month thereafter." *Public Health and Medical Professionals for Transparency v. Food and Drug Administration*. United States District Court for the Northern District of Texas Fort Worth Division case no. 4:21-cv-1058-P, filed February 2, 2022, https://www.phmpt.org/wp-content/uploads/2022/02/Order-February-7-2022.pdf.

2. Pfizer Documents Investigation Team, project director Amy Kelly, *WarRoom/DailyClout Pfizer Documents Analysis Reports: Find Out What Pfizer, FDA Tried to Conceal* (Millerton, NY: DailyClout, 2023).

3. Dr. Christopher Flowers, "Report 11: Pfizer Vaccine—FDA Fails to Mention Risk of Heart Damage in Teens," *DailyClout*, April 7, 2022, https://dailyclout.io/pfizer-vaccine-fda-fails-to-mention-risk-of-heart-damage-in-teens.

4. "Internal Pfizer Documents Prove Knowledge that Lipid Nanoparticles (in Mice Subjects) Do Not Remain in Muscle but 'Were Shown to be Rapidly Distributed in the Blood to the Liver,'" *Daily Clout*, March 13, 2022, https://dailyclout.io/internal

-pfizer-documents-prove-knowledge-that-lipid-nanoparticles-in-mice-subjects-do-not
-remain-in-muscle-but-were-shown-to-be-rapidly-distributed-in-the-blood-to-the-liver.

5. "5.3.6 Cumulative Analysis of Post-Authorization Adverse Event Reports of PF-07302048 (BNT162B2) Received Through 28-Feb-2021," report prepared by Worldwide Safety, Pfizer, April 20, 2021, https://www.phmpt.org/wp-content/uploads/2022/04/reissue_5.3.6-postmarketing-experience.pdf.

6. Cindy Weis, "Report 18: Vaccine 'Shedding': Can This Be Real After All?," *DailyClout*, May 13, 2022, https://dailyclout.io/vaccine-shedding-can-this-be-real-after-all.

7. Etana Hecht, "Vaccinated Women," *Clown World—Honk*, May 25, 2022, https://etana.substack.com/p/vaccinated-women.

8. "A Tissue Distribution Study of a [3H]-Labelled Lipid Nanoparticle-mRNA Formulation Containing ALC-0315 and ALC-0159 Following Intramuscular Administration in Wistar Han Rats," Sponsor: Aceitas Therapeutics, November 9, 2020, https://www.phmpt.org/wp-content/uploads/2022/03/125742_S1_M4_4223_185350.pdf.

9. "Report 07: COVID-19 Vaccines and Pregnancy: Risky Business," *DailyClout*, May 18, 2022, https://dailyclout.io/covid-19-vaccines-pregnancy-risky-business.

10. Yarden Golan et al., "COVID-19 mRNA Vaccination in Lactation: Assessment of Adverse Events and Vaccine Related Antibodies in Mother-Infant Dyads," *Frontiers in Immunology* 12, no. 777103 (November 2021), https://doi.org/10.3389/fimmu.2021.777103.

11. Golan et al., "COVID-19 mRNA Vaccination in Lactation."

12. Amy Kelly, "Report 69: BOMBSHELL—Pfizer and FDA Knew in Early 2021 That Pfizer mRNA COVID "Vaccine" Caused Dire Fetal and Infant Risks, Including Death. They Began an Aggressive Campaign to Vaccinate Pregnant Women Anyway." *DailyClout*, April 29, 2023, https://dailyclout.io/bombshell-pfizer-and-the-fda-knew
-in-early-2021-that-the-pfizer-mrna-covid-vaccine-caused-dire-fetal-and-infant-risks
-they-began-an-aggressive-campaign-to-vaccinate-pregnant-women-anyway.

13. "DOJ Investigating Abbott Plant at the Center of 2022 Baby Formula Shortage," *PBS News Hour*, January 21, 2023, https://www.pbs.org/newshour/nation/doj
-investigating-abbott-plant-at-the-center-of-2022-baby-formula-shortage.

14. Aditi Roy, "Bill Gates' Climate-Change Investment Firm Bets on Lab-Produced Breast Milk," *CNBC*, June 16, 2020, https://www.cnbc.com/2020/06/16/biomilq-raises
-3point5-million-from-bill-gates-investment-firm.html.

15. Milly Chan, "Lab-Grown 'Human Milk' May Be Just Three Years Away," *CNN Business*, May 3, 2022, https://www.cnn.com/2022/05/03/business/lab-grown-human
-milk-biomilq-health-climate-hnk-spc-intl/index.html.

16. Helen McArdle, "Investigation Launched into Abnormal Spike in Newborn Baby Deaths in Scotland," *Herald* (Scotland), November 19, 2021, https://www.heraldscotland.com
/news/19726487.investigation-launched-abnormal-spike-newborn-baby-deaths-scotland.

17. Mark Docherty, "Explosive Ride in Ontario Stillbirths Triggers Parliamentary Questions," *Non Veni Pacem*, December 10, 2021, https://nonvenipacem.com/2021/12/10
/explosive-rise-in-ontario-stillbirths-triggers-parliamentary-questions.

18. Josh Guetzkow, "Stillbirths, Miscarriages, and Abortions in Vaccinated vs. Unvaccinated Women," *Jackanapes Junction* (blog), February 12, 2022, https://jackanapes
.substack.com/p/still-births-miscarriages-and-abortions.

19. AbdulRahman A. Saied, "mRNA Vaccines and Clinical Research in Africa—From Hope to Reality," *International Journal of Surgery* 105, no. 106833 (September 2022), https://doi.org/10.1016%2Fj.ijsu.2022.106833.

20. "Coronavirus (COVID-19) Update: FDA Authorizes Moderna and Pfizer-BioNTech COVID-19 Vaccines for Children Down to 6 Months of Age" (press release), U.S. Food and Drug Administration, June 17, 2022, https://www.fda.gov/news-events/press-announcements/coronavirus-covid-19-update-fda-authorizes-moderna-and-pfizer-biontech-covid-19-vaccines-children.

21. Exodus 11:4–6 (New International Version).

22. Job 2:2 (New International Version).

23. Jeremiah 1:16 (New International Version).

Chapter 11: Facing the Beast

1. Art Moore, "CDC Database Shows Death Risk for Babies of Vaccinated Mothers," *Clark County Today*, June 11, 2022, https://www.clarkcountytoday.com/news/cdc-database-shows-death-risk-for-babies-of-vaccinated-mothers.

2. Paul Alexander, "Etana Hecht, Israeli Scientist Researcher, 'Vaccinated Women Fertility Signals Are Coming Through': 'The FDA and Pfizer Actively Worked to Keep This Data Hidden from Sight for Our Lifetimes,'" *Dr. Paul E. Alexander*, May 30, 2022, https://www.drpaulalexander.com/blogs/news/etana-hecht-israeli-scientist-researcher-vaccinated-women-fertility-signals-are-coming-through-the-fda-pfizer-actively-worked-to-keep-this-data-hidden-from-sight-for-our-lifetimes.

3. Maternal mortality rates almost doubled from prior years' rates, in 2021: Laura Santhanam, "U.S. Maternal Mortality Spiked During the Worst Days of COVID, New Data Shows," PBS.org, March 16, 2023, https://www.pbs.org/newshour/health/u-s-maternal-mortality-spiked-during-the-worst-days-of-covid-new-data-shows.

4. Rajesh Taylor, "Further Disturbing Rates of Disability and Mortality in Life Insurance Data Since Covid Vaccine Rollout," *Rajesh Taylor Journal*, February 5, 2022, updated September 14, 2022, https://journal.rajeshtaylor.com/further-disturbing-rates-of-disability-mortality-in-life-insurance-data-since-covid-vaccine-rollout.

5. Can Li et al., "Intravenous Injection of Coronavirus Disease 2019 (COVID-19) mRNA Vaccine Can Induce Acute Myopericarditis in Mouse Model," *Clinical Infectious Diseases* 74, no. 11 (June 2022): 1933–50, https://doi.org/10.1093/cid/ciab707.

6. BioNTech's SEC filing shows that the memorandum of understanding with Fosun Pharmaceuticals includes an equity investment by Fosun in BioNTech. In other words, the CCP is an equity investor in BioNTech: "As part of the strategic alliance with Shanghai Fosun Pharmaceutical (Group) Co., Ltd ("Fosun Pharma"; Stock Symbol: 600196.SH, 02196.HK) whereby the two companies will work together on the development of BNT162 in China, Fosun agreed to make an equity investment which was received in mid-April 2020. The issuance of 1,580,777 ordinary shares with the nominal amount of k€ 1,581 was registered within the commercial register (*Handelsregister*) as of April 23, 2020." Not only that but: "Ai-Min Hui, President of Global R&D, and Chief Medical Officer of Fosun Pharma said: "We are closely working with BioNTech and regulatory authorities to evaluate the safety and efficacy of the vaccine candidate, in order to synchronize the development process

in China with other countries, and to bring the vaccine to public as soon as possible, if the vaccine succeeds." BioNTech and Fosun Pharma, "BioNTech and Fosun Pharma Announce Start of Clinical Trial of mRNA-based COVID-19 Vaccine Candidate in China" (press release), United States Securities and Exchange Commission, August 5, 2020, https://www.sec.gov/Archives/edgar/data/1776985/000119312520210694/d54613d424b3.htm.

7. "In 2003 Fosun Pharmaceutical acquired 49% stake of Sinopharm Group (Chinese: 国药控股) . . . In 2008, a year before the initial public offering of Sinopharm Group, Fosun Pharmaceutical owned the direct parent company of Sinopharm Group, Sinopharm Industrial Investment (Chinese: 国药产业投资) instead; the majority owner of the joint venture was state-owned China National Pharmaceutical Group (Sinopharm)." 2003年年报 [*2003 Annual Report*] (PDF). Fosun Industrial, April 24, 2004; retrieved 5 August 5, 2018, via Shanghai Stock Exchange website. [国药集团复星联合成立首家混合所有制药企. 企业观察报 (in Chinese (China)), August 4, 2014; retrieved August 5, 2018, via Sina; 2009年年报 [*2009 Annual Report*]. Fosun Pharmaceutical, March 25, 2010; retrieved August 5, 2018, via Shanghai Stock Exchange website. "Connection Transaction" (press release). Shanghai: Fosun International, June 20, 2008.

8. "Fosun Pharma 2021 Annual Results Announcement Accelerating the Globalization," https://fosunpharmausa.com/fosun-pharma-2021-annual-results-announcement.

9. "Fosun Pharma USA Inc: FDA Filings," https://fda.report/Company/Fosun-Pharma-Usa-Inc.

10. Angus Liu, "Pfizer Boosts Paxlovid Manufacturing Capacity as Merck's Rival COVID Pill Hits Surprise Efficacy Setback," *Fierce Pharma*, November 29, 2021, https://www.fiercepharma.com/manufacturing/pfizer-boosts-paxlovid-manufacturing-capacity-as-merck-s-rival-covid-pill-sees.

11. Angus Liu, "Fosun Pharma 'Massively' Fakes API Production Data and Bribes Regulators, Whistleblower Says," *Fierce Pharma*, August 31, 2018, https://www.fiercepharma.com/manufacturing/fosun-pharma-massively-fakes-api-production-data-and-bribes-regulators-whistle-blower.

12. BioNTech, "Performance Targets 2021 Financial Year," BioNTech United States Securities and Exchange Commission Form 6-K, April 2022, https://investors.biontech.de/node/12681/html.

13. Matt Viser, Tom Hamburger, and Craig Timberg, "Inside Hunter Biden's Multimillion-Dollar Deals with a Chinese Energy Company," *Washington Post*, March 30, 2022, https://www.washingtonpost.com/politics/2022/03/30/hunter-biden-china-laptop.

14. Igor Chudov, "New Data from Germany: Births and Even Abortions Are Down!," *Igor's Newsletter*, July 17, 2022, https://www.igor-chudov.com/p/new-data-from-germany-births-and.

15. Igor Chudov, "Dramatic Decline in Births in Germany," *Igor's Newsletter*, June 25, 2022, https://www.igor-chudov.com/p/dramatic-decrease-in-births-in-germany.

Chapter 12: Thanksgiving Gathering

1. "Gilead Sciences Statement on the World Health Organization's Updated Veklury® (Remdesivir) COVID-19 Treatment Guidelines" (press release), Gilead, November 19, 2020, https://www.gilead.com/news-and-press/company-statements/gilead-sciences

-statement-on-updated-veklury-covid19-treatment-guidelines.

2. World Health Organization, "WHO Recommends Against the Use of Remdesivir in COVID-19 Patients," November 20, 2020, https://www.who.int/news-room/feature -stories/detail/who-recommends-against-the-use-of-remdesivir-in-covid-19-patients.

3. "Adverse events were reported in 102 (66%) of 155 patients in the remdesivir group and 50 (64%) of 78 in the control group. . . . More patients in the remdesivir group than the placebo group discontinued the study drug because of adverse events or serious adverse events (18 [12%] in the remdesivir group)." Yeming Wang et al., "Remdesivir in Adults with Severe COVID-19: A Randomised, Double-Blind, Placebo-Controlled, Multicentre Trial," *The Lancet* 395, no. 10236 (May 16, 2020): 1569–78, https://doi.org/10.1016/S0140-6736(20)31022-9.

4. A. E. Housman, *A Shropshire Lad* (New York: Henry Holt and Company, 1924), 3.

Chapter 13: Twenty Will Not Come Again

1. Vigilant Fox, "Yale Exposed, Follow the Money: 'They Need HHS More Than They Need Their Students,'" *Vigilant Fox*, December 9, 2022, https://vigilantfox.substack .com/p/yale-exposed-follow-the-money-they.

2. Dr. Robert W. Chandler, "Report 38: Women Have Two and a Half Times Higher Risk of Adverse Events Than Men. Risk to Female Reproductive Functions Is Higher Still," *DailyClout*, August 20, 2022, https://dailyclout.io/women-have-three-times-the-risk -of-adverse-events-than-men-risk-to-the-reproductive-organs-is-even-greater-report.

3. U.S. Department of Education, "Sex Discrimination: Overview of the Law," https:// www2.ed.gov/policy/rights/guid/ocr/sexoverview.html.

4. Dr. Christopher Flowers, "Report 11: Pfizer Vaccine—FDA Fails to Mention Risk of Heart Damage in Teens," *DailyClout*, April 7, 2022, https://dailyclout.io/pfizer -vaccine-fda-fails-to-mention-risk-of-heart-damage-in-teens.

5. The federal law that defines human trafficking is the Trafficking Victims Protection Act of 2000 (TVPA). The TVPA and its subsequent reauthorizations define "severe forms of trafficking in person" (i.e., human trafficking) as: "the recruitment, harboring, transportation, provision, or obtaining of a person for labor or services, through the use of force, fraud, or coercion for the purpose of subjection to involuntary servitude, peonage, debt bondage, or slavery" (22 U.S.C. § 7102(11)).

6. Michelle Kirby, "Human Trafficking Laws" (research report), Office of Legislative Research, March 3, 2020, https://www.cga.ct.gov/2020/rpt/pdf/2020-R-0005.pdf.

7. Michelle Kirby, "Human Trafficking Laws": "Under Connecticut law trafficking in persons is a stand-alone crime. A person is guilty of trafficking in persons when he or she: 1. uses fraud, coercion, or force (or threat of force) to compel or induce another person to . . . (b) provide labor or services that such person has a legal right to refrain from providing."

8. Ines Chomnalez, "Yale Alum Leads Protest Against University Vaccine Policy," *Yale Daily News*, December 6, 2022, https://yaledailynews.com/blog/2022/12/06/yale -alum-leads-protest-against-university-vaccine-policy.

9. U.S. Department of Health and Human Services Tracking Accountability in Government Grants System (TAGGS) website, https://taggs.hhs.gov.

10. Harvey Oxenhorn, "Body and Soul at Yale," *Malwords Weekly*, December 11, 2022, https://substack.com/inbox/post/90049995.

11. Yale Global Health Equity Scholars Program, "Research Training Sites: Karachi, Pakistan," https://medicine.yale.edu/yigh/ghes/research-training-sites/karachi-pakistan.

12. Ahmed Mushfiq Mobarak and Saad B. Omer, "Send Vaccines Where People Want Them: Developing Nations," *Yale Insights*, July 20, 2021, https://insights.som.yale.edu/insights/send-vaccines-where-people-want-them-developing-nations.

13. Vineet Kumar and Ben Mattison, "To Convince the Vaccine Hesitant, Understand their Underlying Motivations," *Yale Insights*, April 12, 2021, https://insights.som.yale.edu/insights/to-convince-the-vaccine-hesitant-understand-their-underlying-motivations.

14. Yale University, "COVID-19 Vaccine Messaging, Part 1," National Library of Medicine, May 5, 2022, https://clinicaltrials.gov/ct2/show/NCT04460703.

15. Medicine@Yale, "Pfizer and Yale Join Forces for Research and Education," Yale School of Medicine, June/July 2005, https://medicine.yale.edu/news/medicineatyale/article/pfizer-and-yale-join-forces-for-research-and: "At the [Clinical Research Unit] (CRU) . . . , volunteers will take part in studies in which they will receive potential medicines that have cleared several years of safety studies in the laboratory. Although the CRU is *wholly owned and operated by Pfizer*, [italics mine] some studies there will be collaborations between Pfizer and bioimaging experts at the School of Medicine, who will use positron emission tomography (PET) and other technologies to track where and how drugs under study are acting in the body."

Chapter 14: How Lies Killed Books

1. Annabel Gutterman, "The 10 Best Nonfiction Books of 2022," *Time*, December 6, 2022, https://time.com/6238717/best-nonfiction-books-2022.

2. Holly Peterson, "Disco Night at Mar-a-Lago (and Other Tales from Palm Beach's Private Clubs)," *New York Times*, March 17, 2023, https://www.nytimes.com/2023/03/17/style/palm-beach-private-clubs.html.

3. Kathryn Shattuck, "Adam Brody Feels All the Feels with Surfing, 'Avatar' and Cate Le Bon," *New York Times*, March 12, 2023, https://www.nytimes.com/2023/03/12/movies/adam-brody-shazam.html.

4. Catherine Pearson, "How Many Friends Do You Really Need?," *New York Times*, June 22, 2023, https://www.nytimes.com/2022/05/07/well/live/adult-friendships-number.html.

5. Michael D. Shear, "With a Pocket of Shamrocks, Biden Celebrates St. Patrick's Day," *New York Times*, March 17, 2023, https://www.nytimes.com/2023/03/17/us/politics/biden-st-patricks-day.html.

6. Benjamin Mueller, "New Data Links Pandemic's Origins to Raccoon Dogs at Wuhan Market," *New York Times* March 16, 2023, https://www.nytimes.com/2023/03/16/science/covid-wuhan-market-raccoon-dogs-lab-leak.html.

7. Emily Anthes, "What Are Raccoon Dogs?," *New York Times*, March 17, 2023, https://www.nytimes.com/2023/03/17/health/coronavirus-raccoon-dogs.html.

Chapter 15: Rock of Ages

1. "Maoz Tzur," My Jewish Learning.com, https://www.myjewishlearning.com/article/rock-of-ages-maoz-tzur.

Chapter 16: Have the Ancient Gods Returned?

1. The National WWII Museum New Orleans, "The Fascist King: Victor Emmanuel III of Italy," July 14, 2021, https://www.nationalww2museum.org/war/articles/fascist-king-victor-emmanuel-iii-italy.

2. Dwight Jon Zimmerman, "Hitler's Winter Blunder," *Defense Media Network*, December 23, 2018, https://www.defensemedianetwork.com/stories/hitlers-winter-blunder.

3. Richard Cavendish, "Leon Trotsky Assassinated in Mexico," *History Today*, https://www.historytoday.com/archive/months-past/leon-trotsky-assassinated-mexico.

4. Mattias Desmet, *The Psychology of Totalitarianism* (White River Junction, VT: Chelsea Green Publishing, 2022).

5. United States Holocaust Memorial Museum, "Blood Libels in the Middle Ages," https://encyclopedia.ushmm.org/content/en/article/blood-libel.

6. Elizabeth R. Purdy, "Salem Witch Trials," *The First Amendment Encyclopedia*, https://www.mtsu.edu/first-amendment/article/1098/salem-witch-trials.

7. Charles MacKay, *Extraordinary Popular Delusions and the Madness of Crowds* (London: R. Bentley, 1841).

8. Chad Bird, "The Devil in the Details of the Old Testament: Is Satan in the Hebrew Bible?," *Christ for You*, January 18, 2022, https://www.1517.org/articles/the-devil-in-the-details-of-the-old-testament-is-satan-in-the-hebrew-bible.

9. Jonathan Cahn, *The Return of the Gods* (Lake Mary, FL: Charisma House, 2022).

10. "Daemones (Spirits)," *Theoi*, https://www.theoi.com/greek-mythology/personifications.html.

11. John Winthrop, "John Winthrop Dreams of a City on a Hill, 1630," *The American Yawp Reader*, https://www.americanyawp.com/reader/colliding-cultures/john-winthrop-dreams-of-a-city-on-a-hill-1630: "Thus stands the cause between God and us. We are entered into covenant with Him for this work. We have taken out a commission. The Lord hath given us leave to draw our own articles. We have professed to enterprise these and those accounts, upon these and those ends. We have hereupon besought Him of favor and blessing. Now if the Lord shall please to hear us, and bring us in peace to the place we desire, then hath He ratified this covenant and sealed our commission, and will expect a strict performance of the articles contained in it; but if we shall neglect the observation of these articles which are the ends we have propounded, and, dissembling with our God, shall fall to embrace this present world and prosecute our carnal intentions, seeking great things for ourselves and our posterity, the Lord will surely break out in wrath against us, and be revenged of such a people, and make us know the price of the breach of such a covenant. Now the only way to avoid this shipwreck, and to provide for our posterity, is to follow the counsel of Micah, to do justly, to love mercy, to walk humbly with our God."

12. "Discover the 5 Covenants in the Bible," *Olive Tree Blog*, https://www.olivetree.com/blog/discover-5-covenants-bible: "God established the Mosaic covenant just after a significant development anticipated in Gen 15 had taken place: the emancipation of Abraham's descendants from oppression in a foreign land (cf. Gen 15:13–14; Exod 19:4–6; 20:2). The focus at Sinai is less on what Abraham's descendants must do in order to inherit the land and more on how they must conduct themselves within the land as the unique nation that God intended them to be (Exod 19:5–6). In order to be

God's 'treasured possession,' 'kingdom of priests,' and 'holy nation' (Exod 19:5–6), Israel must keep God's covenant by submitting to its requirements (i.e., the stipulations set forth in Exod 20–23). By adhering to these and the subsequent covenant obligations given at Sinai, Israel would be manifestly different from other nations and thus reflect God's wisdom and greatness to surrounding peoples (cf. Deut 4:6–8)."

13. Genesis 9:17; Genesis 9:8, God promises Noah, after the flood: "And God spake unto Noah, and to his sons with him, saying, And I, behold, I establish my covenant with you, and with your seed after you; And with every living creature that is with you, of the fowl, of the cattle, and of every beast of the earth with you; from all that go out of the ark, to every beast of the earth. And I will establish my covenant with you; neither shall all flesh be cut off any more by the waters of a flood; neither shall there any more be a flood to destroy the earth. And God said, This is the token of the covenant which I make between me and you and every living creature that is with you, for perpetual generations: I do set my bow in the cloud, and it shall be for a token of a covenant between me and the earth. And it shall come to pass, when I bring a cloud over the earth, that the bow shall be seen in the cloud: And I will remember my covenant, which is between me and you and every living creature of all flesh; and the waters shall no more become a flood to destroy all flesh. And the bow shall be in the cloud; and I will look upon it, that I may remember the everlasting covenant between God and every living creature of all flesh that is upon the earth. And God said unto Noah, This is the token of the covenant, which I have established between me and all flesh that is upon the earth."

14. There have been times that Yahweh's warnings to us, as the Tribes of Israel, were borne out. A generation that was disobedient to God's instructions, that insisted on worshipping the Golden Calf, was allowed by God to die in exile from the Promised Land; a new, innocent generation had to be born before the Israelites could enter that land. Later, after due warnings from the Lord, and innumerable warnings from His prophets, ranging from Jeremiah to Isaiah, we *did* get deported; the First Temple *was* destroyed; and we *were* sent into exile in Babylon. We *did* weep by the rivers of Babylon, in our exile. Rethe Groenewald, "5 Prophets Warned Israel Regarding Exile," *Faith Writers*, https://www.faithwriters.com/article-details.php?id=164682.

15. We were warned about the destruction of Jerusalem in Luke 13:31–35: "O Jerusalem, Jerusalem, *thou* that killest the prophets, and stonest them which are sent unto thee, how often would I have gathered thy children together, even as a hen gathereth her chickens under *her* wings, and ye would not! Behold, your house is left unto you desolate. For I say unto you, Ye shall not see me henceforth, till ye shall say, Blessed *is* he that cometh in the name of the Lord."

16. Matthew 23:13–14: "But woe unto you, scribes and Pharisees, hypocrites! for ye shut up the kingdom of heaven against men: for ye neither go in *yourselves*, neither suffer ye them that are entering to go in. Woe unto you, scribes and Pharisees, hypocrites! for ye devour widows' houses, and for a pretence make long prayer: therefore ye shall receive the greater damnation."

17. Ephesians 6:12 (King James Version): "For we wrestle not against flesh and blood, but against principalities, against powers, against the rulers of the darkness of this world, against spiritual wickedness in high places."

Notes

Chapter 17: A Fall

1. William Butler Yeats, "Easter, 1916." https://www.poetryfoundation.org/poems/43289/easter-1916.

Chapter 18: Dear Conservatives, I Apologize

1. Sri Ravipati, "McCarthy Defends Releasing Jan. 6 Footage to Tucker Carlson," *Axios*, March 7, 2023. https://www.axios.com/2023/03/08/mccarthy-defends-jan-6-footage-tucker-carlson-fox-news.

2. Ella Lee, "Fact Check: Nancy Pelosi Wasn't 'In Charge" of Capitol Police on Jan 6," *USA Today*, July 27, 2021, https://www.usatoday.com/story/news/factcheck/2021/07/27/fact-check-nancy-pelosi-isnt-in-charge-capitol-police/8082088002.

3. "Oversight," United States Police Capitol Police, https://www.uscp.gov/the-department/oversight.

4. "Medical Examiner Finds USCP Officer Brian Sicknick Died of Natural Causes" (press release), United States Capitol Police, April 19, 2021, https://www.uscp.gov/media-center/press-releases/medical-examiner-finds-uscp-officer-brian-sicknick-died-natural-causes.

5. Adam Klasfeld, "Capitol Police Officer Brian Sicknick Died of Natural Causes After Suffering Two Strokes Day After Jan. 6: D.C. Medical Examiner," *Law & Crime*, April 19, 2021, https://lawandcrime.com/u-s-capitol-siege/capitol-police-officer-brian-sicknick-died-of-natural-causes-after-suffering-two-strokes-day-after-jan-6-report.

6. Richard Luscombe, "Chuck Schumer Attacks 'Shameful' Fox News Over Use of January 6 Footage—As It Happened," *Guardian*, March 7, 2023, https://www.theguardian.com/us-news/live/2023/mar/07/biden-medicare-taxes-desantis-trump-2024-live-updates.

7. "Senator McConnell Calls Tucker Carlson's Depiction of January 6 Attack a 'Mistake,'" *C-SPAN*, March 7, 2023, https://www.c-span.org/video/?c5060662/senator-mcconnell-calls-tucker-carlsons-depiction-january-6-attack-mistake.

8. Emily Brooks et al., "Tucker Carlson Shows the First of His Jan. 6 Footage, Calls It 'Mostly Peaceful Chaos,'" *The Hill*, March 6, 2023, https://thehill.com/homenews/media/3887103-tucker-carlson-shows-the-first-of-his-jan-6-footage-calls-it-mostly-peaceful-chaos.

9. "About the National Archives of the United States: General Information Leaflet, Number 1," National Archives Publications, https://www.archives.gov/publications/general-info-leaflets/1-about-archives.html.

10. Brandon R. Burnette, "Daniel Ellsberg," *The First Amendment Encyclopedia*, https://www.mtsu.edu/first-amendment/article/1435/daniel-ellsberg.

11. Joseph A. Wulfsohn, "Tucker Carlson Talks Exclusively with Key Capitol Police Officer Ignored by Jan. 6 Panel Amid Footage Release," *Fox News*, March 8, 2023, https://www.foxnews.com/media/tucker-carlson-talks-exclusively-key-capitol-police-officer-ignored-by-jan-6-panel-amid-footage-release.

12. Julia Pierson, "Written Testimony of USSS Director Julia Pierson for a House Committee on Oversight and Government Reform Hearing Titled 'White House Perimeter Breach: New Concerns About the Secret Service,'" Department of Homeland Security: Testimony, September 30, 2014, https://www.dhs.gov/news/2014/09/30/written-testimony-usss-director-house-committee-oversight-and-government-reform.

13. Joseph A. Wulfsohn, "Former Lawyer for 'QAnon Shaman' Says Jan. 6 Footage Wasn't Shown to Client, Calls Prison Sentence a 'Tragedy,'" *Fox News*, March 9, 2023, https://www.foxnews.com/media/former-lawyer-qanon-shaman-says-jan-6-footage -I-shown-client-calls-prison-sentence-tragedy.

14. "Watching Congress in Session," U.S. Capitol Visitor Center, https://www .visitthecapitol.gov/visit/know-before-you-go/watching-congress-in-session.

15. "Visiting the Capitol Galleries," United States Senate, https://www.senate.gov /visiting/common/generic/visiting_galleries.htm.

16. "Gallery Level," History, Art & Archives, United States House of Representatives, https:// history.house.gov/Exhibitions-and-Publications/Capitol/1857-1950/Gallery-Level/.

17. Scott Bomboy, "Looking Back: The Electoral Commission of 1877," *National Constitution Center*, January 4, 2021, https://constitutioncenter.org/blog/looking-back-the -electoral-commission-of-1877.

18. "Historical Artifacts: Passes," History, Art & Archives, United States House of Representatives, https://history.house.gov/Collection/Search?Term=Search &Classifications=Historical+Artifacts%3A+Passes.

19. History.Com Editors, "Andrew Jackson Holds 'Open House' at the White House," *History*, March 3, 2020, https://www.history.com/this-day-in-history/jackson-holds -open-house-at-the-white-house.

20. Paul Dickson, "The Bonus Army," *Bill of Rights Institute*, https://billofrightsinstitute .org/essays/the-bonus-army.

21. John McLaughlin, "Hunter Biden Story Is Russian Disinformation, Dozens of Former Intel Officials Say," citing *Politico* story, October 20, 2020, https://sais.jhu.edu/news -press/hunter-biden-story-russian-disinformation-dozens-former-intel-officials-say; Natasha Bertrand, "Hunter Biden Story Is Russian Disinfo, Dozens of Former Intel Officials Say," *Politico*, October 19. 2020, https://www.politico.com/news/2020/10 /19/hunter-biden-story-russian-disinfo-430276.

22. "Did Trump Spread Russian Disinformation During the Debate?," *CNN Politics Facts First*, https://www.cnn.com/factsfirst/politics/factcheck_036fb62c-377f-4c68 -8fa5-b98418e4bb9c.

23. "Mueller Finds No Collusion with Russia, Leaves Obstruction Question Open" (press release), American Bar Association, March 25, 2019, https://www.americanbar.org /news/abanews/aba-news-archives/2019/03/mueller-concludes-investigation.

24. David Smith, "'The Perfect Target': Russia Cultivated Trump as Asset for 40 Years— ex-KGB spy," *Guardian*, January 29, 2021, https://www.theguardian.com/us-news /2021/jan/29/trump-russia-asset-claims-former-kgb-spy-new-book.

25. Jennifer Jacobs and Mark Niquette, "Trump Team Hoping 'Peacefully and Patriotically' Will Be Shield," *Bloomberg*, February 10, 2021, https://www.bloomberg.com/news /articles/2021-02-11/trump-team-hoping-peacefully-and-patriotically-will-be-shield.

26. "Trump-Russia Steele Dossier Source Acquitted of Lying to FBI," *BBC News*, October 18, 2022, https://www.bbc.com/news/world-us-canada-63305382.

Chapter 19: Red Sparkly Shoes

1. Wilhelm Reich, *The Mass Psychology of Fascism* (New York: Farrar, Straus and Giroux, 1980).

2. Susan Sugarman, *What Freud Really Meant: A Chronological Reconstruction of His Theory of Mind* (Cambridge, UK: Cambridge University Press, 2016).

3. Mattias Desmet, *The Psychology of Totalitarianism* (White River Junction, VT: Chelsea Green Publishing, 2022).

4. Hannah Arendt, *The Origins of Totalitarianism* (New York: Harcourt, Brace & Co., 1951).

5. Sylvia Plath, "Daddy." First published in *Ariel*, 1965. Reprinted in *The Collected Poems* (New York: HarperCollins, 1999), https://www.poetryfoundation.org/poems/48999/daddy-56d22aafa45b2.

6. The Zimbardo experiment in 1971, at Stanford University, found that formerly normal groups of people could very quickly, when assigned roles of "prisoner" or "guard," become obsessive about rules and internalize their assigned roles to the point of both cruelty and of submission to cruelty. Saul Mcleod, "Stanford Prison Experiment: Zimbardo's Famous Study," *Simply Psychology*, May 18, 2023, https://www.simplypsychology.org/zimbardo.html.

Chapter 20: The Last Taboo

1. Ora Nadrich, *Time to Awaken: Changing the World with Conscious Awareness* (Seattle: Amazon Digital Services, 2022).

2. Ephesians 6:12 (King James Version).

3. "When Does Kali Yuga End? Symptoms of the Age of Kali," *Popular Vedic Science*, July 30, 2022, https://popularvedicscience.com/history/yugas/when-does-kali-yuga-end.

4. Celeste Longacre, "What Is the Age of Aquarius?," *Almanac*, April 3, 2023, https://www.almanac.com/what-age-aquarius.

5. "Counting: Tomorrow, The Day After Tomorrow," *Explore Mesolore*, http://www.mesolore.org/tutorials/learn/18/Counting-Tomorrow-The-Day-After-Tomorrow/48/Ages-of-Creation.

6. Homer, *The Odyssey* (Cambridge, MA: Harvard University Press, 1919), book 1, line 178.

7. Christopher Hall, "Blue Is the Rarest Color: Language and Visual Perception," *Burnaway*, August 30, 2018, https://burnaway.org/magazine/blue-language-visual-perception: "One of the first people to seriously study Homer's use of color was the 19th-century classics scholar and British Prime Minister William Gladstone. In 1858, Gladstone published a seminal 1,700-page study of Homer's epic poetry, which included a 30-page statistical analysis of Homer's use of color. Gladstone notes that, compared to modern writers, Homer rarely mentions color, and what is mentioned is mostly limited to shades of black and white, with red, yellow, and green making only occasional appearances. Black is mentioned almost 200 times, white about 100. Red is mentioned fewer than 15 times, and yellow and green fewer than 10. Moreover, Homer's descriptions of color can be, at times, completely bizarre: skies the color of bronze, stars are an iron or copper hue, sheep wool and ox skin appear purple, horses and lions are red, and honey glows green. Most conspicuous, however, Gladstone noted the complete absence of the color blue. Nothing is ever described as 'blue.'"

8. Gary Lupyan et al., "Effects of Language on Visual Perception," *Trends in Cognitive Sciences* 24, no. 11 (2020): 930–44, https://doi.org/10.1016/j.tics.2020.08.005.

9. Dan Cohn-Sherbok, "Mystical Explanations for the Existence of Evil," *My Jewish Learning*, https://www.myjewishlearning.com/article/mystical-explanations -for-the-existence-of-evil.

10. Geoffrey W. Dennis, "What Is Kabbalah?," *Reform Judaism*, https://reformjudaism.org /beliefs-practices/spirituality/what-kabbalah.

11. "Mysticism: Saint Teresa of Ávila—The Ironic Doctor by Francine Prose," *The Value of Sparrows*, January 12, 2013, https://thevalueofsparrows.wordpress.com/2013/01 /12/mystical-women-saint-teresa-of-avila-the-ironic-doctor.

12. "5 Powerful Tips to Get Rid of the Negative Energy Attached to You," *Times of India*, April 11, 2020, https://timesofindia.indiatimes.com/life-style/health-fitness /de-stress/5-powerful-tips-to-get-rid-of-the-negative-energy-attached-to-you /photostory/75082932.cms.

13. "But then Pharaoh called the wise men and sorcerers—the magicians of Egypt, and they also did the same thing by their occult practices. Each one threw down his staff, and it became a serpent. But Aaron's staff swallowed their staffs." Exodus 7:11–12 (King James Version).

14. Mark A. Wrathall, ed., *The Cambridge Heidegger Lexicon* (Cambridge, UK: Cambridge University Press, 2021), https://www.cambridge.org/core/books/cambridge -heidegger-lexicon/AADB99E1404A1EF2961658F9C6242205.

15. Maria Cohut, "Synesthesia: Hearing Colors and Tasting Sounds," *Medical News Today*, August 17, 2018, https://www.medicalnewstoday.com/articles/322807.

16. William Blake, "Auguries of Innocence," in *Auguries of Innocence* (Gehenna Press, 1959).

17. Walt Whitman, "Song of Myself (1892 version)," from *Leaves of Grass* (New York: Norton, 1973). Source: *Leaves of Grass* (final "Death-Bed" edition, 1891–92, David McKay, 1892), https://www.poetryfoundation.org/poems/45477/song-of-myself -1892-version.

18. Taylor Orth, "Two Thirds of Americans Say They've Had a Paranormal Encounter," *YouGov*, October 20, 2022, https://today.yougov.com/topics/society/articles-reports /2022/10/20/americans-describe-paranormal-encounters-poll.

19. Russell Heimlich, "Mystical Experiences," Pew Research Center, December 29, 2009, https://www.pewresearch.org/short-reads/2009/12/29/mystical-experiences.

20. Chabad.org staff, "The Rebbe: A Brief Biography," *The Rebbe*, https://www.chabad .org/therebbe/article_cdo/aid/244372/jewish/The-Rebbe-A-Brief-Biography.htm.

21. Chabad.Org staff, "The Rebbe."

22. Barry Dunford, "Iona: Sacred Isle of the West," *Sacred Connections Scotland*, https:// sacredconnections.co.uk/index.php/iona-sacred-isle.

Chapter 21: Not Dead Yet

1. Cindy Weis, "Report 18: Vaccine 'Shedding': Can This Be Real After All?" *DailyClout*, May 13, 2022. https://dailyclout.io/vaccine-shedding-can-this-be-real-after-all.

2. Ioannis P. Trougakos et al., "Adverse Effects of COVID-19 mRNA Vaccines: The Spike Hypothesis," *Trends in Molecular Medicine* vol. 28, no. 7 (April 20, 2022): 542–54, https://doi.org/10.1016/j.molmed.2022.04.007.

Notes

3. "Vehi SheAmdah": "And This Is That Promise," Hebrewsongs.com, https://www
.hebrewsongs.com/?song=vehisheamdah.

Epilogue

1. Oscar Francis, "Revealed: Police Used Sound Cannons Against Parliament Protesters,"
New Zealand Herald, June 28, 2022, https://www.nzherald.co.nz/nz/revealed-police-used
-sound-cannons-against-parliament-protesters/PIBFZEHRIOEADS7SK4Y4SWM464.

2. Katherine Fung, "Banks Have Begun Freezing Accounts Linked to Trucker Protest,"
Newsweek, February 18 2022, https://www.newsweek.com/banks-have-begun
-freezing-accounts-linked-trucker-protest-1680649.

3. "U.S. to End COVID-19 Vaccination Requirement for International Visitors Arriving
by Air or Land," *Snowbird Advisor*, May 8, 2023, https://www.snowbirdadvisor.ca
/news/us-end-covid-19-vaccination-requirement-international-visitors-arriving-air
-and-land-2023-05.

4. "Sweden's Birth Rate Falls to Lowest in 17 Years," *News@thelocal.SE*, February 22, 2023,
https://www.thelocal.se/20230222/swedens-birth-rate-falls-to-lowest-in-17-years.

5. Naomi Wolf, "The Covenant of Death," *Outspoken*, August 26, 2023, https://
naomiwolf.substack.com/p/the-covenant-of-death.

6. Veena Raleigh, "What Is Driving Excess Deaths in England and Wales?" *British Medical
Journal* 379 (October 20, 2022), https://doi.org/10.1136/bmj.o2524.

7. "Excess Mortality: Cumulative Deaths from All Causes Compared to Projection
Based on Previous Years," *Our World in Data*, https://ourworldindata.org/grapher
/cumulative-excess-deaths-covid.

8. Ed Dowd, "Cause Unknown: The Epidemic of Sudden Deaths," *LondonReal*, March 29,
2023, https://londonreal.tv/ed-dowd-cause-unknown-the-epidemic-of-sudden-deaths.

9. Luisa Colón, "The New COVID EG.5 Variant Symptoms to Watch For, According to
Experts," *GoodHousekeeping.com*, August 27, 2023, https://www.goodhousekeeping
.com/health/a44913133/eris-eg5-covid-symptoms.

10. Tina Reed, "Pfizer Signals Future Cuts Amid Waning COVID Demand," *Axios*, August 2,
2023, https://www.axios.com/2023/08/02/pfizer-covid-vaccine-revenue-down.

11. Allison Gatlin, "Moderna's Game Over? Not Quite, As Company Boosts Its 2023
Outlook," *Investor's Business Daily*, August 3, 2023, https://www.investors.com/news
/technology/mrna-stock-moderna-earnings-q2-2023.

12. Fox 5 Atlanta Digital Team, "Morris Brown College Implements Two-Week COVID-19
Mask Mandate as Cases Climb," *Fox 5*, August 22, 2023, https://www.fox5atlanta.com
/news/morris-brown-college-implements-two-week-covid-19-mask-mandate
-as-cases-climb.

13. Elizabeth Prann, "Rutgers Will Still Require COVID-19 Vaccine, Masks," *KXAN.com*,
August 22, 2023, https://www.kxan.com/news/national-news/rutgers-will-still
-require-covid-19-vaccine-masks.

14. Charlotte Nickerson, "Learned Helplessness Theory in Psychology (Seligman): Examples & Coping," *Simply Psychology*, April 20, 2023, https://www.simplypsychology
.org/learned-helplessness.html.

ABOUT THE AUTHOR

Brian W. O'Shea

Naomi Wolf's books include the *New York Times* bestsellers *Vagina*, *The End of America*, and *Give Me Liberty*, in addition to *The Beauty Myth*, which the *New York Times* called "one of the most important books of the 20th century." A former Rhodes Scholar, she completed a doctorate in English language and literature from the University of Oxford in 2015, was a research fellow at Barnard College and the University of Oxford, and taught rhetoric at the George Washington University and Victorian studies at Stony Brook University. She is cofounder and CEO of DailyClout.io, a successful civic tech company, and currently reaches more than 70,000 subscribers with her Substack column, *Outspoken*. Wolf lives with her husband, intelligence analyst Brian O'Shea, in the Hudson Valley.

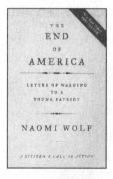
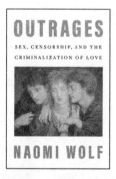
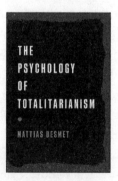